# PLANNING
# AND
# MANAGING
# SCHOOL FACILITIES

# PLANNING
# AND
# MANAGING
# SCHOOL FACILITIES

Theodore J. Kowalski

LIBRARY

PRAEGER

New York
Westport, Connecticut
London

**Library of Congress Cataloging-in-Publication Data**

Kowalski, Theodore J.
    Planning and managing school facilities / Theodore J. Kowalski.
        p.    cm.
    Bibliography: p.
    Includes index.
    ISBN 0–275–93279–6 (alk. paper)
    1. School facilities—United States—Planning.    2. School plant
management—United States.    I. Title.
    LB3218.A1K638    1989
    371.6'8'0973—dc20          89–16078

Library of Congress Catalog Card Number: 89–16078
ISBN: 0–275–93279–6

First published in 1989

Praeger Publishers, One Madison Avenue, New York, NY 10010
A division of Greenwood Press, Inc.

Printed in the United States of America

∞™

The paper used in this book complies with the
Permanent Paper Standard issued by the National
Information Standards Organization (Z39.48–1984).

10 9 8 7 6 5 4 3 2 1

# CONTENTS

# PREFACE

Planning and managing school facilities are two of the most neglected areas of school administration. Some preparatory programs for school administrators do not even offer a separate course of study on these critical topics. Yet, school buildings are multimillion dollar investments and school superintendents and other educational leaders are expected to help shape them and keep them operational once they are constructed. Not infrequently, success or failure of an administrative team can be linked to some aspect of facility administration.

Two circumstances in particular are intensifying practitioner interest in school facilities. First, education in the United States faces an unprecedented dilemma with regard to physical plants. Decades of neglect, poor planning, cost-cutting, and deferred maintenance have created a situation in which a significant portion of America's school buildings are in need of major repair or replacement. This problem extends from kindergarten to graduate and professional schools at some of the nation's most prestigious universities. Second, interest in school facility planning and management is fueled by the realization that costs related to repair and replacement have escalated significantly in the past 20 years. In some parts of the country, a new high school for 2,000 students may cost as much as $40 million.

This book addresses both planning and management. Planning is discussed from the perspective of individual facility projects as well as more comprehensive efforts, such as district-wide strategic planning. A systems analysis approach that is based upon high-level data integration and used in conjunction with a vision-driven model of goal development is advocated. Particular attention is given to potential participants of planning, alternative planning paradigms, and possible pitfalls of various approaches.

The management of existing facilities is a topic that has been even more ignored than planning in the professional literature. This fact was weighed heavily in designing this text. This book addresses the responsibilities associated with administering school buildings from two perspectives: (1) the school district program, and (2) the individual school program. Separate chapters are devoted to these two perspectives. A third chapter examines the major contemporary problems associated with school facility management.

Appreciation is expressed to Diana Meyer for assisting with technical tasks related to preparing this manuscript, to Cheryl King for developing the graphics, and to Steve Dickerson, my doctoral fellow at Ball State University, for assisting with the research and literature searches. Additionally, I am grateful for the association I have with three outstanding colleagues: Dr. Alex Moody of Indiana State University, Dr. Everett Nicholson of Purdue University, and Dr. William Wilkerson of Indiana University. Each has taught me a great deal about school facility planning and management, and my experiences with them as a professional consultant have been invaluable in preparing this book. Finally, I thank my wife, Mary Anne, and children, Catherine, Christopher, Timothy, and Thomas, for always being supportive.

# PLANNING
# AND
# MANAGING
# SCHOOL FACILITIES

# AN EVOLUTIONARY PROCESS

A high school in Virginia is plagued by vandalism. An elementary school in Missouri is destroyed by a tornado. The bids for a new middle school in Florida are 35 percent above the architect's estimate. A construction project for a new community college in California is delayed 14 months because of labor disputes. These are but a few of the multitude of problems that can surface in planning and managing school facilities. In the early years of American education, school buildings were less elaborate, less expensive, and less important. Today, they are multimillion dollar investments playing a critical role in the educational process. As such, taxpayers and educators alike recognize that they require expert management.

The quality and design of contemporary educational structures are the products of a host of contributing factors, ranging from federal legislation to research in the behavioral sciences. Today's school plants are expected to be modern, accessible, inviting, flexible, durable, and efficient. Often they are focal points in a community, standing proudly as testaments of citizen commitment to education. The schools we erect today reflect our priorities as a people (Boyer, 1989). It is neither surprising nor disappointing that school boards frequently devote significant attention to establishing policies for planning and managing these public structures. Given the value of these public investments, preparing school administrators to adequately address the issues of school facility planning has become a higher priority of schools of education.

This book is devoted to the administrative procedures associated with planning and managing school facilities. This chapter focuses upon two introductory topics. The first is the history of school facilities. In working to either plan or manage school facilities, knowledge of the evolutionary nature of this component of school management is useful. The second topic is planning. The administrator needs to comprehend and accept the value of careful planning before venturing into the more detailed study of facilities management. Despite all the literature devoted to the importance of systemic planning, many practitioners continue to rely upon instinct or to merely copy the efforts of others.

## THE EVOLUTION OF SCHOOL FACILITIES

In ancient times, education was a much more informal activity than it is today. Instruction occurred in open spaces or in shelters designed for purposes other than teaching and learning. In Greece, for example, the use of open-air classrooms and temples was common. The Romans also used a variety of environments for schooling. One of the most prevalent was the veranda—an area which provided shelter, yet was outdoors. Another "school" in Rome was the taberna. This was nothing more than a simple lean-to located off a street (Brubaker, 1947).

In the United States, the earliest schools reflected the belief that buildings per se were of little consequence. They were constructed as shelters, the products of artless designs expected to protect occupants from the elements. Their lack of importance was also established by their location. Wasteland or dusty crossroads undesirable for farming were typical sites. Brubaker (1947) chronicled these drab conditions by offering the following description: "Ceilings were low; ventilation bad; lighting unsatisfactory; heating uneven; and sanitary arrangements often unmentionable" (p. 594). In summary, most early schools were constructed with wood, had unattractive and unimaginative designs, and were situated on undesirable land.

Few architects were available to assist with the planning and construction of schools in the early settlements. Even if they had been present in needed numbers, the nature of those who occupied the colonies was such that their services probably would not have been used. The early Americans were self-governing adventurers not prone to seeking advice for tasks they believed could be mastered independently (Brooks, Conrad, & Griffith, 1980). As public schools became more prevalent (most of the earliest schools were private) and as enrollments began to surge, the school building took on greater importance.

Several factors were critical in the establishment of a new philosophy for educational environments. Urbanization was one of the most significant. The concentration of people in developing cities spawned new interests in cultural activities, technology, and education (Kowalski, 1983). Some cities, such as Boston, erected schools that were much more than the mere shelters of colonial times. In early America, the large-city school systems provided models for administrative practice—they were the "trend setters" of their day. Given the immense problems now faced by urban schools, it is hard to imagine that these districts were once prestigious lighthouses of educational innovation.

Additionally, elementary and secondary schools were affected by the industrial revolution and the expanding base of knowledge in the world. In the early

1900s, thoughtful educators perceived the need for a fundamental education that went beyond the traditional three ''R's.'' Health education and physical education exemplified components of an expanding curriculum. Trade and industrial education placed new demands upon schooling. These accumulating initiatives produced larger and more diversified facilities as the structures were required to accommodate a broadening curriculum.

The federal government exerted influence upon educational buildings as well. The most notable example can be found in the Public Works Administration (Butts & Cremin, 1953). In an effort to create jobs during the economic depression, millions of federal dollars were made available for constructing public buildings. These structures, many still standing today, were more complex and sturdy than their predecessors. They included some special use areas such as libraries, special instructional areas, and laboratories.

State departments of education also played a critical role in developing a new posture toward educational settings. Prior to the twentieth century, these agencies exercised little control over local schools. With the passage of compulsory attendance laws and laws mandating that certain subjects be taught, the state departments of education became a greater governance force (Spring, 1985). As part of this expansion of authority, these agencies became active participants in the creation of schoolhouses by monitoring quality and adequacy. Their role typically centered on the tasks related to establishing minimum standards for design and construction. This contribution was in keeping with the state's responsibility to govern public education—a responsibility that is delegated to local school boards (in all states except Hawaii). Given what had been the view of school buildings in colonial times, the impact of state department intervention is truly noteworthy. These agencies had the authority to regulate local school board decisions, and via this influence, state officials established criteria for school construction such as mandated health and safety standards (e.g., fire codes, health department codes).

Research in disciplines such as educational psychology and sociology produced linkages between the instructional environment and learning. The inclusion of these findings in professional journals led educators to seek environments which could (1) accommodate specific teaching tasks, and (2) assure that design features were congruent with the physical stature of the children. The acceptance of the theory that environmental factors (e.g., color schema, lighting, and the like) influence learning, however, did not occur spontaneously. Historical depictions verify that until approximately 1950, the school building was given little consideration as a potential facilitator of effective teaching. After World War II and during the early 1960s, the association of environment and learning emerged as a more cogent planning consideration. During that era, Leu (1965) wrote the following:

Recent school buildings reflect an increasing concern with the environmental effects of the physical space on teaching and learning. School buildings are being scaled to the ages, interests, and behavioral traits of children. (p. 5)

Although educational practitioners readily accept the importance of physical space, many taxpayers remain skeptical. Even today, remonstrators frequently attack attempts to make schools responsive to the psychological, social, and emotional needs of young children—especially where such planning decisions result in observable cost increases.

One of the truly interesting evolutionary stages of school facilities occurred as a result of school district reorganization. In 1940, there were over 223,000 elementary and secondary schools in the United States. By 1977, this figure had fallen to 106,000 (Hentschke, 1986). Obviously, reorganization resulted in mergers between small, often single-township schools in rural areas in order to create larger units. The movement was influenced by (1) a need for broader secondary school curricula, and (2) the growing dominance of bureaucratic behavior in American industry. There is little doubt that efficiency was a primary objective of those who coerced small districts to be dissolved. Larger organizations are perceived not only as more economical, but also as more capable of responding to wide ranges of student needs. The union of small school systems gave birth to the need for larger and more modern school facilities, especially at the secondary level. As a result, the modest one-room schoolhouses were eventually abandoned. Their replacements were: (1) bigger, in order to accommodate larger enrollments, (2) constructed at times when curricular mandates and student needs were growing, and (3) developed at a time when state departments of education were exercising increased scrutiny over capital development projects.

School district reorganization continues to generate controversy. Even today the debate whether ''bigger is better'' continues. As Ornstein (1989) writes:

One can make a case for either large or small school districts. I do think, however, more people who attended small schools, if surveyed, would prefer to repeat their experiences as opposed to people who attended large schools. (pp. 42–43)

In many states (e.g., Nebraska and Illinois) hundreds of small districts remain. The political, economic, and educational issues associated with school reorganization are still a cogent topic for facility planners. From an historical perspective, consolidations brought about by school district reorganization gave rise to thousands of school construction projects.

The rapid development of technology after World War II also contributed to a changing attitude about school buildings. The effects of technology are exhibited in two ways. First, better building materials were produced (e.g., brick and mortar replaced wood in many building projects). Second, new instructional equipment made its way into the schoolhouse, requiring special considerations for lighting, electricity, and security. Movie projectors and other early forms of audio-visual equipment exemplify those teaching aides. Today, in an era of sophisticated computers, this fact seems relatively unimportant. In essence, the introduction of audio-visual equipment was a discernible step toward closer ties between school design and instructional practices.

The final and probably most significant influence upon changing values related to school design was the addition of architects to the planning process. Professional input markedly increased the aesthetics, functionality, and flexibility of school buildings. Architects possessed specialized knowledge that simply improved the quality of educational environments, making it possible, for example, to establish realistic building codes addressing the health and safety needs of teachers and students. Most noteworthy, the contributions of architects were largely responsible for eradicating two barriers to effective school design—ignorance and an obsession with frugality. Today, school design has become a specialized area of practice and the American Institute of Architects maintains a separate committee to address this task.

## THE NEED FOR PLANNING

The need to enter into a facility project can be perceived as a product of change. That is, some factor, either within the school, the school district, or the community, is altered, creating a facility deficiency. It would be comforting if change were always the product of administrative initiatives. But this is certainly not the case. Unanticipated change accounts for most facility projects—often in the form of emergencies (Campbell, Corbally, and Nystrand, 1983). Reacting to change, as opposed to initiating it, is a disadvantage and makes the use of comprehensive planning less likely.

Planning is nothing more than a formalized procedure used to create programs. It could be argued that all school facility projects involve some degree of planning, if for no other reason than the laws and specific administrative regulations of most states mandate that school facilities meet established standards. These planning requirements, however, usually set forth only minimum expectations. Today, mounting costs for construction and the expanding missions of contemporary schools have heightened practitioner interests in going beyond minima; progressive leaders are seeking comprehensive and integrated planning paradigms.

Imagine a school district in which the administrators are thinking of building a new high school. Some of the questions expected to emerge almost immediately are the following:

1. What will the high school cost?
2. How much will taxes be increased?
3. Where will it be located?
4. What will be the school's name?
5. Will the school have certain "special" features (e.g., an auditorium, a swimming pool, a planetarium)?
6. When will the project be started; how long will it take to complete construction?

Obviously, these are not all the inquiries that will emerge. Since schools represent long-term public investments, administrators will be faced with additional queries. But simply answering the public may not suffice. In a growing number of communities, many individuals want to participate in the process of formulating the answers to their own questions. Not all administrators or specialists employed to assist with a facility project may be enthusiastic about sharing decision-making authority. After all, conflict becomes much more likely when there are "too many cooks in the kitchen." Despite this concern, experts are increasingly pointing out the benefits of having added insights from teachers, parents, and others (Graves, 1986). Accessing and managing participatory planning is no simple matter. These tasks require a knowledge base as well as administrative skills.

Integrated, participatory planning serves three major purposes: (1) it creates a procedure for widespread input; (2) it addresses a myriad of issues hopefully touching all the needs and objectives of the building project; and (3) it integrates the single act of designing a school facility with the overall philosophy and missions of the school system. In the absence of these considerations, errors and omission are more likely. Since it is the school board that ultimately makes decisions about participation, and since it is the administration that advises the board on such matters, the values and beliefs of both parties toward participatory planning are pivotal.

It is ironic that the availability of more specialized assistance for facility projects has lulled some school administrators into myopically believing that the responsibilities associated with planning can be delegated entirely to consultants, architects, engineers, and attorneys. These administrators painfully learn that accountability and public expectations do not disappear simply because of professional service contracts. Regardless of how many specialized personnel are employed to assist with a facility project, the superintendent and his or her team are expected to set the tone for planning, establish educational priorities, and protect the interests of the public. This inescapable fact illuminates the need for school administrators to possess the planning skills necessary to direct multi-million dollar projects.

Planning for school facilities takes place at several levels. Some states, for example, develop a plan for addressing the needs of all school districts under their jurisdiction (a state-wide plan). School systems may develop district-wide plans identifying when and how individual projects will be accomplished. However, facility planning most often encompasses the procedures associated with a single project (a plan that addresses only one school). All three levels are extremely important, and where all three levels exist, planning is the most comprehensive.

One concept common in planning literature is strategic planning. Typically, this term refers to long-range planning (i.e., beyond two or three years) and focuses upon proposed actions by which administrators systematically evaluate organizational opportunities and the potential impacts of environmental changes in an effort to fulfill the missions of the organization (Justis, Judd, & Stephens, 1985). Cooper (1985) describes this function as follows:

Strategic planning is the method by which an organization identifies relevant trends in its environment, analyzes their potential implications, and projects an integrated strategy to address these future events and their contingencies. (p. 1)

For a school district, this could mean a process for assessing needs, wants, and interests of the community and preparing programs (and the support services) to address these issues. Accordingly, school systems engaging in strategic planning already have a mechanism for identifying facility needs (such needs periodically emerge as planning progresses). Because of the continuous state of assessment and goal setting, these districts are much more likely to be proactive rather than reactive in satisfying facility needs.

Chapter 3 provides a more detailed discussion of planning procedures. The point being stressed here is that administering school facilities requires planning skills. The requirement for these skills is ubiquitous; they are needed in all phases of the task. As a result, a good portion of this book is devoted to planning activities. Just like educational leadership in general, school facility administration is neither all theory nor all "common sense." It is a combination of academic knowledge and craft knowledge—amalgams of theory and practice that are most effective when used in the context of purposeful planning.

## SUMMARY

School administration is a complex responsibility that includes the planning and management of facilities. These tasks have become even more demanding due to the growing cost and expanding uses of school buildings. In colonial America schools were little more than shelters. Urbanization, expanding curricula, creation of state departments of education, reorganization of schools, the infusion of technology, and the inclusion of architects in planning exemplify factors that contributed to a new philosophy about school buildings.

Good school facilities are the products of good planning. Although some degree of forethought is required for all projects, the best planning occurs when there is a commitment to the process by the educational leaders and when it occurs in an integrated and comprehensive fashion. School systems engaged in strategic planning are much more likely to institute proactive plans to meet facility needs.

## ISSUES FOR DISCUSSION

1. Many of the earliest schools in America were private. Did this fact have any impact upon the quality of early school buildings?
2. In addition to those listed in this chapter, what other factors influenced a changing philosophy about the importance of school facilities?
3. Identify whether your existing laws, codes, or regulations require an approval from the

state department of education for a facility project by a local school district. If they do, obtain a copy of the relevant material for discussion purposes.

4. Identify a recent facility project in your community (or a neighboring community). Find out who was involved in the planning process.

5. Differentiate between short-range and long-range planning.

6. Why is the superintendent's philosophy important with regard to a facility project?

7. Why do some taxpayers object to school facility projects?

8. What values and beliefs are associated with participatory planning?

# 2

# CONTEMPORARY ISSUES

The present state of school facility planning is affected by a myriad of regulations, needs, wants, and changing priorities. For the most part, these factors emerged after 1970. As with all organizations, schools are susceptible to national, state, and local influences such as legislation, economic conditions, and changing needs and attitudes. Automobile manufacturers, for example, cannot ignore national laws pertaining to emission standards; chemical companies must comply with toxic waste statutes. In like manner, school districts must also be responsive to forces in the environment (i.e., forces external to the organization) that suggest that change is needed. This is especially true because public schools belong to the taxpayers, and as service institutions, taxpayers anticipate that schools will be sensitive to public needs and wants to a greater extent than private businesses.

The environmental circumstances influencing contemporary facility planning have been dramatic. An ever-expanding vision of civil rights, a continuing concern for energy, and the inclusion of health and safety concerns in all public buildings serve as examples. This chapter focuses upon some of the more potent issues serving to give direction to school construction projects.

## BARRIER-FREE ENVIRONMENTS

The passage of federal civil rights legislation in the early 1960s was only the first of several major laws designed to address individual rights. In the 1970s, additional acts were promulgated concentrating on handicapped individuals. These initiatives required public buildings to be barrier-free, that is, accessible to all including the handicapped. A discussion of this topic is more meaningful if key terms are defined.

**Basic Definitions**

The first term that needs to be understood with regard to laws for barrier-free schools is *school environments*. This term refers to the entire setting in which education programs are presented under the direction of the school system. All interior and exterior features of schoolhouses and support buildings (e.g., storage buildings) are included. Accordingly, sidewalks, parking lots, and playgrounds are as much a part of the school environment as is the classroom.

A *barrier-free school environment* is a setting free of architectural and equipment barriers. An architectural impediment is an element of design or construction that prevents a handicapped person exerting reasonable effort from entering and/or making use of a building or school facility with reasonable effort (Erekson, 1980). An equipment barrier places the same restrictions on a handicapped person due to the nature or design of a piece of equipment in a school.

A third term requiring description is *handicapped person*. Perhaps the best definition for purposes here is the one incorporated in Section 504 of Public Law 93-516:

a handicapped individual is defined as any person who (A) has a physical or mental impairment which substantially limits one or more person's major life activities, (B) has a record of such impairment or (C) is regarded as having such an impairment.

The term "handicapped" is sometimes used synonomously with the term "exceptional." Doing so can create confusion. Meyen (1978) noted that the lay public, for instance, often associate "exceptional" solely with gifted individuals. In an attempt to clarify this issue, he pointed out that exceptionality may be based upon intellectual, physical, and/or sensory conditions.

With reference to school facilities, the following handicapping conditions are most relevant: hardness of hearing, deafness, visual impairment, blindness, orthopedic impairment, and multiple handicaps (e.g., deafness and blindness). To a lesser degree, mental retardation, learning disabilities, and emotional disturbances also need to be considered. Public Law 94-142 identified an additional category referred to as "other health impaired." The definition of this category, located in Section 121a.5(7) of that Act, is:

"Other health impaired" means limited strength, vitality, or alertness, due to chronic or acute health problems such as a health condition, tuberculosis, rheumatic fever, nephritis, asthma, sickle cell anemia, hemophelia, epilepsy, lead poisoning, leukemia, or diabetes, which adversely affects a child's educational performance.

Three associated terms provide further clarification:

*non-ambulatory:* a person confined to a wheelchair;

*semi-ambulatory:* a person whose physical impairment(s) cause the person to walk with insecurity or difficulty; and

*coordination handicap:* a person experiencing impairments of muscle control of the limbs.

## Legal Mandates

The requirements for barrier-free public buildings stem from several separate pieces of legislation. School buildings are covered by general legislation directed toward all public buildings as well as by more specific enactments directed to the services of special education.

*Section 504, Rehabilitation Act of 1973.* Section 504 guarantees the civil rights of all handicapped individuals. It was put into effect on June 3, 1977, and applies to all handicapped citizens regardless of age. Of primary importance to the area of facilities is the concept of "program accessibility." This concept does not mean that all buildings must be totally free of barriers. It does not require that every school building, or sub-parts of school buildings, be accessible to the handicapped. What the law does require is that the entire school program be accessible to handicapped individuals.

This idea of program accessibility is frequently misinterpreted. For example, assume an elementary school has three first-grade classrooms. Would each room need to be made accessible? The answer is no. What matters is that the student is not deprived of participation in a regular first-grade program due to a handicapping condition. If just one of the rooms is accommodating, the student could be placed in that classroom and exclusion would not be an issue. But if all three rooms were inaccessible (e.g., they are all on the second floor and no elevator is present), the student could not be placed in a regular first-grade program. In this instance, the school would be in violation of the law.

*Public Law 93-380.* PL 93-380 was passed in 1974 as an extension of the Elementary and Secondary Education Act of 1965. It essentially reaffirmed the high priority of equal educational opportunity and established the goal of providing full educational opportunity to all handicapped children. In addition, this law sets forth procedural rights for the handicapped.

*Public Law 93-516.* PL 93-516 is an amendment passed by the United States Congress that broadened the application of Section 504 of the Rehabilitation Act of 1973 to include educational services. This law also clarifies some issues with regard to barrier-free environments in schools.

*Public Law 94-142.* PL 94-142 is entitled "The Education for All Handicapped Children Act of 1975," and it amended PL 93-380. Goodman (1976) properly cited its importance by describing it as the "Bill of Rights for the Handicapped." Five major concepts are included in the law:

- a right to a free appropriate public education for all handicapped,
- nondiscriminatory evaluation,
- procedural due process,
- individualized educational programs (IEP), and
- least restrictive environment.

The concept of least restrictive environment is especially cogent to barrier-free schools. The concept promotes placement of handicapped children in the most appropriate environments as determined by the individualized program (IEP). Therefore, a child confined to a wheelchair, for example, could not be placed in a room for physically handicapped children if the IEP identified regular classroom placement as the least restrictive environment. In this respect, mainstreaming (the common term of placing children in the least restrictive environment) is associated with facility problems. It is the child's needs, as expressed in the IEP, that determine program needs. The school is required to meet these needs.

*Public Law 99-457*. PL 99-457 was passed in October 1986. This legislation mandates services for handicapped individuals from birth to age five by state and local educational agencies starting in 1990 (Blackburn and Campbell, 1988–89). This law raises questions that are yet to be fully answered regarding the impact upon educational facilities. Since the ''normal'' educational environment for very young children is not the elementary school, it is quite possible that these services will be provided in some environment other than in existing school buildings.

### Related Information

It is estimated that approximately 10 to 12 percent of the population has some type of handicap. More than a decade after the passage of laws targeted for handicapped persons, most school officials are familiar with the essence of legislation that assures civil rights for these citizens. School officials and architects have the primary responsibility of assuring that educational environments are free of hazards and barriers, and no planner can continue to justify the existence of potential or actual problems in these areas (Castaldi, 1987).

The effects of barrier-free legislation are visible in new school construction projects as well as in major renovations. There is little doubt that such requirements have increased costs; however, in a society that emphasizes the rights of all citizens, the added expenses are justified and defensible. A listing of common barriers is found in Appendix B.

### THE ECONOMY

Shifts in the economy can have a dramatic impact upon public construction projects. These consequences are both explicit and implicit. During the late 1970s and early 1980s, for example, inflation was a particular problem for public schools contemplating facility projects. The effects of this economic condition were visible in three key areas: the cost of professional services, the cost of materials, and interest costs. Inflation fueled escalating interest rates. At one point in the late 1970s, construction costs in some areas of the country were rising as fast as 1 percent per month.

Deflation in recent years has produced a reverse effect for school districts. Lower interest rates offer a more encouraging economic environment for long-term indebtedness. Unfortunately, the improved conditions arrived at a time when many school systems no longer perceived a need for facility projects due to stabilized or declining enrollments. Despite these demographic conditions, some progressive school districts utilized favorable economic conditions to modernize and alter existing facilities as long-term investments. Will favorable economic conditions continue into the next decade? Predicting future trends is extremely difficult. Even the most noted economists often disagree about future inflationary trends. Thus, school superintendents are never really sure if better economic conditions are on the horizon.

The economy affects more than interest rates and the costs of services and materials. Psychologically, it conditions the thinking of taxpayers about public projects. In many states, voter approval, via referenda, is required to execute school building construction. In a negative economy, voters are less likely to support initiatives that will raise their taxes. States maintaining finance systems that place all or most of the burden for facility costs on local revenues are especially vulnerable to negative attitudes generated by a lackluster economy.

Fluctuations in the economy have made school officials more sensitive to timing with regard to facility planning. More enlightened leaders are not willing to rely on kismet to determine if a referendum will pass or if favorable interest rates can be obtained. Rather, they actively seek information which facilitates planning. As a result, projects are scheduled with a keen eye on economic conditions and master plans are adjusted to take advantage of the most favorable market conditions.

## ENERGY AND THE ENVIRONMENT

In a single year, 1979 to 1980, the Consumer Price Index for energy increased from 250.2 to 358.8 (Bureau of Labor Statistics, 1980). Of course, this dramatic jump occurred in a period of high inflation. But the cost increase to the consumer was also a product of supply and demand conditions in the energy market. This latter issue is even more pervasive today than it was a decade ago. The periodic shortages in crude oil remind Americans how dependent the nation has become upon other countries for meeting energy needs.

Many of the schools in use today were erected when energy conservation was not a primary consideration. Poor insulation, high ceilings, and single-pane windows are common features of these buildings—even in geographic areas with harsh winters. The cost of energy was so low when these schools were designed that savings related to initial construction costs dominated the planning process. The planners obviously did not accurately predict the rising cost of energy nor did they weigh the initial savings in construction against long-term operating expenses. Low initial costs evolved into high operating costs.

Today, terms such as *energy management, energy audits,* and *cost-effective energy* are used by school administrators. Those working in energy management are becoming accustomed to comparing options by calculating various formulas designed to produce cost/benefit analyses (Hansen, 1986). Given that public buildings are a major consumer of energy in this society, budgetary constraints and accountability are two realities forcing increased scrutiny in energy management. In this respect, energy is truly a force for change in educational facility planning (Rankin, 1987). Contemporary architects are stressing the fact that there are many design features that can contribute to an energy efficient building. Furthermore, approximately 80 percent of these energy design elements can be achieved with no increase in the cost of traditional construction (Lawrence, 1984).

Closely related to energy considerations are concerns for the environment. Air, water, and ground pollution, acid rain, and the disposal of wastes are factors not unrelated to energy usage. As scientists illuminate the dangers of poisoning the atmosphere, the reactions of governmental agencies circuitously shape decisions about school buildings. Usually, state regulatory agencies must approve projects to assure that designs and specifications are in compliance with existing statutes and codes. One positive outcome of environmental dangers has been the creative use of natural conditions to support school operations. Solar energy is a good example. Additionally, concern for the environment has generated more scrutiny for a multitude of health and safety issues, resulting in school designs that provide cleaner and safer classrooms.

## PROBLEMS DURING CONSTRUCTION

Construction delays have become an even greater concern for school administrators in recent years. In part, this growing disquietude can be attributed to the "emergency" nature of many educational facility projects—projects where even the slightest delay can be critical. To a larger extent, however, the problems stem from more demanding standards and labor-related issues. The shift to a worldwide economy also needs to be considered. This condition creates markets where construction materials are often purchased from foreign manufacturers. The attraction may be lower initial costs but delivery delays and adjudication of product defects may eradicate this benefit.

Construction timetables are most likely to be upset by *change orders*. These decisions require alterations in the approved construction documents. They may be caused by: (1) a change of mind by the school officials, (2) architectural errors, (3) unanticipated conditions that affect the original construction plans (e.g., discovering a problem with soil quality requiring an alteration), (4) a decision to substitute materials for those originally specified, or (5) changes in key personnel (either in the school district or in the architectural firm).

Construction can also be delayed by the following factors:

- strikes (or other work stoppages)
- unanticipated damages at the work site (e.g., tornadoes, fire)
- poor workmanship (requiring a segment of the project to be repaired or completely redone)

- improper time scheduling (resulting in delay of the entire project)
- inability of one or more contractors or subcontractors to perform (e.g., bankruptcy)
- unavailability of materials (specified construction materials not being available or not being delivered as scheduled)
- poor working relationships or communications (various parties engaged in the project not working well with each other).

Because there are so many potential problems, school districts are exercising greater caution in developing plans to manage construction. One outgrowth of this concern has been the use of construction managers—specialists who serve as the owner's agent throughout the project. A second product of the concern for construction delays has been the creation of larger contingency funds. These funds are established by the owner (school district) to provide resources that may be necessary for unanticipated problems. Finally, the potentiality of construction delays causes many school officials to demand detailed schedules for construction and to utilize penalty clauses in construction contracts (stipulations that place a financial penalty upon contractors if their work assignments are not finished by mutually agreed upon dates). Although the inclusion of penalty clauses could have an inflationary effect on bids, they are advantageous in situations where educational programming will be hampered by construction delays.

## CHANGING INSTRUCTIONAL PRIORITIES AND TECHNOLOGY

Some argue that the more things change, the more they stay the same. In elementary and secondary schools, radical alterations in philosophy and priorities have not been uncommon during the twentieth century. Consider the proposals enacted in the mid to late 1960s. Open-space schools, mini-courses, nongraded schools, team teaching, and schools without bells were ideas which many believed would change education forever. Nothing was further from the truth. Some open-space schools had not even opened yet when the general public and school boards were denouncing them as counter-productive to "basic" educational values. Radical departures from traditional teaching usually create a public perception of chaos.

In truth, American schools have always exhibited a proclivity to change. Alternating concerns for academic achievement and social issues are largely responsible. Schools are truly mirrors of society and the shifts in priorities often represent the reactive nature of public education to social, political, and economic dynamics. Eisner (1985) likens schools to "a giant gyroscope" striving to remain upright in a windblown sea. The effects of this instability are typically recognized by architects specializing in the design of educational environments. Knowing that directions are apt to change two or three times in the life of a building, flexibility and adaptability become highly prized concepts. Although predicting future instructional initiatives and designing environments to support these practices are extremely difficult, contemporary planning procedures do take into account the inevitability of change. That is, one can plan for change without knowing exactly what change will occur, thereby at least accommodating the need for flexibility.

No single factor has had greater influence upon instructional practices in the last decade than technology. In particular, the microcomputer has altered classroom behaviors and curricula. Designing a school today without a computer laboratory is like designing a school without a media center 20 years ago. Fiber optics and coaxial cable, too, are relatively common features of current construction projects. Much like the uncertainty surrounding instructional initiatives, no one is really sure how much technology will dominate the schools of the future. Today, there already exist some electronic classrooms—environments where the teacher can use computerized systems to bring the media center and elements of the world into the classroom.

Educators can only speculate about what the school environment will look like in the year 2010. Many different perceptions are being painted by various futurists. There are few arguments, however, about the fact that the development of technology is occurring at an accelerated pace. This rapid materialization indicates that the impact of technology upon the school environment will become even more dramatic in the future.

## DEMOGRAPHIC TRENDS

One of the most obvious conditions related to school facility planning is enrollment trends. Following World War II, virtually all communities in the United States experienced growth. This was especially true in the 1950s and 1960s as the "baby boomers" moved through the elementary and secondary schools. This period of expansion was followed by a sharp decline in birth rates starting in the 1970s. This, of course, led to an eventual drop in elementary school enrollments. Many administrators are now wondering if the decline has ended.

In 1985, slight but actual increases in elementary school enrollments were noted in the United States. In looking at a forecast for the period of 1988 to 1992, public school enrollment in grades kindergarten through eight is expected to increase 6.1 percent, from 28.4 million in 1988 to 30.2 million in 1992. By contrast, enrollment in high schools (grades 9–12) is projected to decrease from 11.8 million in 1988 to 11.4 million in 1990. This trend is expected to reverse in 1991 and climb to 11.7 million in 1992 (U.S. Department of Education, 1988).

Facility planners pay much more attention to demographic trends today than in the past. Attempts are now made to localize population studies. National figures, although important, provide only a partial clue to local needs. States vary significantly in population trends, and locations within given states likewise exhibit marked variance. Later in this book, techniques for projecting enrollments are reviewed.

## EXPANDING USES OF SCHOOLS

Another factor serving to direct contemporary facility planning is the usage of school facilities. In many communities, the school serves several purposes in addition to the education of children. Recreational programs, adult education classes, and civic meetings are but three examples.

The expanding usage of schools is driven by two considerations. First, escalating taxes move many citizens to expect more benefits for their investment. Why should schools stand idle a good bit of the time when they can be serving needs of the community? This question has prompted many administrators and school boards to adopt enabling policies granting community groups access to school buildings in non-school hours. Second, the growing acceptance of lifelong learning and the recognition that schools and society are really inseparable give birth to new values and beliefs. Community education is a prime example. This philosophy promotes the use of all community resources, including schools, to address community needs and improve community life (Kowalski and Fallon, 1986). A model for such programs is found in Flint, Michigan, where assistance from the Mott Foundation has created a true community education program.

Using schools for more than the "traditional school program" expands the scope of planning. Added space, parking, access, and security are examples of issues that must be studied in detail. Another prime consideration for community usage is linked to a topic already discussed in this chapter—energy consumption. Undoubtedly, using the school plant beyond the normal school day is apt to increase energy consumption. When the benefits of community use are weighed against the added costs, however, those added costs appear to be minimal. A 1980 study, for example, found that extending the school day to accommodate more services reduced per-hour costs of operation. The study concluded that increased building use (the benefit) was greater than the cost (increased energy consumption) (Council of Educational Facility Planners, International, 1980). Increasingly, educational planners and architects take such matters into account in designing modern schools.

## BETTER PLANNING MODELS

The days when schools were planned by a relatively small number of administrators and school board members are past in most school districts. Teacher empowerment, new theories about administration in public organizations, and changing community values are but three influences increasing the popularity of participatory planning. Including more people in the process has benefits—but it also has potential pitfalls. The next chapter is devoted to the topic of paradigms for facility planning and looks more closely at the advantages and disadvantages of citizen and teacher participation.

Participation is not the only reason why more attention is being devoted to properly organizing a planning format for a facility project. Systematic and integrated planning helps reduce errors. Schools are complex structures and the potential for mistakes is pervasive. Craft knowledge (the collective experiences gained through practice) elucidates this reality and encourages practitioners to seek out and use proven planning models. Past mistakes are the best encouragement for better planning.

## THE GROWING USE OF TECHNOLOGY

In the past decade, there has been a dramatic increase in the use of technology to assist with school building designs. The availability of mainframes and micro-computers has resulted in a number of software packages and programs that are revolutionizing the design of school buildings. As a result, several technology-related terms are now an ordinary part of the professional language of architects:

- Computer Assisted Design (CAD)
- Computer Assisted Design and Drafting (CADD) (in some instances referred to as Computer-Aided Design and Drafting)
- Computer Assisted Facility Management (CAFM)
- Management Information Control System (MICS)

CADD is a process that has revolutionized facility design. Given the advantages, the process is relatively low in cost. CADD not only is a significant advancement in design, but is also an effective management tool. In the design phase, the process permits multiple layouts that can be studied and shared with school officials. This advantage facilitates communications between the architect and client. Once the building is constructed, the working drawings can be loaded into a facilities management program. This procedure offers the school system a distinct advantage, especially if the district is engaging in preventive maintenance (Skypeck, 1988). Documents created in the design phase are utilized throughout the life of the facility.

## SUMMARY

This chapter explored circumstances giving direction to contemporary facility planning. The following received focused attention:

- barrier-free environments
- the economy

- energy and the environment
- growing concern for construction delays
- changing instructional practices and technology
- expanding uses of school facilities
- demographic patterns
- more detailed planning
- greater use of technology

Each of these factors has had a pronounced effect upon decisions related to school buildings.

The influences discussed here are frequently interrelated. For example, energy cost and usage have implications for air quality (pollution). An uncertain economy and ever-changing population patterns serve to heighten interest in comprehensive planning models. The cumulative product of these conditions is the conviction that facility planning is a demanding administrative responsibility.

## ISSUES FOR DISCUSSION

1. Examine the rationale behind the concept of "least restrictive environment." Cite examples of how this concept could be dependent upon a barrier-free environment.

2. What would be the impact upon facility projects if the American economy enters into another cycle of high inflation?

3. In what ways are current reform efforts for elementary and secondary schools affecting decisions regarding school buildings?

4. Try to identify a school system utilizing an energy management system. Find out the details regarding its use.

5. What are some of the reasons why school officials in past years were often opposed to wide-spread participation in planning school buildings?

6. Identify a school system involved with community education. What are the distinguishing features of the program?

7. Discuss the issues of benefits outweighing added costs when school usage is extended to meet community needs.

8. In what ways will a global shortage of crude oil affect the operations of schools?

9. Compare the advantages of using word processing to write an essay with the advantages of using CADD to design a school building. Are there similarities and differences?

10. In what ways would it be an advantage to have working drawings for a school building infused into a facilities management software package?

# 3

# PLANNING MODELS

In some unfortunate situations, superintendents and school boards have charged forward with facility projects not knowing exactly how all the pieces of the task would fit together. Decisions are made on a day-to-day basis, frequently the products of instincts alone. This form of administration is, to say the least, the high-risk path to facility planning. Three essential decisions should be made before commencing a facility project: (1) the purpose of the facility project, (2) the selection of a planning format, and (3) a determination of the groups and individuals who will be involved in the planning process. Facility projects are most often sparked by obvious needs, such as adding classroom space or replacing a deteriorating facility. But school construction projects may also be generated by conscious attempts to institute change. For instance, a desire to employ a new curriculum or different instructional methodologies may require a change in the environment (Hoy and Miskel, 1982).

After establishing the purpose, the administration moves forward to select a planning format. Although there are literally hundreds of planning models, it is critical to recognize that no single paradigm is best for all tasks and all situations. For this reason, the practitioner needs to be familiar with the range of available options. Each planning model has some potential value—and each has potential pitfalls. Likewise, it is important to recognize that leadership and planning models are highly interrelated. Failure often results from mistakes, not from a poor paradigm (Sawyer, 1986). For this reason alone, the administrator(s) should select a planning format that he or she understands.

Simply using a planning model does not guarantee success. Selecting the right type of model given the circumstances is critically important. Essentially, planning models fall along two distinct continua:

nonintegrated_____integrated

nonlinear_____linear

The concepts of integration and linear planning are basic selection criteria. Before examining these factors, two guiding principles should be understood.

The first is efficiency. This refers to the degree to which the process can be completed with a reasonable balance between cost and benefit, without a serious strain on the human or material resources of the school system, and in a required or desired time period. The second principle is comprehensive planning. That is, the process should include all relevant data.

## INTEGRATED VS. NONINTEGRATED PLANNING

One of the primary considerations for planning models is the attribute of integration. This property entails the association of given planning components to each other and to the task as a whole. Leaders in public organizations experience a constant friction between two conflicting public demands—low costs and better services. This mentality often pressures school administrators to minimize planning costs. As a result, some corners are cut, key issues are ignored, and the input of consultants or other professionals is labeled "unnecessary."

### Nonintegrated Paradigms

Isolation is the distinguishing feature of nonintegrated models. That is, these models create situations where planning occurs with restricted participation and focus. Accordingly, there is no conscious attempt to amalgamate the specific task (planning the facility) with other factors such as the environment or the organization (Kowalski, 1988). Imagine a school district where only the superintendent and several school board members make all the decisions related to a facility project. No one else is allowed to have input. This is not only politically dangerous, but is also a precarious management decision. Administrators are driven by dissimilar convictions and inspired by different visions, and as such, a variety of solutions may result from the same set of circumstances (Plante, 1987). Should a school district make major decisions based upon the values and perceptions of a select few?

In addition to restricted input, suppose further that in planning the school, the needs of the community and total school district are never really identified. Isolated input, plus concentration on an individual school without regard for the organizational and community contexts, exemplifies nonintegrated planning at its worst. The illustration in Figure 3.1 exhibits how the nonintegrative planning process repels attempts at intervention from a variety of influences in the environment and in the organization.

The obvious advantage of a nonintegrated approach is efficiency. The planner is not burdened by conflicting input; as a result, time need not be devoted to

**Figure 3.1**
**The Closed-Planning Process**

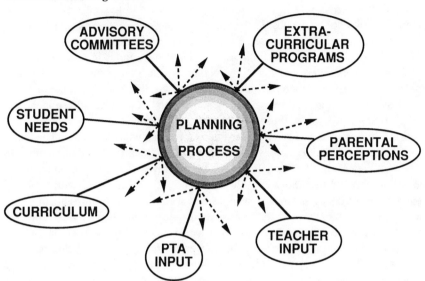

reaching compromises or determining that one option is better than others. But this option also has disadvantages. By accepting a narrow vision for the task (i.e., the task is viewed as an isolated need), the process fails to incorporate information that may be vital. Information about students, other facilities in the school district, budgets, and community needs are inputs that may be ignored. Two examples of errors related to nonintegrated planning are described here:

*Example A:* A school district erects a new high school that is designed to use electricity as the sole source of energy. The new facility is 45 percent larger in square feet than the school it is replacing. Because no effort was made to look at energy costs or available funds to pay such costs, a deficit of one million dollars occurs in the first year of occupancy. This occurs because the operating budget was based upon the myopic assumption that utility costs would remain the same.

*Example B:* A rural elementary school is designed without input from the faculty or community. After opening, the patrons are infuriated because the facility lacks adequate parking, interior security zoning, and other features which would accommodate community-based meetings and other activities that were conducted at the "old" school.

In both examples, problems could have been avoided if more information (input) had been integrated into the planning process. If, in the first case, detailed study had been made of the cost of electricity, projections made of energy usage, and calculations made with regard to budgetary constraints, the problem might have been avoided. Community input in the second case would have revealed expectations and needs beyond those of the school program.

Nonintegrated approaches are typically the product of two conditions: (1) the administration not consciously selecting a planning model, and as a result, using a nonintegrated approach by default; (2) the superintendent and board deciding that only a select number of individuals should have input in order to control efficiency. This latter decision is frequently driven by bureaucratic values that place the highest priority on avoiding conflict. By restricting inputs, the planners are less apt to engage opposing values and beliefs. American culture is largely based upon power (i.e., those that have it make the decisions). Thoughts and actions, however, can be altered when people interact with each other (Theobald, 1987). Imagine an individual who decides to retain the services of an architect to design a new family home. If only one person gives direction and input (e.g., either the husband or the wife), the architect will not be faced with differing perceptions of needs and wants even though such differences may actually exist among family members. This limited input permits the task to be completed more rapidly—but efficiency has its price. What if this one person fails to communicate accurately the needs of the entire family? What if this person's perceptions are incongruent with the remainder of the family? Recognition of the potential problems of nonintegrated approaches leads most planning experts to reject them.

### Integrated Planning

Integrated planning approaches are more complicated and difficult to use than nonintegrated models, yet they are more precise and typically produce a higher quality of information. The growing use of integrated paradigms stems largely from the realization that organizations are complex entities possessing numerous elements (Holloway, 1986). Systems analysis is one of the best known integrated concepts. A system is defined as a set of elements standing in relation among themselves and with the environment. Systems analysis is a way of viewing an existing whole by breaking it down into its constituent parts. This dissection is critical to complex tasks such as facility planning. By using a systems approach, interactions and relationships of the parts of the whole and to each other in various combinations can be analyzed. This activity is the nucleus of general systems theory. The planners think through options in terms of objectives, goals, and the independent activities required to achieve these goals (Hill, 1972).

This concept is easier to understand if one examines its origin. Ludwig Von Bertalanffy is commonly credited with the greatest contribution to general systems theory (Laszlo, 1972). A scientist who studied organisms, he became intensely interested in how they interact with larger entities (e.g., the entire body, the environment). Eventually, he applied his work to other areas of study, such as psychology, and the basics of general systems theory were developed. The concept is also congruent with the methods of developmental theorists such as John Dewey. Dewey was a proponent of clarifying ideas and subjecting them to the simple test of tracing concrete consequences. A more comprehensive explanation of systems analysis as a tool for decision-making can be found in the work of McNamara and Chisolm (1988). Their analysis of research into the relationship of human behavior and organizational problem-solving provides an explanation of how systems analysis culminates in a framework for administrative action.

With regard to facility planning, a systems approach attempts to integrate a host of considerations into the planning model with the express intent of goal achievement. It takes the form of a delivery system capable of identifying, relating, and ordering parts. Since the process breaks a whole into parts, assessment of differential influences on outcomes is possible. A systems model for facility planning is presented in Figure 3.2.

*Needs and Philosophy.* Two primary factors provide the origin for the process: (1) *philosophy,* and (2) *needs.* A philosophy contains both values and beliefs. Values essentially have three dimensions. The first is an affective domain which relates to emotions accompanying an idea. The second is a behavioral domain focusing on overt and/or covert actions. And the final dimension is the cognitive domain where integration with situations, objects, or people occurs (Worell & Stilwell, 1981). Everyone—school board members, administrators, parents, and students—has values with respect to education. These values interact with needs to achieve confluence regarding initial desires. The following example illustrates this point. A school board member believes that school buildings are extremely

**Figure 3.2**
**A Systems Model for Facility Planning**

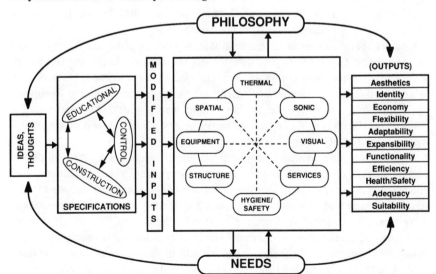

important to the learning process and a reflection of the quality of community life (an emotion). This school board member actively works for the approval of a new school building which will reflect outstanding design, educational relevance, and aesthetic qualities (an action). The beliefs and actions expressed in the facility project affect the board member's attitudes toward curriculum decisions, selection of faculty, and other related decisions for the new school (cognitive mediation).

Needs are nothing more than the gaps between what is and what is needed. Many needs are so obvious that they surface even in the absence of formal assessment activities. For example, a school district desperately short of classroom space does not need to conduct a detailed survey to confirm this fact. The shortage is manifested in a host of related concerns that affect day-to-day operations. Yet the absence of a formal needs assessment may result in "tunnel vision." That is, the school district sees only the most obvious needs while other equally important deficiencies go undetected. Both needs and needs assessment will be discussed later in greater detail.

*Specifications.* Specifications constitute refined inputs. Philosophy and needs are filtered through three sets of specifications in the systems model. The first is educational specifications (also referred to as performance specifications). Educational specifications provide qualitative and quantitative statements detailing what individuals (educators) want the facility to do. They include decisions relative to the number, type, size, layout, association, location, and content of spaces. Educational specifications bring needs and philosophy face-to-face with wants. Two problems are common in educational specifications: (1) they result in a "wish list" completed without adequate consideration of the project budget, or (2) they are overly specific with descriptions of wainscots heights or U-values of windows (Affleck and Fuller, 1988). Given that educational specifications are a difficult component of the total planning process, the document is usually prepared by a skilled educational consultant.

*Control specifications* are concerned with regulating problems related to setting standards, fixing limits, and determining feasibilities. Legal and fiscal controls are two of the most common. Also included are organizational factors such as size of the school district, site selection, and resources available to support operations (e.g., maintenance budgets, maintenance staff). An example of a control specification is placing a limit on the cost of a building or requiring that it meet fire and safety codes.

*Construction specifications* deal with interpretive engineering through design and material decisions. These documents are dependent upon educational and control specifications. They are interpretations of the other two documents and result in design and engineering drawings and related construction decisions.

*Systems Components.* As Figure 3.2 exhibits, there are eight systems components: spatial, sonic, visual, thermal, service, hygiene/safety, equipment, and structural components. In facility planning, six of the eight are usually considered simultaneously. In ordering the parts, the spatial arrangements are typically determined first and the structural elements are dependent upon the other seven. As interaction occurs among these considerations, alterations and adaptations are not uncommon. These systems components not only interact with each other, but are also touched by the initial inputs (philosophy and needs) as well as the modified inputs (specifications).

Spatial relationships include association, accessibility, arrangement, and fluidity of space. The shape and size of spaces, adaptability of given spaces, accommodations for traffic patterns, and the location of spaces are the paramount issues. For example, locating all the first-grade classrooms in the same wing of an elementary school might be critical. Or, locating high-noise areas (shops, gymnasium, music) in certain locations of a high school may increase the building's effectiveness. Spatial considerations evolve from planned functions—that is, decisions are predicated upon what is needed or desired in a given area.

The sonic component obviously relates to sound. Quality, reduction, and control are three key goals. Acoustical treatments are a good example of a sonic consideration. Sound control addresses both air-borne and structure-borne transmissions. Design decisions such as suppression and isolation of noise fall within this category. Acoustical treatments should result in a good listening environment accomplished by:

properly balanced reverberation time, the use of appropriately absorptive and reflective materials, adequate sound isolation and control of unwanted heating, ventilation and air conditioning noise and vibration. (Paoletti, 1989, p. 22)

The visual qualities of a school are more detailed than one might imagine. Light and color are two examples of visual decisions. Proper lighting in a school serves a myriad of purposes such as reduction of physical tension, conservation of energy, and increased work efficiency. Color schema complement light by improving sight conditions and providing aesthetic qualities to space. Acting together, color and light can stimulate, relax, and provide an expression of warmth. Both natural and artificial lighting fall into this category. Additionally, the visual component addresses light control in spaces (e.g., dimmers in classrooms to permit the use of audio-visual equipment).

Heating, ventilation, cooling, and humidity control are aspects of the thermal component. The importance of thermal control is most readily observed by visiting an older school on a hot September school day. Without air conditioning or a highly effective ventilation system, the school environment becomes a detriment to instruction. Given that school buildings are massive structures, thermal control is one of the most common problems reported by school principals. The concern for energy consumption, in particular, has increased awareness of this portion of facility planning. Thermal factors, such as relative humidity and temperature, need to be considered collectively. For example, a relative humidity range of 40 to 60 percent is considered comfortable. At 70 degrees farenheit, a 60 percent relative humidity would be acceptable. As the temperature increases, however, the relative humidity has to decrease to remain in the comfort zone (Knirk, 1979).

The services system element includes provisions for improving the operation/utilization of the building. Included are such factors as housecleaning, security systems, communication systems, and shipping/receiving areas. Utilities also fall under this category. Power, water, fuel, and sewage are examples. Many of the considerations for handicapped individuals (e.g., elevators, larger entryways) fall within the realm of the service system component.

Hygiene and safety play a much more important role in school design today than was true 30 years ago. Restrooms, lockers, and drinking fountains are features that are reviewed in this segment of the planning model. Proper storage provisions are another critical element. Chemicals, cleaning materials, and the like need to be placed in areas where they do not present a danger. Internal and external traffic designs also have obvious relevance to safety.

Equipment selection for a facility project is rarely given proper importance. Administrators often decide to delay such decisions or to assume that they will "take care of themselves" as the project evolves. Equipment is vital. Improper equipment planning can attenuate the effectiveness of an otherwise well-designed facility. Durability, repairability, and appropriateness (with regard to decor) are some of the concepts that are integrated into this segment of planning.

Finally, the structural component entails decisions regarding the enclosure of space, use of materials, reductions of maintenance, and the interfacing of space. Expansion of the structure, fire-proofing, ability to withstand high winds, and load-bearing features exemplify aspects of structural decisions.

*Outputs.* The final part of the systems model for facility planning deals with outputs. A good facility should be expected to meet certain tests:

| | |
|---|---|
| aesthetics | functionality |
| identity | efficiency |
| economy | healthfulness and safety |
| flexibility | adequacy |
| adaptability | suitability |
| expansibility | |

Each provides a measuring stick for determining the extent to which inputs and systems components have contributed to a quality product.

A school facility is aesthetically pleasing when it has a pleasurable and inspiring effect upon users and viewers. A school having this quality exudes warmth and beauty. A school should not have an "institutional" appearance. Elementary schools in particular should be inviting and non-threatening.

A school should be proudly identified as a resource which adds to the quality of community life. In this respect, it improves the character and image of the community. A building scoring high in this output is one that relays the message,

"This community cares about children, youth, adults, and learning." Schools designed to serve as cultural and service centers, as well as educational environments, are most likely to have a proudly identifiable aspect.

When is a school economically defensible? A facility meets this output test when the fiscal output is appropriate. That is, the building cost neither drained the community nor produced an inexpensive shelter incongruent with the community's ability to support education. This measure also includes consideration for running the school once it is operational.

Flexibility refers to a building's ability to serve changing purposes without altering the structural system of the facility. For example, a school would be flexible if it could be modified from an open-space facility to a traditional classroom building.

Adaptability is an attribute that permits given spaces to serve varying purposes. This does not entail redesign. For example, a classroom is adaptable if it can serve varying modes of instruction without significant alterations to the interior arrangements of space.

Expansibility entails the ability to expand a facility. Given the uncertainty of the future, expansibility is often an overt planning decision (i.e., the architect clearly stipulates how the building will be expanded if necessary).

Functionality deals with the degree to which the building accommodates a wide variety of teaching, learning, and service activities. The stations and equipment should fit user requirements. Resources should be available when they are needed. If a school meets these output tests, it is considered functionally appropriate.

A school is operationally efficient when mechanical services and energy sources are adequate and easily serviced. Design and structural features should provide a reasonably maintenance-free environment. Maintenance in an operationally efficient school is not an undue burden.

Healthful and safe schools provide a host of services such as climate control, sanitary conditions, visual control, sound control, and proper storage facilities. Traffic flows, alarm systems, public address systems, driveways, sidewalks, and other similar features fall into this output category.

Adequacy is a measure of how well the school really meets the needs of the community and of the school district. Adequacy and functionality are similar; adequacy, however, deals more specifically with addressing needs inputs.

Finally, suitability refers to the appropriateness of the environment. Do color schemes, equipment, and special use spaces meet the physical, emotional, and educational needs of the students housed there? Suitability is often a problem when secondary schools are converted to elementary schools without major renovations (e.g., the chalk boards are not at the proper height).

*Summary of the Systems Model.* A system is an ordered grouping which identifies and relates parts. In the model for facility planning presented here, inputs are modified, related to systems components, and measured as outputs. Again, the value of the paradigm is that it raises the planner's consciousness regarding the untold number of factors that can bear upon a facility project. By concentrating on the "whole" organization in relation to its ecosystem, the planner is able to take a proactive stance toward managing (Cope, 1987). Individual components can be weighed against each other and against the project as a whole. Such detailed analysis reduces errors and omissions in facility planning.

## LINEAR VS. NONLINEAR PARADIGMS

In cooking and baking, recipes provide a tool for satisfactory completion of the task. Not only are ingredients and their quantities listed, but each is typically ordered so that the cook knows what to do in proper sequence. Obviously, the more inexperienced the cook, the more vital is the use of recipes. This analogy has application to facility planning. School administrators 50 to 100 years ago knew little about formal planning and even less about school facilities. They relied heavily upon recipes which outlined the tasks that needed to be performed. These recipes were early versions of linear planning models.

### Linear Planning

There are two common characteristics to linear planning models. First, the specific tasks to be completed are identified. Second, they are sequenced. Linear models traditionally dominated most planning functions in education. In curriculum or general program planning, educators believed that there was consensus as to what formal steps were needed for specific tasks. In 1965, one of the leading books in school facility planning was entitled *Step by Step to Better School Facilities* (Boles, 1965). This work designated 11 critical steps to planning a school building project.

One example of a linear model for planning is presented in Figure 3.3. The importance of the example is the time relationships among the many tasks, not the tasks themselves. In any given facility project, these tasks may vary. Explicitly, this paradigm suggests that each phase is a step—a component that must be completed before moving to the next assignment. Thus, acquiring a site is completed before curriculum planning begins. Any malfunction is apt to delay the entire project.

Some planning specialists refer to the linear process as "institutional planning" (Brookfield, 1986). Since sequencing is critical, tasks are usually assigned only to administrative personnel. One of the shortcomings of this decision is the tendency to place total emphasis on the philosophy, needs, and wants of the organization (at least on how the administrators interpret these factors). The obsession with efficiency (every step must be completed on time) may result in the administrators paying little attention to the needs and wants of individuals who are affected by the planning decisions (e.g., faculty, students, parents). Additionally, linear paradigms do not recognize that resources, prevailing conditions, and needs among school districts vary markedly. For this reason, a sequen-

**Figure 3.3**
**An Example of a Linear Planning Model**

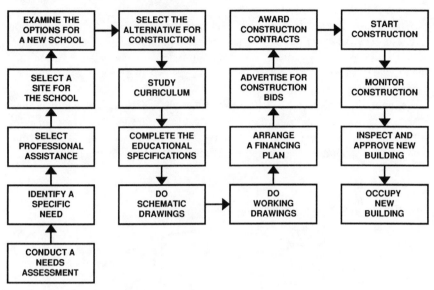

tial planning format that is successful for one school district may be a disaster for another. Additionally, the step-by-step approaches have the circuitous effect of standardizing objectives. That is, administrators who use them tend to believe that the goals and objectives of every building project are essentially the same. Some argue that objectives are never precise and that critical alterations in goals occur during the planning deliberations themselves (Eisner, 1985). Being preoccupied with the completion of the planning phases may inhibit the creative thoughts which can emerge as a variety of individuals are exposed to information by virtue of participation.

Despite the shortcomings, linear models prevail as the common mode for planning today. One reason for this continued popularity lies with the fact that they do serve a purpose. They guide the planner through critical steps. For inexperienced planners with limited specialized consultation, a linear model, despite its deficiencies, may prove to be a wise choice.

### Nonlinear Planning

Some administrators fail to use any planning paradigm. This is like baking a cake without a recipe. If you have done it before, perhaps memory and experience will guide you. But even for the most experienced administrators, the probability for errors increases when instinct, feelings, and hunches are the basis for decisions. Nonlinear planning is not a process of moving forward without a formal structure. Rather, it is a model that does not rely upon the sequencing aspect of linear approaches. Simply because a paradigm is nonlinear does not mean it is helter-skelter.

An example of a nonlinear model is exhibited in Figure 3.4. As this illustration suggests, several functions can be addressed simultaneously. Each major function has an association with all other planning functions. For instance, a committee can be working on site selection at the same time that another is working on performance specifications.

School facility projects, however, usually require more sequencing than other tasks with which the administrator has contact (e.g., designing a new course for high school students). This is true in large measure because state laws, regulations, and codes often require approvals at various stages of the project. Thus,

**Figure 3.4**
**An Example of a Nonlinear Planning Model**

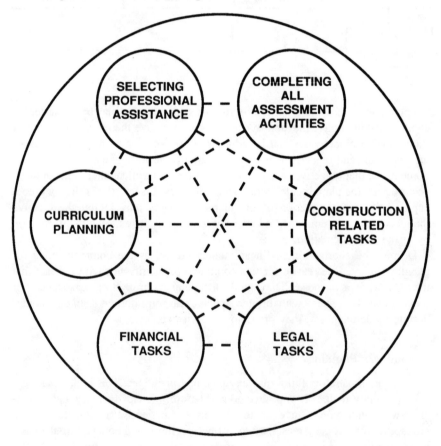

planning paradigms for school facilities nearly always have some degree of linearity.

One advantage of nonlinear tactics is that the situation dictates which components will be initiated at any given time (Murk and Galbraith, 1986). Thus, the process is flexible. Additionally, nonlinear models may require both more time and more participants. This alternative tends to place less emphasis on efficiency. These paradigms are especially accommodating for planning situations where large numbers of persons will be involved (i.e., it allows for the formation of several committees that work simultaneously). Since it is more complex than the highly structured approaches, coordination by the administration is more demanding.

One example of nonlinear decision-making is found in the project method of management. Structured organizations tend to make decisions in sequenced manners and to delegate authority for decisions to specific divisions of the organization. For example, fiscal decisions might be delegated to the assistant superintendent of business and performance specifications to the assistant superintendent for instruction. By contrast, the project method brings together a team to complete a specific task without regard for the bureaucratic boundaries of the organization. For instance, fiscal planning might be assigned to a committee that is composed of representatives of the school district's total community. This permits some of the projects to be completed simultaneously. Nonlinear approaches recognize that some tasks in planning are pervasive—they have no clear beginning or ending point (Kowalski, 1988).

## COMBINING INTEGRATION AND LINEARITY

As previously mentioned, planning models fall along two continua of integration and linearity. A more precise manner of visualizing this is presented in Figure 3.5. Four different planning alternatives are plotted on this grid. Program A is highly integrated and nonlinear. That means that many factors are infused into the process and at least some tasks are not executed in a lock-step fashion. Program B is highly integrated and linear. That is, the process relies on a sequential format but infuses a variety of inputs. Low integration is found in Programs C and D. The difference between the two is that C is linear and D is not.

A project which is planned by a superintendent, the board, and the architect (without additional input) following a step-by-step procedure would be classified as a nonintegrated linear approach. Historically, this option has been widely used despite the fact that it is likely to produce errors. Beyond potential omissions and errors, nonintegrated approaches spawn negative political by-products. Taxpayers, teachers, and even students do not like being left out of the planning process.

If conditions are appropriate, a highly integrated paradigm that provides flexi-

**Figure 3.5**
**Planning Alternatives**

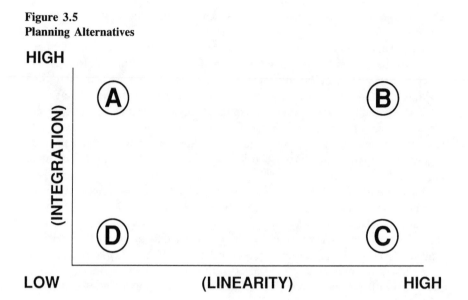

**HIGH**

(INTEGRATION)

Ⓐ                                            Ⓑ

Ⓓ                                            Ⓒ

**LOW**                    **(LINEARITY)**                    **HIGH**

ble planning decisions (i.e., some degree of nonlinear planning) can be extremely effective. But no one option is superior for all situations. The most difficult decision the administrator must make is to determine which option best fits the conditions surrounding an individual project.

## SUMMARY

This chapter explored planning paradigms for school facility projects. These models can be plotted on continua addressing the integration and linearity of the processes. Historically, administrators have relied heavily upon nonintegrated and linear models. Today, integration is becoming a more accepted option.

Facility planning, because of its very nature, cannot be totally free of linear considerations. Despite this fact, some stages of planning—especially the early stages, can be done simultaneously. This not only increases participation, it makes the entire process more flexible. Unanticipated information, new ideas, and necessary compromises are more likely to be infused into the planning process.

## ISSUES FOR DISCUSSION

1. Identify some common factors related to planning for a new school that could vary from one school district to another.
2. Why is efficiency enhanced when planning input is restricted?
3. What are the advantages and disadvantages of using committees in planning?

4. Identify requirements in your state that would prevent or restrict the use of nonlinear planning models.

5. Describe why high levels of integration typically result in more comprehensive planning.

6. Try to find an example of where restricted planning contributed to a problem with a facility project.

7. Identify a school district that recently planned a facility project. Determine who was involved in the process.

8. Discuss the advantages and disadvantages of the ''project method'' of management.

9. What conditions would favor the use of a linear model of planning?

10. What conditions would favor the use of a nonintegrated model of planning?

# 4

# ASSESSMENT ACTIVITIES

Sound planning is most likely to evolve when it is erected on a solid foundation. This foundation, an amalgam of several key components, does not rely on any single element. For example, choosing the right planning format is indeed an important decision, but a paradigm by itself is relatively useless. In addition to an effective and relevant model for making decisions, planning also relies upon accurate data that provide the inputs for the process. Often school administrators and/or school board members are tempted to leap directly into planning a facility without generating foundational information (i.e., the needs and wants related to facilities). This most often occurs for three reasons: (1) the accurate accumulation and description of needs and wants are deemed too time consuming or costly; (2) the school district lacks the human or material resources necessary to complete the task; and/or (3) the officials believe they already know the wants and needs and decide that a formal assessment is not necessary. Whatever the reasons for the omission, ignoring the assessment stages of facility planning constitutes a critical planning error.

Assessment activities can be viewed as having four potential dimensions as illustrated in Figure 4.1. The distinct information sources are:

1. general needs assessment data,
2. educational planning data,
3. school facility appraisal, and
4. performance specification data.

As previously mentioned, the temptation is often great to bypass the assessment stages in a facility project. School districts frequently fall prey to time manage-

**Figure 4.1**

**Information Sources for Facility Planning**

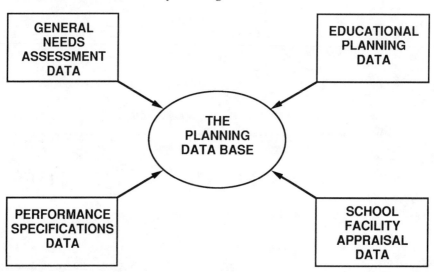

ment problems. Put simply, the needs related to facilities become so acute that adequate time cannot be allocated for comprehensive planning and detailed studies. The penalties for skipping assessment tasks are confusion, uncertainty, and needless errors.

Some needs are rather obvious with regard to facility management. Take, for example, a school district that has a rapidly growing population. The justification for an additional elementary school may be apparent to the entire community. The superintendent may conclude, "I don't need any study to tell me I need a school." What this administrator fails to realize is that comprehensive data-gathering entails more than the mere collection of facts. It also categorizes data to be used systematically as planning occurs, and makes it more probable that a systems approach will be used in creating new school buildings.

## NEEDS ASSESSMENT

For school districts engaged in strategic planning, needs assessments are usually completed on an annual or bi-annual basis. This occurs because the process is an element of organized, detailed, long-range studies. In fact, school facility planning experts recommend that long-range plans remain in a flexible format (e.g., a three-ring binder) and be updated annually to assure that data remain current (Graves, 1989). Some authors refer to needs assessment as school surveys (Castaldi, 1987). This label is somewhat restricted and is often interpreted to refer solely to the needs of individual schools or facilities. In practice, needs assessments typically include community information as well as input from individual schools. When data are collected in this latter context (e.g., as part of strategic planning for the total school district), the term, "needs assessment," is more appropriate.

Needs are essentially gaps between what is and what is needed. Society has needs; communities have needs; school districts have needs; and, individuals have needs. A comprehensive planning effort attempts to address all of these simultaneously. Adjectives commonly attached to the word "needs" can create confusion. Terms such as real needs, felt needs, and ascribed needs are found in the literature, occasionally without adequate explanation. A real need is defined as the difference between present and desired performance; a felt need is a self-identified need; while contrast, an ascribed need is the difference between the actual and desired need determined by an objective assessment specialist. The literature on needs assessment also uses the term educational needs. Wlodowski (1985) defines an educational need as the distance between aspiration and reality. Although each of these terms is important, the critical definition for facility planning is that a need represents the difference between existing facilities and requirements for the present and/or future.

Frequently, needs and wants are confused. Wants involve motivation—the predisposition to achieve something. Alone, wants do not fully reflect needs. For example, a school district may desperately need to close a school because of declining enrollment; however, the board and administration are not motivated to do this. Thus, the need exists but the want does not. In facility planning, wants are usually expressed in performance specification documents.

### Instrumentation

There are a number of different tools available for conducting a needs assessment. The most common is the *questionnaire*. These instruments come in many forms; the most widely used is the checklist. Completion of this form of questionnaire entails the placement of a checkmark to indicate response choice for each item. Likert-type scales are also used in school needs assessments. Here the person responding reacts to a statement by selecting a response option provided within the questionnaire (e.g., indicating strong agreement, agreement, disagreement, strong disagreement, or no opinion).

Frequently, the terms *open* and *closed* are used in conjunction with questionnaires. Open questionnaires are designed to allow the respondent to make clarifying comments. By contrast, closed instruments do not permit this alternative. Obviously, open questionnaires produce more information, but they are more difficult to administer, score, and report. Among the advantages of the questionnaire are that it: permits wide coverage (many persons can be included); is relatively easy to use; tends to be less expensive than other options, and allows consistency in the presentation of questions. The questionnaire's disadvantages are that: it is impersonal; it often does not offer appropriate or sufficient response choices, and its users tend to employ it without establishing the reliability and validity of the instrument. The critical issue in selecting a questionnaire for a needs assessment focuses on determining if the instrument can indeed generate the data that are needed. For instance, a questionnaire may be effective for identifying prevailing attitudes, but may be ineffective with regard to establishing quantitative differences.

*Interviews* are a second option for needs assessment. Similar in purpose to the questionnaire, this instrument entails direct interaction between the assessor and the assessee. Interviews may be conducted with a single individual or with groups. They may be either structured (predetermined and constant content and procedures) or unstructured (the conversational approach). Structured interviews typically require more work, but offer greater reliability. The advantages of the interview technique for needs assessment include: the opportunity to probe responses, the ability of the assessee to ask questions, and the opportunity for skilled assessors to gain added information from nonverbal behaviors that occur during the interaction.

The debilities of this process include:

• the possibility that the biases of the assessor can affect responses/judgments,

• the time it can consume, and

• the expense, especially when compared to the questionnaire.

For the most part, comprehensive needs assessments for school districts usually rely either on questionnaires or interviews or a combination of the two. There are additional instruments that may be used to add data. They include:

• job analyses (e.g., reviewing job expectations, observations, performance and program evaluations),

• tests (e.g., standardized tests, energy consumption tests, air quality tests),

• national or state surveys (e.g., census data, vital statistics, consumer price indices),

• trend reports (e.g., studies of common needs in a community), and

• information from advisory committees.

The last option, data from advisory committees, is becoming more common in school districts. School administrators who recognize the political dimensions of large capital outlay projects are prone to establish such groups.

## Procedures

Each school district should base its needs assessment process on the uniqueness of circumstances surrounding the task. It should be remembered that no two facility projects are ever alike (Brubaker, 1988). Fortunately, there are some standard components that provide a basic framework for assessment as illustrated in Figure 4.2. The first is the identification of purpose. The school board,

**Figure 4.2**
**Key Decisions in Establishing an Assessment Procedure**

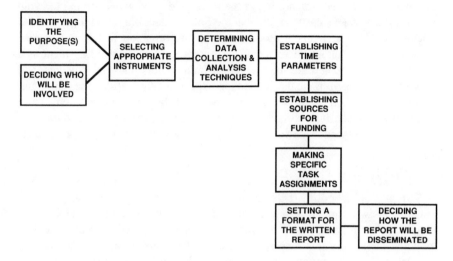

administration, and entire school community should have a clear perception of why the process is being used. The second is the scope of the process. Who will be involved? What issues will be covered? The first two decisions provide a foundation for the third element, the selection of appropriate instrumentation. The fourth component is the selection of data collection and analysis procedures, while the next essential element is the establishment of time parameters. Decisions are also needed regarding funding the process; an adequate budget should be established to assure necessary resources to complete the assessment. In addition, the designation of task responsibilities should be assigned, while finally, a format for the final report and decisions pertaining to the distribution and use of the final report needs to be established.

One process involving needs assessment that is gaining popularity is the *community survey*. Typically, this iteration of data-gathering utilizes a questionnaire to obtain information from a random sample of the community. The process proves to be especially beneficial when conflicts seem inevitable with regard to a project (e.g., the community seems to be divided over building a new school). Not infrequently, outcomes of community surveys clarify needs, dispel rumors and misperceptions, and provide information useful for establishing planning contingencies. It is highly recommended that a community survey culminate in a written document that provides the data collected, an analysis of that data, conclusions, and recommendations. The results of the community survey can be attenuated if there are suspicions related to credibility, objectivity, validity, reliability, or purpose.

A number of school districts have unsuccessfully experimented with needs assessment. Discontinuance typically results from an unfavorable balance between costs and benefits. In other words, the administration and/or board decide that what was gained was not worth the price paid. One way of trying to avoid this result is to take steps to assure that the final product is a relevant and useable document. If the assessment produces obscure information written in technical language, many school board members are apt to view needs assessment as a waste of money. Likewise, the teachers, administrators, citizens, students, and consultants engaged in the data collection expect that their efforts are important. If the fruits of their input are ignored, there will be a reluctance to engage in future assessments. It is extremely important to have a clear perspective of what is to be accomplished at the very outset if needs assessments are to be productive.

## EDUCATIONAL PLANNING

Virtually all school districts engage in some form of educational planning. Whether it is designing a new curriculum or merely revising a syllabus for a single course, instructional programs demand some degree of forethought. It is assumed commonly that new school projects (or renovations) are spawned by inadequate space or antiquated conditions. Although this assumption is accurate in many instances, some progressive school systems also weigh carefully the degree to which educational objectives are being met and the extent to which the physical environment plays a positive or negative role in goal attainment.

Sustained and systematic curriculum planning are vital to sound facility planning. The most common approach to assessing educational programs is *curriculum evaluation*. Curriculum evaluation is essentially that segment of planning that focuses on what is currently occurring in a school. Schubert (1986) chronicled the evolution of this procedure in American education, correctly noting that the options for completing a curriculum evaluation are numerous. Included are such distinct practices as the use of teacher grades, goal-based evaluation, testing, and naturalistic evaluation.

There are three essential questions related to a school's curriculum: (1) exactly what is the curriculum, (2) how is it sequenced and implemented, and (3) to what extent is it successful? Answering these questions is more likely when a comprehensive evaluation system is employed. An inclusive assessment also creates a cyclical relationship among the three questions. For example, answers to the query regarding outcomes (i.e., to what degree are students meeting current objectives), automatically creates a data base for alterations to curricular content (what should be taught) and instructional methodology (how should it be taught). In general, curricular evaluation is a planning component pinpointing needs and guiding the selection of new materials, procedures, and organizational patterns (McNeil, 1985).

Entire graduate courses are devoted to the subjects of curriculum planning and evaluation. A complete discussion of these topics here is not practical. The administrator should realize, nevertheless, that curriculum evaluation is an indispensable element of educational facility planning. If one accepts the following two premises, the responsibility is fundamental:

1. *Form should follow function in school facilities.*
2. *The primary purpose of a school building is to enhance achievement of educational goals.*

Put simply, planning decisions for school buildings should be governed, first and foremost, by needs and wants related to the educational practices that will occur in the environment. Proceeding with a facility project in the absence of curriculum evaluation data abates the potentialities of even the best planning paradigm.

## SCHOOL FACILITY ASSESSMENT

A more specific form of assessment is the school building survey. Here the focus is upon an evaluation of a specific structure. The procedure is based upon a uniform rating of existing conditions against some established standard(s) (e.g., safety codes, recommended standards for schools). All assessments, whether for the site or for the building, should be based upon both qualitative and quantitative standards. Thus, for example, the report should clearly convey if there is an adequate number of classrooms, if the classrooms are of adequate size, and if the location and general condition of classrooms are acceptable.

The term "school facility assessment," can be misleading. In actuality, it is an evaluation of the site and facility. Common items to be assessed with regard to the site include:

- location
- relative freedom from noise and pollution
- relative freedom from hazards
- vehicular access
- pedestrian access
- size
- access to public utilities
- playgrounds
- sidewalks
- roads
- landscaping
- soil quality and drainage
- outdoor instructional capabilities (e.g., physical education, science)
- parking for faculty, guests
- security provisions (e.g., lighting, fencing)

This list is not intended to be exhaustive, but it does communicate the complexity of assessing the site itself.

Assessment of the school facility itself is also an entangled task. Every aspect of the building, from its exterior walls to the size of classrooms to the quality of corridors to the number of restrooms, needs to be included. Two contemporary dimensions of school facility assessment are: (1) determining whether the facility is barrier-free, and (2) whether the facility is void of asbestos problems.

School facility assessments are best completed by a team of experts including at least one architect and one educational consultant. Having a range of expertise permits mechanical and structural elements of the school to be evaluated along with the educational dimensions. Some commercial guides for school facility assessment are available (e.g., *Guide for School Facility Appraisal* by Hawkins and Lilley, 1986); however, the consumer should be aware that many code standards vary from one state to another. Therefore, the use of a commercially produced guide for facility assessment should be preceded by a careful examination of the qualitative and quantitative standards employed in the specific instrument.

A key element of facility assessment is the conscious linkage of these data to evaluative information produced by the curriculum assessment. Hawkins and Overbaugh (1988) developed an interface profile to express the desired relationship between a school environment and learning:

*Student Learning is enhanced when a facility:*

is an integral part of the community reflecting

- community pride
- community involvement
- broad utilization

is adaptable to the user's needs through

- a controllable physical environment
- provision for varied and ample storage
- flexible instructional space for teaching and learning styles
- walls, floor, fenestration that serve the learning process

permits teachers to function as professionals with

- a reasonable control of the learning environment
- space which permits work-related dialogue
- appropriate space for preparation of instruction
- a motivational environment conducive to professionalism

fosters communication

- through the appropriate use of technology
- through the use of "learning surfaces"
- about the school at points of entry
- that emphasizes student achievement
- that is demonstrated as important to students

creates an appropriate behavioral setting

- with an emphasis on aesthetics
- that encourages student interaction
- that provides a stimulating atmosphere for learning
- that is a comprehensive laboratory for learning

accommodates a variety of learning styles

- through hands-on experiences that result from building design
- that foster fine arts appreciation
- that result from student interaction
- through well-designed and well-equipped space
- that are related to individual needs and interest (p. 7)

School facilities are supposed to enhance the educational process—to be an asset. This relationship requires an awareness of (1) what the educational program is supposed to accomplish, (2) how these goals and objectives are to be accomplished, and (3) the degree to which they are being accomplished. Just in the past 30 years, American public schools have experienced a number of dramatic changes in curriculum and instructional procedures. From the post-Sputnik emphasis on science and mathematics to the era of mini-courses and open-concept schools in the late 1960s to the Back to Basics movement to the current era of reform and accountability, elementary and secondary schools have meandered between concerns for learning and concerns for social/psychological adjustment. Educational experts warned that school buildings erected in the 1960s and 1970s should be expected to accommodate decisive and abrupt alterations in programming priorities. In truth, most buildings were not designed to meet this challenge.

School facility surveys should produce data that reveal more than just information about the size of a school or its current state of repair. The evaluation should also generate judgments that permit an interface between the findings of the educational programming assessment and the evaluation of the environment.

## PERFORMANCE SPECIFICATIONS

The third component of comprehensive planning is the development of *performance specifications* (also referred to as *educational specifications*). Just as the needs assessment process identifies deficiencies in the school district, the performance specification document identifies the desired functions of an individual school. There is no universally accepted formula for completing this document, but in general, the effort should provide written statements about the educational program, extracurricular activities, and other intended uses which will permit the architects to begin design activities. This process is distinctively different from needs assessments. Whereas needs assessment may lead to a conclusion that a new facility is required, performance specifications outline what is desired in that facility (remember the distinction between needs and wants).

Every building project involves creating or reshaping spaces. Accordingly, the professionals who will work in the environment provide the primary source of input for the specifications. Most often the tasks of soliciting, collecting, and analyzing inputs are assigned to the educational consultant. The consultant meets with teachers and administrators and filters their wants through two screens: (1) educational feasibilities, and (2) financial feasibilities. Thus, the competent consultant does far more than collate employee "wish lists."

Some facility planning experts suggest the establishment of an educational specifications task force (The Council of Educational Facility Planners, 1985). This more elaborate process includes not only the consultant, but the architect, board of education, administration, and working committee as well. If this more comprehensive option is employed, it is critical that roles and responsibilities of each party are carefully defined. Time parameters also need to be considered since the use of a committee is likely to be more lengthy than relying upon the more standard option of using a single consultant.

The common elements of performance specifications include:

- a description of the project which addresses the issue of need
- a listing of control specifications (as discussed under systems analysis planning)
- statements regarding the overall educational program (curriculum, instruction, and extracurricular programs)
- a listing of grade levels and/or subjects to be accommodated
- a description of the purpose and objectives of each grade level or subject area
- a description of special uses of the facility (e.g., community uses)
- a listing of required spaces
- a description of spaces and the relationship of spaces
- identification of specifics for each space (e.g., lighting, seating, wall surfaces, floor surfaces, acoustical treatment, storage, chalkboards, display areas, etc.)
- a summary of space requirements
- an estimate of square footage for each area and the entire project.

In essence, this collective information constitutes a description of what is to occur in the school building.

Educational specifications are not supposed to provide design decisions. Teachers and administrators are often tempted to "play" architect and create drawings of what they want their work environment to be. Function, not design, is the nucleus of educational specifications. The specifications are expected to transmit to the design architect clear statements of what is expected to take place in the school environment. The architect then uses this information to generate potential designs.

Before becoming a final product, those who contributed information, especially the administrators, teachers, and staff involved, should have the opportunity to review the content of the specifications. Errors and misinterpretations should be corrected as a matter of course. Disagreements that are substantive, however, should be adjudicated between the superintendent and consultant. It is essential that the specifications document receive formal approval by the school board prior to being transmitted to the architects. This assures that the information is correct and is supported by the policy body of the school district.

## SUMMARY

Facility planning includes a multitude of tasks. The earliest stages are often the most difficult and cumbersome because they require extensive data that frequently are not viewed by administrators and school board members as critical. As such, there is a temptation to leap directly to the decision phase of planning for a school facility without first erecting a data base.

Assessment activities are divided into three categories: needs assessments; educational assessments; and performance specifications. Needs assessments are frequently completed as a component of school district strategic planning. They provide general information about needs for the entire school system, including facility needs. Educational assessments relate to curriculum evaluation. Determining the content of curriculum, the methodology for implementation, and the degree to which the curriculum meets its objectives are valuable inputs for individual school facility projects. Finally, educational specifications provide a statement outlining the expected activities within a facility. As such, they represent wants rather than needs; however, they are more accurately described as an amalgamation of wants and needs.

## ISSUES FOR DISCUSSION

1. What are the advantages and disadvantages of having a consultant identify the needs in a school district?

2. Identify the reasons why so many school districts do not engage in strategic planning.

3. Discuss the advantages and disadvantages of teachers and administrators visiting other schools prior to providing input for the development of educational specifications.

4. Defend the decision to use a community survey as part of assessment activities (or, take the opposite position).

5. Do you believe that most school districts wait too long before entering into facility projects (i.e., they only move forward once they are in a crisis or near crisis situation)?

6. Discuss the advantages and disadvantages of completing educational specifications for a new facility without the assistance of a consultant.

7. Why would a curriculum evaluation be important with regard to determining facility needs?

8. In addition to employing an educational consultant, what other options are available for completing educational specifications? What are the advantages and disadvantages of each of these approaches.

# 5

# THE ELEMENTARY
# SCHOOL

The grade organization of elementary schools (also called primary schools) has not remained constant in the United States. At one time, most of these schools included grades kindergarten through eight. As early as 1910, junior high schools, typically grades 7–9, emerged as a protest against the prevailing 8–4 organizational pattern. In many school systems, especially in urban areas, a 6–3–3 pattern evolved. Most recently, the popularity of the middle school has affected the organization of elementary schools. Since middle schools have varying grade configurations (e.g., 5–8; 6–8; 4–8; 7–8), their impact upon elementary schools varies from one district to another.

Ideally, curriculum and instructional strategies should be the factors determining a school's grade level parameters. In reality, this is the exception rather than the rule. Fluctuations in enrollments and economic considerations are commonly the catalysts spawning grade reorganization. A school district experiencing growth in enrollment, for example, may find it convenient and fiscally feasible to change grade configurations to accommodate an increased number of students rather than building another school. Imagine a school district with three K–6 elementary schools, a 7–8 middle school, and a 9–12 high school. The middle school has a capacity of 800 but only 500 are currently enrolled. By changing the middle school to a 6–8 organizational pattern, the superintendent is able to create space in the elementary schools by removing the sixth grades from them (the elementaries now become K–5). In selecting this option, the superintendent is able to accommodate the enrollment growth without building another elementary school or expanding any of the existing facilities. Such examples of reorganization are not uncommon.

Today, there are numerous grade groupings within schools that are labeled "elementary." They range all the way from kindergarten centers (schools which house only the grade of kindergarten) to some remaining K–8 schools. The K–6 configuration continues to be the most popular, although K–5 schools are gaining, largely due to the middle school concept. During the 1960s and early 1970s, there was a great deal of experimentation at the elementary school level. Much of this activity was spawned by national concerns (e.g., the war in Viet Nam, concern for social justice). This experimentation included attempted alterations to the organizational patterns of elementary schools. By the start of the 1980s, however, the organizational experimentation resulting from philosophical factors slowed considerably (Jarolimek & Foster, 1981).

Historically, elementary school facilities have not received the attention or fiscal support given to secondary schools. In fact, many elementary schools in existence today are dated structures that were originally erected as high schools and converted to elementary schools as new high schools came into existence. Two reasons for this condition are quite prevalent. Many educators and citizens view the elementary school as having less complex environmental needs (i.e., a standard classroom is the basic unit of space and a relatively small number of special spaces is required). In a secondary school, by contrast, a number of special areas is needed (e.g., laboratories, shops, and the like). This reality permits conversions of secondary schools to elementaries for less cost than the reverse. In addition, a high school is often the "showpiece" of a school system. When a school district is faced with several facility projects, it is probable that the high school needs will be addressed first.

## CURRENT CURRICULA AND INSTRUCTIONAL PRACTICES

The needs of a modern elementary school are best expressed by its curriculum and instructional strategies. Although many still function using the self-contained classroom concept (i.e., a teacher teaching multiple subjects in the same classroom), that trend is being modified by new initiatives and the inclusion of additional subjects in the elementary school program. No single pattern of organization, either for grade levels or for curriculum, fits all situations in elementary schools. The needs and abilities of students, along with available resources and the educational environment (the facility), combine to determine the best organizational approach (Wiles & Bondi, 1984).

As previously described, educational philosophy (values and beliefs about education) does not remain constant. As a result, American education experiences changes in programming practices that eventually have implications for facilities. Ideally, facility design and programming initiatives ought to be intertwined. But this is not always the case. Perhaps the best example of inadequate linkage between educational philosophy and facility design is found in the *open concept school*. In the late 1960s and early 1970s, many new elementary schools were designed to be open environments where children would sense warmth and be spared the "closed" feeling attributed to institutional-like structures. Thus, interior walls were essentially removed. This design was adopted from national programs that were being advocated by innovative educators. But opening up school environments was often not accompanied by changes in philosophy or teaching methods at the school district or at individual school levels. The faculty in some elementary schools continued to teach the standard curriculum using their standard methods but did so in a nontraditional environment. By the late 1970s, the national focus on schooling was altered in the direction of increased accountability and open schools came under even more intense criticism (e.g., they were perceived as noisy, permissive, and unstructured environments). This example illustrates the extent to which philosophy, curriculum, instruction, and facility planning are interrelated.

## Curriculum

The core of an elementary school curriculum has not changed much in the past four or five decades. Language arts (reading, writing), mathematics, science, and social studies remain the essential components. Elementary schools also offer instruction in physical education, health, art, and general music. Most often the elementary school emphasizes a vertical structure to subject matter. That is, the curriculum is based upon grade levels and children are exposed to new subject matter as they move upward in grade placement. In some schools, emphasis is placed on both vertical and horizontal curricular organization. Horizontal patterns concentrate on the distribution of subject matter at the same grade or age level (Shepard & Ragan, 1982). Three relatively new components found in some schools are computer science, foreign language, and instrumental music. Many elementary schools also offer programming in special education. The most commonly identified programs in this area are for the mentally handicapped, speech and hearing impaired, emotionally disturbed, and learning disabled (a rapidly growing program).

Specialized programming for gifted and talented students has become increasingly popular in the United States in the past ten years. These programs can be based upon acceleration and/or enrichment of the curriculum and are operated either in a self-contained classroom or in a resource room. Gifted and talented education will be one of the rapid growth areas for schools in the next decade.

## Instruction

Although the self-contained classroom remains the norm in elementary schools, departmentalized teaching is one variation growing in popularity. In a departmentalized format, children do not remain with the same teacher for all subjects. One teacher in fifth grade, for example, may teach all of the mathematics while another teaches science and yet another teaches language arts. Departmentalized formats can, and often do, affect facility needs for an elementary school. For example, departmentalized instruction may require that one classroom be designed as a science laboratory.

Instructional aides are being used with greater frequency in grades K–6. This is partially the result of special initiatives, such as Chapter One programs, that provide supplemental fiscal resources. Most existing elementary buildings were not designed in anticipation of aides working with individual students or small groups. As a result, aides are often forced to work in hallways, under stairs, or in other undesirable and congested spaces.

Instructional practices in an elementary school typically fall into three realms: (1) class instruction, (2) small group instruction, and (3) individual instruction (one instructor and one student). Less common is large group instruction where two or more classes may be combined. Ability grouping within classrooms remains a common practice in the elementary schools (Hessong & Weeks, 1987). It is estimated that about 77 percent of all school districts engage in some form of grouping (Drake & Roe, 1986). This instructional practice requires that space within the classroom environment be flexible and adaptable. Grouping is most often done on the basis of achievement and ability levels, but is also done occasionally for other reasons (e.g., special interests, special projects). One form of grouping that is experiencing popularity is cooperative learning. In this format, groups are structured heterogeneously rather than homogeneously so that students with varying abilities and needs can help each other (Johnson et al., 1984). Regardless of the criterion for grouping, the facility planner must recognize that the practice of small group instruction is prevalent in elementary school environments.

Specialized instruction in art, music, and physical education has increased in popularity. This popularity is more than a passing fancy. Changing values and lifestyles in American society create the need for cultural and physical activities in the curriculum. As a result, more and more elementary schools employ specially prepared teachers in art, music, and physical education. Since virtually every elementary school has a gymnasium, specialized instruction in physical education does not typically generate additional space needs. The conditions for art and music are quite different. Frequently, specialized instruction in these subjects is restrained or prevented by space restrictions.

The newest instructional practice in elementary schools involves supplementing curricular experiences in mathematics and language arts (and possibly other subjects) with computers. The proliferation of computer usage in schools is attributable to a number of circumstances, but among the more prominent are: (1) the availability of the microcomputer, and (2) the organizational support systems that have emerged to assist teachers who employ computers in their instructional activities (Baker, 1982). A modern elementary school should have a computer laboratory large enough to permit an entire class (up to about 26 students) to receive instruction simultaneously. Where this is not possible, effort should be made to put several microcomputers in the regular classroom environment.

## SPACES WITHIN AN ELEMENTARY SCHOOL

Spaces in an elementary school can be divided into three categories. The first includes standard classrooms (kindergarten through upper grade levels). The second is special instruction areas such as art, music, physical education, and the media center. The last category is made up of those spaces providing general support services for the school (e.g., administration, cafeteria). The descriptions of these areas presented here are not intended to be exhaustive. They do, nevertheless, profile the range of rooms found in an elementary school.

Before examining each of these three categories, it is helpful to review certain considerations that apply to all instructional spaces in a modern school. The more cogent ones are listed here:

- All instructional areas require adequate electrical outlets. Many older schools were not designed to accommodate the use of audio-visual equipment and computers. Although the quantity of outlets needed will vary depending upon function, at least two double outlets on each wall are recommended.

- The use of interactive television is a growing practice in organized education. New facilities should have coaxial cable and fiber optics installed in original construction. If this is not possible, at the very least the conduit required for subsequent installation should be included in the original design.

- All instructional areas require light control. This includes control of natural and artificial light.

- Air conditioning is highly recommended for most climates. Lengthening of the school year and greater use of school facilities by communities are but two of the reasons for this feature. Increasingly, teachers are also requesting windows (with screens) that can be opened to permit ventilation at times when mechanical cooling is not warranted.

- Storage is usually a problem for most teachers and administrators. Modern schools should provide ample storage to accommodate the increasing amount of equipment and materials used in the instructional and extracurricular programs.

- It is common practice to keep classrooms housing the same grade level clustered. Thus, all first-grade rooms should be located in the same area of the facility unless there exist compelling reasons to do otherwise. Likewise, primary grades are typically kept in one part of the building while intermediate grades are in another.

- Every school should have some flexibility of space to accommodate large group instruction. An acoustically treated movable wall between two standard classrooms is the most common method of meeting this requirement.

### Standard Classrooms

*Kindergarten classrooms* should be different from standard classrooms. They ought to be larger and provide flexible space. Separate student restrooms are highly advisable in kindergartens (i.e., separate rooms designed within the classroom which are accessed without leaving the classroom). A carpeted area adds to the warmth of the room and permits students to sit on the floor for certain activities. Most kindergarten rooms have a special area permitting the teacher to read to all of the students at the same time (e.g., either a story pit or risers in one of the corners). A sink and counter space are commonly included and provisions for students' coats, boots, and the like are most often provided directly in the classroom environment. Kindergarten rooms are generally designed to accommodate 18 to 25 students at a given time. Accordingly, a room of approximately 1,100 to 1,300 square feet is needed. Increasingly, kindergarten programs are infusing readiness activities, such as penmanship into the curriculum. Chalkboard, at least half of which is permanently lined, is a common feature. It is also noteworthy that kindergarten is generally a half-day program; thus, two sections occupy a single room each day (an A.M. kindergarten and a P.M. kindergarten). Since all-day kindergarten is a possibility for the future, expansibility should be considered in the original design. That is, additional kindergartens can be built as part of an addition so that they will be next to the existing kindergarten rooms. Easy access to transportation areas and the playgrounds is also a prime consideration with regard to location within the facility.

Regular classrooms are used for grades above kindergarten. In the primary grades (grades 1 and 2), special attention is given to including some permanently lined chalkboard and placement of chalkboards and counter space at appropriate heights. Many school administrators and teachers desire separate restrooms in the classrooms for the primary grades, especially for first grade. Coat storage is most often provided in the classroom environment; some elementary schools, however, do opt for hall lockers. Regular classrooms in an elementary school are usually designed to accommodate approximately 25 students and are usually about 800 to 1,000 square feet.

## Special Instructional Spaces

Two frequently identified special instructional spaces in an elementary school are art and music rooms. Not all schools that use special teachers in these areas have special rooms. Where these rooms are lacking, the teachers simply move from classroom to classroom to provide instruction. It is far more desirable to have rooms designed especially for art and music for at least two reasons: (1) the teacher does not have to limit instructional activities based upon equipment that can be moved from classroom to classroom, and (2) the additional rooms tend to reduce overall utilization levels within the school, providing greater programming flexibility. Some educators also contend that separate art and music rooms provide a transitional experience for young children that prepares them to eventually encounter departmentalized instruction.

An art room in an elementary school functions best with ample storage. The room ought to be located so as to provide relatively easy access for all children in the building. Access for the youngest children is especially important. Carpeting is usually avoided in this room and the inclusion of a kiln is becoming quite common. Art rooms should have at least two sinks. One accommodates the need of children to wash their hands and the other accommodates the cleaning of equipment and materials. Artificial and natural lighting are also important considerations. Art rooms generally are between 1,000 and 1,500 square feet (depending on whether an office and/or a separate storage room is included). Some art rooms are designed to provide direct access between the room and the outdoors. This design feature facilitates outdoor drawing and other activities that may be part of the curriculum.

Music rooms in elementary schools vary markedly depending upon the scope of programming. Beyond general music instruction, some elementary schools depend upon this space for instrumental music. When both general and instrumental music are taught in the same room, it is not uncommon to incorporate several small practice rooms into the music complex. Some instructors prefer to have risers in the room while others do not. If flexibility is a high priority, portable risers may be advisable (as opposed to the fixed type). The music room should be located away from low noise areas in the school, yet should not be isolated to the extent that the smaller children will have difficulty finding it. Often music rooms are located next to the facility having a stage (e.g., the gym, an auditorium) to accommodate special shows. Elementary school music rooms also vary in size from about 900 to 1,500 square feet depending upon the features provided.

A third specialized instructional space that is becoming common in elementary schools is the computer laboratory. This area ought to be designed to accommodate an entire class at one given time. Thus, a laboratory usually includes about 26 stations. Writing boards made for felt-tipped pens are often preferred to chalkboards in these rooms because they do not generate chalk dust. A central location in the building is usually preferred; perhaps the most common placement of the computer laboratory is next to the media center. A computer laboratory is generally about 900 to 1,100 square feet.

Other special areas include the speech and hearing clinic and special education classrooms. Rooms used to house self-contained special education programs such as those for the learning disabled or the mentally handicapped are generally about 900 square feet. Classrooms housing programs for more severe disabilities ought to have a self-contained restroom(s). If special education classes function in a resource room, they are generally about half the size of a regular classroom. Speech and hearing clinics range from about 150 to 300 square feet, as anywhere from one to seven students may be receiving therapy at any given time.

By far the most common instructional support space in an elementary school is the library or media center. Although the terms "library" and "media center" are used interchangeably by most educators, the latter term refers to a comprehensive program that includes both library functions and media services (e.g., audio-visual equipment, films). The elementary school media centers vary markedly in size and design; however, the following spaces are common:

- an office for library/media personnel (especially for the director)
- a workroom for repairs, cataloguing, and so forth
- a storage room for audio-visual and other materials
- a main reading room (library)
- a storytelling area in the main reading room

A media center should be a focal point within a school. It should be a warm and inviting area—clearly transmitting the message that learning is both pleasurable and important. A central location is generally recommended unless instructional strategies suggest an alternative. One consideration that deserves special attention is whether the media center should be designed as an "open" or "closed" space. An open media center is designed so that access is gained without going through doors—meaning that there are virtually no walls. The advantage of this approach is that it gives an inviting appearance to the area. The disadvantage is that it presents security problems. Both open and closed designs are widely used in elementary schools, and principals and librarians usually have a strong preference as to which option should be used in their school. Media centers vary markedly in size in an elementary school. Some may be as large as 2,500 square feet. As a standard rule, it is recommended that a minimum of 10 percent of the school's enrollment be able to sit in the library at any given time.

One option for meeting the space needs of instructional aides is the creation of an instructional support complex. This space, usually adjoining the media center, provides offices and instructional rooms where teachers and aides can work with children individually or in small groups. This concept is especially popular in schools where teachers prefer that the aides work with children outside of the regular classroom environment. If such a complex is included in the design, it should provide flexible spaces to meet a variety of special needs.

Virtually all elementary schools have a gymnasium. This area serves at least two major functions: (1) a space for instruction in physical education, and (2) a space for recreation (indoor recess or intramural sports). Budgetary considerations cause many school districts to utilize the concept of a multipurpose room instead of the standard gymnasium. A multipurpose room usually is designed to accommodate the combined functions of a gymnasium and cafeteria. For instance, the room is used as a gym except during those time periods when meals are being served. Although this concept has definite financial benefits, it does restrict educational programming—and the larger the school's enrollment, the more restrictive it is. In some instances, the multipurpose area serves a third function. By including a stage, the area is also used for plays, assemblies, and the like.

Critical questions related to an elementary gymnasium include:

- Will the facility be used by individuals other than the school population (e.g., athletic practices for middle and high schools, community recreation programs)?
- Is spectator seating required? If yes, in what amount? (Note: Spectator seating is often justified in order to hold student assemblies in the gymnasium. Having one area where the entire student body can be assembled is recommended.)
- What type of floor surface should be used (wood, synthetic, tile, carpeting)?
- Should locker rooms be provided?
- Should a faculty office be provided?
- How much storage area is required?

There are additional questions pertaining to items such as lighting, a scoreboard, bulletin boards, and water fountains. The size of the elementary gymnasium depends upon several factors including whether or not a standard basketball court is specified, whether seating is required, whether locker rooms and storage are included, and the scope of programs that are to occur in this space. Since most elementary schools do not have an auditorium, a stage is usually placed in a gymnasium so that special programs can occur there. If a permanent stage is not included, a portable stage is recommended. The location of the gymnasium should take into consideration access to the outdoors, isolation from the low noise areas of the facility, and security zoning if the facility is to be used during evenings and/or weekends.

### General Support Area

The *cafeteria* is one of the more obvious general support areas in a school. Unless a school has a multipurpose room, separate dining facilities for the children and faculty/staff are required. Increasingly, new schools include a dining room for adults. This permits teachers and staff to be away from the children for at least a small part of the day. Key questions related to a cafeteria include: Will food be prepared on-site or satellited from elsewhere? How many lunch periods will there be—or what should be the capacity of the cafeteria? What type of service lines need to be designed? How many individuals will work in the food service operation? Will the cafeteria serve purposes other than dining; if so, what are they?

Other questions about access, types of tables, storage, wall surfaces and the like are equally important. The cafeteria should be located away from low noise areas and provide relatively easy access to the outdoors since children often go directly to the playground after lunch.

Many older schools were designed without areas specifically designated for teacher workrooms and lounges. In a contemporary elementary school, a workroom should be considered a necessity rather than a luxury. The work day of the elementary teacher is complex and demanding. Faculty members need an area where they can prepare materials and lessons and have access to support literature (books, journals). The inclusion of specialized teachers (art, music, physical education) generates some released time for regular classroom teachers, and this situation makes a workroom an even more necessary concept. In many schools, a single room is designated as a workroom/lounge. Where possible, this concept should be avoided. The workroom should be an environment which is quiet and the lounge should be a place for casual conversation and relaxation.

The *administrative complex* is another visible support area. This typically includes the principal's office (and possibly an office for an assistant principal), a reception area, a workroom, adult restrooms, a conference room, a bookstore/storage area, a guidance office, and a health suite. The *health suite* houses the school nurse and provides space for children who become ill at school. A restroom(s) is required in this area. At least two privacy areas for sick students should be included. In many states the school nurse is charged with the responsibility of conducting vision testing. In planning a health suite, a determination should be made if this testing will occur in this specific area. If so, adequate space for such testing must be provided.

The administrative complex should also provide space for record-keeping (files and other materials), and a fireproof safe is highly desirable. The administrative complex is centrally located near the main entrance to the school unless there is a compelling reason to do otherwise.

*Restrooms* should be properly dispersed throughout the school. Typically, student restrooms are designed to permit the primary grades to use one set and the intermediate grades to use another. This allows the fixtures to accommodate the physical size of the children. Adult restrooms are also necessary so that faculty, staff, and visitors are not forced to use student restrooms. The number of facilities required for students in an elementary school may be determined using the following formula developed by Hawkins & Lilley, (1986):

**Lavatories:**

1 for every 30 students if total enrollment is below 300

1 for every 40 students if total enrollment is above 300

**Water Closets:**

1 for every 40 boys plus 1 urinal for every 30 boys

1 for every 35 girls

Other areas that must be considered for an elementary school include a *mechanical/service area, general storage,* and *articulation spaces* (hallways). The actual development of these spaces becomes less cumbersome when an educational consultant and architect participate in the planning. Table 5.1 provides a summary of recommended space requirements for elementary schools. Keep in mind that actual needs will vary depending upon the size and location of the school. School districts must meet codes for their respective states, and this factor alone can cause significant variance in standards for room sizes.

### Special Considerations

Three additional points deserve mention with regard to elementary school environments. One is the variance in the physical stature of children who occupy the school. A kindergarten student, for example, could weigh as little as 46 pounds. By contrast, a sixth grader could weigh over 160 pounds—over three times as much. Likewise, a small kindergarten student may be less than four feet tall, while a sixth grader could be over five feet-eight inches. These are significant differences that deserve more than casual reflection in designing the school.

**Table 5.1**
**Summary of Recommended Room Sizes for an Elementary School**

| room | suggested size in sq. ft. | comments |
|---|---|---|
| kindergarten | 1,000 to 1,300 | includes restrooms |
| standard classroom | 800 to 1,000 | based upon 25 pupils |
| art room | 1,000 to 1,500 | depends on office/storage |
| music room | 900 to 1,200 | depends on office/practice rooms |
| media center | 1,300 to 1,800 | depends on special features |
| computer laboratory | 900 to 1,100 | depends on class size, office area |
| gymnasium | 6,000 to 8,000 | depends on seating, locker rooms |
| instructional support area | 800 to 1,600 | depends on number of units |
| cafeteria | 12 sq. ft. p/pupil | kitchen/storage areas not included |
| learning disability | 900 | if self contained |
| learning disability | 400 to 600 | if resource room |
| mentally handicapped | 900 to 1,100 | depends upon class size & restrooms |
| speech and hearing clinic | 150 to 300 | depends on size of therapy groups |
| administration | | |
| principal's office | 200 to 250 | should have 2 entry/exits |
| reception area | 250 to 450 | depends on number of secretaries |
| health suite | 400 to 700 | depends on size of school |
| other offices | 120 to 150 | asst. principal; counselor |
| conference room | 250 to 400 | depends on size desired |

Such consideration is especially needed for the common areas of the building that all students are likely to use.

Second, elementary schools are definitely becoming larger and more costly in most parts of the United States. They are becoming larger because of the addition of specialized facilities such as computer laboratories and guidance offices. There are many existing elementary schools that have about 100 square feet per pupil. Today, some elementary schools reach 160 or 170 square feet per pupil— a size that used to be considered appropriate for a high school. Space allocations within a school, regardless of whether an elementary or secondary school, are the products of more than curricular decisions. Geographic location also plays a part in determining total school size. In warm, rural areas, for example, some schools might have as little as 80 square feet per pupil. By contrast, some schools in cold, urban areas have more than 200 square feet per pupil (Brubaker, 1988).

In an era of unstable enrollments, administrators and board members frequently inquire about the optimum size for an elementary school. Unfortunately, there is no magic formula. Size, the third issue deserving mention, is a factor subject to differing values and beliefs. Two questions serve to guide this critical decision: (1) Is the school large enough to permit flexibility with curriculum and instructional grouping?, and (2) Is the school so large that it becomes a threat for some students or limits student participation in school functions?

In general, elementary schools that have between two and four sections per grade level present the best mix with regard to these queries. Spencer (1988) believes that elementary schools should be somewhat larger and states that they are most effective when they are between 500 and 700 pupils. There are many excellent elementary schools that have but one section per grade level and others that have as many as five or six. When a school is smaller than two sections per grade level or larger than four, some measures can be taken to compensate for potential problems. For example, providing special teachers (art, music, physical education) is more expensive if it is done in a one-section school than in a three-section school, yet a school board may be willing to make this commitment in deciding to erect a one-section school in order to assure that the children will not be deprived of services.

Young children should find school to be warm and inviting. The issue of size ought to be reviewed thoroughly in the early stages of planning. Keep in mind that elementary schools, more so than secondary schools, retain neighborhood identities. For this reason, the size of the school can be affected by community usage of the building and political considerations (e.g., a strong desire by the taxpayers to keep the school in the neighborhood). Comprehensive needs assessment activities should reveal both the needs of the children and the needs of the community to the planners. Far too often, these inputs do not receive ample consideration, and under such conditions, cost often becomes the sole determining factor related to size decisions.

## SUMMARY

There is no standard organizational pattern for elementary schools. They range from centers that house only kindergarten programs to some remaining K–8 facilities. Curriculum is broadening in many elementary schools. Foreign language, computer literacy, and instrumental music are three examples of expansion. Instructional methodology also is dynamic. Grouping remains a prevalent practice; however, other forms of instruction are also used. Unique instructional programs for students with special needs are becoming much more common as well (e.g., in areas such as learning disabilities and gifted and talented education).

Much of an elementary school is composed of standard classrooms. Specialized spaces, such as computer laboratories and art rooms, have emerged in the past two decades. As a result, elementary schools are becoming more elaborate and more costly. The design of an elementary school should take into account several critical factors. Philosophy, curriculum, instructional methods, desired location, and cost are some of the more important. Since elementary schools tend to have distinct neighborhood identities, the political realities associated with this linkage ought not be overlooked in making planning decisions.

## ISSUES FOR DISCUSSION

1. Why is it so difficult to define the elementary school today?
2. Discuss why many communities tend to place more emphasis on high school facilities than they do on elementary school facilities.
3. What factors influenced the grade organization of elementary schools in the United States? That is, why were some K–8, some K–6?
4. Discuss the differences between horizontal and vertical articulation in an elementary school curriculum. How does each affect the facility needs of a school?
5. What were the beliefs and values that gave rise to the open concept school? What caused a decline in its popularity?
6. Discuss the advantages and disadvantages of providing both a teachers' lounge and a teachers' workroom in an elementary school.
7. Discuss the merits of elementary schools below two sections per grade level and those above four sections per grade level.
8. State your philosophy regarding the ideal grade organization and curriculum for an elementary school.
9. Why is the identification with neighborhoods so prevalent among elementary schools?
10. Should political considerations ever determine facility decisions?

# 6

# SECONDARY SCHOOLS

The purpose of this chapter is to explore the more important aspects of secondary schools as they relate to facility planning. One should keep in mind that an exhaustive review of all such programs and needs would simply be too lengthy for a book of this type. The material here focuses upon key topics that usually fall within the planning process.

Secondary schools are identified by three common labels in the United States: middle schools, junior high schools, and high schools. Technically, there is a fourth category—the combined junior–senior high school that still exists in rural or less populated areas. Some high schools are known as "senior high schools," differentiating them from junior high schools. Secondary schools do not have standard grade organizations. The determinants of organization include factors such as size, philosophy, economics, tradition, and available facilities. Accordingly, some high schools include grades 9–12; others include grades 10–12; and still others might include only grades 11–12. Likewise, junior high schools may include grades 7–9, only grades 7–8, or only grades 8–9. Schools using the title of middle school are more likely to include one or more grades below the common starting point of the traditional junior high school (e.g., 5–8; 6–8).

Primarily because of the diversity of curricula (including all experiences provided by the school), secondary schools are usually more expensive to erect than elementary schools. Size also plays a critical role in facility cost. Senior high schools usually have the largest enrollments of any of the attendance centers in a district; thus, they simply are larger buildings. This chapter examines the curricula and instructional practices of these schools.

## THE SCHOOLS IN THE MIDDLE

The junior high school emerged as the result of several major studies of the vertical organization of schooling. One of the most influential of these study groups was the Commission on the Reorganization of Secondary Education which concluded in its report, issued in 1918, that American schools should move away from the 8–4 pattern to a 6–6 configuration (i.e., six years of elementary education and six years of secondary education). The junior high school was advanced largely by the following arguments:

1. they would provide a more suitable environment for young adolescents;
2. students in seventh and eighth grades would be exposed to a broader curriculum;
3. the students would have better opportunities to participate in activities;
4. students would study with teachers who have more in-depth preparation in subject areas (i.e., more so than in K–8 elementary schools);
5. students would receive better guidance services; and
6. the schools would offer a better transition period from the self-contained classroom to departmentalized teaching (Anderson & Van Dyke, 1963).

Junior high schools emerged throughout the United States, especially as school districts reorganized to become larger administrative units. Merging two or more school districts was a difficult task and political considerations played an important role. A common compromise was to allow elementary and junior high schools to remain in their current locations (the respective communities) and to erect a centrally located high school to serve the reorganized district.

Eventually, critics charged that junior high schools had become miniature versions of high schools. The organization of subject matter, teaching methods, administrative practices, and even extracurricular activities were modeled from high schools. Of more importance junior high schools were often perceived as less desirable working environments than high schools. Students in grades 7, 8, and 9 exhibit tremendous diversity in maturation levels (and behavior). This situation creates a wide range of student needs both inside and outside of the classroom. Many teachers and administrators accept positions in these schools in hopes of eventually "moving up" to the high school level. Many teach as though they were in a high school, further fueling charges that the junior high school fails to provide the desired transition between the self-contained elementary school and the diverse curricula of the high school.

In the early 1970s, American education was experiencing unstable conditions, due largely to an outgrowth of social-political concerns that led to the questioning of values, priorities, and even the basic purposes of long-standing institutions. It was during this era of introspection that the middle school grew in popularity. Some argue that the emergence of the concept was the unintended product of two circumstances: first, a growing dissatisfaction with the junior high school, which encouraged educators to seek alternatives, and second, economic and demographic manifestations which made the reorganization of schools possible. Some observers of the advent of the middle school noted that these schools came into being more for administrative reasons than for educational initiatives (e.g., Alexander & Kealy, 1969). And even today, economic considerations more often than philosophical convictions spawn the creation of middle schools (Schubert, 1986). Despite this reality, the middle school abounds with potential. The ideals on which the concept is based are challenging and interesting and provide unlimited potentialities (Henson, 1988).

When middle schools are the product of expediency rather than educational planning, they often do not differ much from junior high schools. Observers sadly note that many existing middle schools do not exemplify the ideals and standards advanced in professional journals and books as the very foundation of this concept. Principles such as integration, exploration, guidance, differentiation, socialization, and articulation recur in writings supporting the concept, yet these qualities are not always present in middle schools. When discussing the junior high school and the middle school, the facility planner must recognize this condition. From an educational perspective, the middle school is intended to be a truly unique entity; in reality, many middle schools planned and designed in the absence of purposeful educational objectives are, de facto, junior high schools.

## Curriculum and Instruction

The curricula of junior high schools and middle schools essentially consist of two components: (1) required courses and (2) electives. In most states, a good portion of the curriculum is mandated by state requirements (laws and regulations). The elective courses are at times referred to as exploratory courses. Typically, students are required to take social studies, language arts, mathematics, science, physical education and health. Additional courses common at the middle level schools include art, music, foreign language, home economics, typing, and industrial education (technology). Since these schools vary widely in purpose and scope, the planner must be extremely careful to identify all aspects of the curriculum. The extracurricular programs of junior high schools are usually well developed and reflect a range of athletic and club activities. Middle schools may also have this broad range of opportunities; however, some middle schools deemphasize competitiveness to allow more students to participate in extracurricular activities.

Instructionally, schools in the middle exhibit marked differences from elementary schools. Departmentalized teaching replaces the self-contained classroom. In some junior high schools and middle schools, the concept of core classes is employed. Core classes, sometimes referred to as block-time scheduling, entails combining two or more subject areas. For example, social studies and language arts are combined and the student is assigned the same teacher for both subjects in a single block of time. Mathematics and science are likewise often joined. The core class provides a transition between the self-contained classroom and departmentalized teaching.

There is a conscious attempt to make the learner more independent after the elementary school. As a result, individual learning activities are emphasized and individual student use of special resources such as the media center becomes more prevalent. In elementary schools, ability grouping usually occurs within classrooms. In the schools in the middle, ability grouping is usually accomplished by arranging separate classes based upon student needs (e.g., there might be three different levels of eighth grade mathematics). The junior high school and the middle school were centers of instructional experimentation during the 1960s and 1970s. Team teaching and non-graded concepts were two ideas that were tried during that era. Although some of these instructional approaches continue today, many schools have returned to more traditional teaching methods and organizational patterns.

Contemporary schools in the middle are putting forth additional effort to address the needs of all students, especially those at the ends of the continuum. Special education programming is broadening and new programs for the gifted and talented are emerging. One outgrowth of more specialized instruction is the need for more diverse instructional spaces.

### Space Needs

Because the scope of programming becomes more complex after elementary school, schools in the middle require more square feet per pupil than schools relying upon self-contained classrooms. As might be expected, space requirements for middle schools are continuing to increase. Among the factors driving this escalation are the addition of computer laboratories, a more diverse curriculum, equal opportunities for girls in extracurricular activities, more student support services (e.g., guidance, social work), and a demand for more diversified extracurricular activities. An average of 160 to 180 square feet per pupil in a contemporary middle school is not uncommon.

Table 6.1 identifies some basic considerations for the various spaces in a middle school. Subjects that utilize standard classrooms obviously entail less complicated considerations.

Specificity of program needs is appropriately developed through careful planning on a project-to-project basis. This is why a comprehensive set of educational specifications should be developed for every new or renovated facility. Generalizations about special environmental needs is a particularly risky planning tactic. Assuming that features viewed in other schools will suffice in planning a new plant often results in disappointments or serious utilization problems. Table 6.2 contains recommended space allocations for a middle school. Table 6.3 contains additional recommendations regarding spaces for a secondary school.

**Table 6.1**
**Considerations for Middle School Instructional Spaces**

| Space | Considerations |
| --- | --- |
| language arts & social studies | what courses are included; will there be core periods; extent of special instruction |
| mathematics | what courses are included; need for computer lab; will there be core periods; extent of special instruction |
| science | what courses are included; what types of laboratories are required; number of teaching stations in each lab; scope of security and storage provisions; will there be core periods |
| art | scope of the curriculum; number of students enrolling at each grade level; special equipment and design considerations; number of student stations in the room; office and storage provisions |
| music | need for instrumental and vocal rooms; scope of the curriculum; number of students enrolling at each grade level and each course; special equipment and design considerations; number of students to be accommodated at any given time; storage and office areas; practice rooms |
| home economics | number and type of laboratories required; scope of the curriculum; number of teaching stations in each lab; number of students enrolling in each grade level and each course; special equipment and design considerations; storage and office area |
| industrial education | special shops vs. unit shops; scope of the curriculum; number of teaching stations shops; number of students enrolling in each grade/each course; special equipment and design of spaces; storage/office area; security/safety |

**Table 6.2**
**Suggested Space Requirements: Middle School**

| area/room | space required (sq. ft.) | comments |
|---|---|---|
| standard classroom | 900 | |
| art room | 1,200-1,500 | depends on storage/office |
| science labs | 900-1,100 | depends on storage in room |
| home economics | | |
| foods | 1,000-1,300 | depends on number of stations |
| clothing | 1,000-1,200 | depends on number of stations |
| combined | 1,200-1,500 | depends on number of stations |
| computer lab | 900-1,100 | depends on number of stations |
| music | | |
| instrumental | 1,200-1,600 | may need risers |
| vocal | 1,100-1,400 | may need risers |
| practice room(s) | 50-125 | depends on individual or group |
| office | 100-150 | |
| storage | 300-500 | depends on total amount stored |
| physical education | | |
| gymnasium | 7,000-8,000 | depends on seating and number teaching |

station

| | | |
|---|---|---|
| locker rooms | 400-600 (each) | |
| office | 150-300 | depends on number sharing space |
| storage | 400-600 | |

industrial education

| | | |
|---|---|---|
| unit shop | 1,700-2,000 | a general shop area |
| wood shop | 1,400-1,600 | depends on number of stations |
| metal shop | 1,400-1,600 | depends on number of stations |

media center

| | | |
|---|---|---|
| reading room | 10-15 percent of student body at 25 square feet p/pupil | |
| office | 120-200 | |
| workroom | 120-300 | |
| storage | 250-500 | |

| | | |
|---|---|---|
| cafeteria | 12-16 square feet p/pupil seated at one time | |
| speech therapy | 250-300 | |

auditorium

| | | |
|---|---|---|
| stage | 1,500-1,800 | |
| seating | 10 square feet p/occupant | |

**Table 6.3**
**Size Guidelines for Spaces in a High School**

| area/room | recommended size (sq. ft.) | comments |
|---|---|---|
| standard classroom | 800-900 | |
| art | 1,400-2,000 | depends on storage/office; whether there is more than one art room |
| science | | |
| biology lab | 1,000-1,300 | depends on number of stations |
| chemistry | 1,000-1,300 | depends on number of stations |
| physics | 1,000-1,200 | depends on number of stations |
| physics/chemistry | 1,300-1,600 | combined for small school, |
| physical science | 1,000-1,200 | earth science |
| storage | about 10 percent of classroom/lab spaces | |
| music | | |
| instrumental | 1,400-2,000 | depends on size of program |
| vocal | 1,200-1,800 | depends on size of program |
| practice rooms | 50-150 | individual or group |
| storage | 500-700 | for instruments, uniforms, etc. |
| office | 100-200 | |
| physical education | | |
| gymnasium | 8,000-10,000 | depends on seating; number teaching stations |
| auxiliary gym | 5,000-6,000 | |
| athletic locker rooms | 700-900 | at least two needed |
| p.e. locker rooms | 700-900 | at least two needed |
| office | 200-350 | depends on number sharing |
| storage | 500-800 | should accommodate large equipment |
| wrestling room | 600-900 | proper ventilation required |
| weight room | 300-600 | avoid wood floors |
| training room | 250-400 | access to locker rooms |
| industrial technology | | |
| unit shop concept | 2,500-5,000 | all shops in one area |
| wood shop | 1,600-2,000 | depends on number of stations |
| metals shop | 1,600-2,000 | depends on number of stations |
| electronics | 1,100-1,500 | depends on number of stations |
| drawing lab | 1,000-1,300 | depends on number of stations |
| office | 150-200 | centrally locate in department |

**Table 6.3 cont.**

| area/room | recommended size (sq. ft.) | comments |
|---|---|---|
| industrial technology (cont.) | | |
| agriculture shop | 2,000-3,000 | access for large machinery/equipment |
| auto shop | 1,800-2,500 | access for autos, small trucks |
| business education | | |
| typing room | 900-1,000 | depends on number of stations |
| office practice | 900-1,000 | depends on number of stations |
| computer laboratory | 1,000-1,200 | depends on number of stations |
| home economics | | |
| foods laboratory | 1,200-1,400 | depends on number of stations |
| clothing laboratory | 1,100-1,300 | depends on number of stations |
| home living area | 600-900 | living room/dining room |
| office | 100-200 | centrally locate in department |
| administration | | |
| principal's office | 200-300 | should have 2 entrances/exits |
| asst principal's office | 120-200 | |
| bookkeeper office | 100-150 | |
| counselor's office | 120-150 | one provided for each |
| conference room | 250-500 | should accommodate 12-15 adults |
| workroom | 150-300 | sink provided |
| reception area | 300-600 | includes secretarial spaces |
| faculty workroom | 400-800 | sink provided |
| departmental offices | 250-500 | depends on size of department |
| health suite | 500-800 | includes one or two restrooms |
| media center | | |
| library | 10-15 percent of study body at 25-30 sq. ft. p/pupil | |
| office | 150-200 | access to workwoom |
| workroom | 200-300 | sink provided |
| storage | 500-900 | climate control important |
| auditorium | | |
| stage | 2,000-2,200 | |
| seating | 10 sq. ft. p/person | |
| cafeteria | | |
| student dining room | 13-16 sq. ft. p/pupil seated at one time | |
| faculty dining room | 300-600 depends on size of school | |

Many middle and junior high schools now in existence were not erected as such. They were converted from high schools. Regardless of whether renovation or new construction is the task, it is critical to realize that schools in the middle are the least standardized educational environments. That is, grade organization, instructional format, and extracurricular programs are apt to vary more than at either elementary or high school levels, resulting in unique facility needs.

## THE HIGH SCHOOL

The high school is the focal point in many communities (or in neighborhoods in larger cities). Being the capstone experience offered by local school systems, many high school programs have prominence and are the source of community pride. Basically, high schools in America have one of two standard grade plans: 9–12 or 10–12 (there are some 11–12 schools but they are far less common).

Today, high schools are becoming increasingly "academically oriented." This trend is occurring after several decades of altered economic conditions, changing values in society, and a decline in public confidence (Perrone, 1985). However, the renewed emphasis upon academics does not necessarily portend stability. It is anticipated that the need to revise curriculum will continue to accelerate as the result of new knowledge and technology (Roberts & Cawelti, 1984). Every time priorities change, the demands placed on educational environments are altered.

For many communities, declining enrollments at the high school level have become a serious problem. This is especially true in school districts where facility needs were overestimated as a result of the "baby boomers" passing through secondary schools during the 1960s. Not surprisingly, the size of high schools has become a major issue in these communities if they are still maintaining more than one high school. In large school districts, high schools may reach 3,000 to 5,000 pupils. In rural areas, some enroll less than 100. Basically, high schools below 800 pupils in four grades have some difficulty in providing a broad curriculum. At the other end of the spectrum, schools that go beyond 1,500 students often must address concerns such as alienation and limited access to extracurricular activities. Brooks, Conrad, and Griffith (1980) suggest the following parameters:

| | |
|---|---|
| minimum size | 500 students |
| optimum size | 1,000 to 1,200 students |
| maximum size | 1,500 students. |

Spencer (1988) reported similar parameters for middle and high school size:

| | |
|---|---|
| middle school optimum size | 600 to 800 students |
| high school optimum size | 1,000 to 1,200 students. |

Despite such guidelines, it is widely recognized that some quality high schools exist with enrollments below 500 or above 1,500. The key is the degree to which the administrators take positive steps to alleviate the problems associated with size.

## Curriculum and Instruction

Despite the experimentations of the 1960s and 1970s, the high school continues to embrace the subject-oriented curriculum. That is, study is divided by basic groupings (departments) and divided further by subgroupings (courses). The reluctance to change curricular structure can be attributed to such factors as teacher preparation, licensing of teachers, and the continuing reliance upon standard credits and units for graduation (Kowalski, 1981). The subject curriculum also helps to simplify facility planning in secondary schools. Because subject matter is divided into neat compartments, the structure lends itself to departmental designs.

Compared to middle and junior high schools, the high school has a more diverse curriculum. Students are able to take many more electives and are exposed to a wider range of courses. In most high schools, students can pursue several courses of study (e.g., college preparatory, vocational); these alternatives further broaden the total scope of course offerings. Extracurricular activities, too, are much more developed in high schools than at previous levels. As mentioned with schools in the middle, equality for girls' athletics and the growing demand for even more sports programs produces an expanded extracurricular program. This pattern holds true for the high school as well.

Instructional methodology is diverse in most high schools. Large group instruction and independent study, for example, are widely used. The inclusion of modern technology has had a dramatic impact upon school facilities. Most high schools have responded to the computer revolution and have done so in a timely fashion (Walker, 1985). In some progressive schools, the "electronic classroom" (a classroom environment incorporating modern technology for functions such as interactive television and other media usage) has become a reality. The advances of technology affect curriculum as well as instruction. Perhaps the best example can be found in industrial education. Once a "hands on" program delivered in specialized shops, experts in this field now advocate a technology curriculum that focuses on problem solving (Bensen, 1988).

A number of alterations serves as indicators that the high school curriculum certainly is not stable. Table 6.4 identifies some of the more cogent transformations and their causes. The listing in Table 6.4 is by no means exhaustive, but the issues do exemplify the fact that the secondary school in America remains in transition.

Interactive television is already having a dramatic impact upon instruction in high schools. Small schools in particular have need to obtain programming in specialized courses for low incidence needs (e.g., enrichment activities for gifted

**Table 6.4**
**Selected Changes in High School Curriculum/Instruction**

| change | causes | implications |
|---|---|---|
| industrial education to technology | less emphasis on vocational | rethinking shop needs; from "hands-on" to concepts |
| reduction of interest in home economics | changing values; academic orientations | less need for labs in home economics |
| increasing interest in foreign languages | world economy; demand for bilingual workers | better designed labs and resources in language study |
| more special programs | recognition of special student needs | more programs at the extremes (e.g., gifted) |
| more emphasis upon "hard" sciences | competition for entry to best colleges/professions | more and better science labs |
| reduced demand for business education | technology; changing values for females | fewer business labs; more computer labs |
| infusion of technology | availability of and demand for micro-computers | computer labs; other special equipment |

students). Technology coupled with rising energy costs may make it more feasible to link schools with each other via interactive television than to rely on the old method—consolidation of schools. Several universities (e.g., Oklahoma State and Ball State) offer high school courses via television to rural high schools. The practice, now commonly referred to as *distance learning* in the literature, undoubtedly will assist small schools to continue operating.

The microcomputer has had an irreversible effect on American schooling. Computer laboratories, in some form, are now found in virtually all high schools in the United States. True, many of these laboratories were created by converting standard classrooms (or other spaces). True, many of the laboratories were established hastily—some schools purchased equipment even prior to establishing instructional goals and objectives (Walker, 1985). But nevertheless, most high schools now have spaces designated for computer usage. The acceptance of microcomputer laboratories is resulting in better instructional techniques and more refined specifications for space, environmental controls (e.g., climate, acoustical treatment), and support areas (e.g., repair areas). As older schools are replaced, better designed computer facilities evolve. Computer labs may have a variety of designs; most often, that design is a product of educational objectives, available finances, and/or the personality of the lab coordinator (Lane & Lane, 1988). Since all schools do not use computers in the same way, decisions about purchasing computers and creating spaces for their use need to be site specific (Henson, 1988). The design of the laboratory should reflect needs and wants that are articulated in the educational specifications.

### Space Needs

The space needs for a given high school depend upon enrollment and scope of the curriculum (including extracurricular programming). Some schools, for example, participate in area vocational school programs. Others participate in special education cooperatives. These arrangements either reduce space needs (if the students go elsewhere for programming) or increase them (if the cooperative programs are offered in the school). The formula presented for calculating middle school room needs is valid here as well. The standard classroom remains the primary space in a high school; however, more specialized spaces are needed than at the middle or junior high school. The diversification of instructional methods requires more than flexibility in space—it necessitates certain provisions being designed into the facility such as more independent study areas in the media center or several lecture rooms to accommodate several hundred students at one time.

Some guidelines for room sizes were provided in Table 6.3. Keep in mind that variance in space allocations is probably greatest at the high school level.

### Estimating Classroom Requirements

In secondary schools, the standard classroom remains the basic environment for instruction. But there is also need for numerous special instructional spaces. Unlike schools utilizing self-contained classrooms, the departmentalized secondary school requires a more complex method of estimating the number of needed instructional spaces. This process can be accomplished in several ways. In using any formula, it is important to recognize the factor of utilization. This refers to the amount of time a given space will be scheduled for classes. Although it may appear that a 100 percent utilization is efficient and desirable, a lesser percent is recommended. Utilization levels of 80 to 90 percent permit some spaces to be used for special purposes not included in the master schedule (e.g., club meetings). Such flexibility is considered essential for modern high schools.

The first formula presented here focuses on determining the number of teacher stations required for a school and was developed by Nelson (1972). The calculation is as follows:

$$TSS = (AE \times TW)/(ND \times CS \times TO)$$

where:     TSS = teacher stations required for a subject

AE = anticipated enrollment (total number to be accommodated in this subject; it is determined from actual needs or estimates (e.g., 70 percent of 1,000 need to take mathematics; thus, 700 is the AE)

TW = time distribution per week (number of periods the class meets per week)

ND = number divisions (number of activities to be carried out in a single space at the same time, e.g., if a gym had a divider and housed two classes of physical education during the same period, the ND would be 2)

CS = class size (largest class size anticipated)

TO = time occupied (represents the extent to which a station is to be utilized for a given activity, i.e., periods per week less periods per week that room is to be free)

### Example

A high school has an enrollment of 1,000. All students are expected to take English. English classes meet five times per week for 50 minutes. There are seven periods in the school day and only one class will meet in a room at a given time. The maximum class size is 30 and the classroom utilization is desired to be 90 percent (i.e., that rooms are to be unassigned 10 percent of the time). Accordingly, the formula would be:

$$\begin{aligned}
TSS &= (1,000 \times 5)/(1 \times 30 \times (35 \times .9)) \text{ or} \\
&\quad 5,000/(30 \times 31.5) \text{ or} \\
&\quad 5,000/945 = 5.29 \text{ or} \\
&\quad 6 \text{ classrooms}
\end{aligned}$$

Nelson's formula is especially useful for schools using nontraditional scheduling such as modules. It allows calculations for large group instruction (via the ND factor) and varying time utilizations (via the TO factor) which are not possible in more basic formulas.

An alternative, and more basic, formula may be more useful for traditional programming formats. The one that follows is widely used by planners:

$$NR = (1.15 \times (ns/cs)) \times (npw/swp)$$

where:     NR = number of rooms required

ns = number of students taking a course

cs = desired class size

npw = number of periods per week that the class meets

swp = number of school week periods

1.15 = some allowance for variance

## Example

There are 306 students who need to take eighth grade science. The science labs can accommodate a maximum of 26 students. The class meets five days per week. The school has seven periods each school day with 45 minutes in each period. Therefore, the formula for determining how many labs are needed is as follows:

$$1.15 \times (306/26) \times (5/35)$$
or
$$(1.15 \times 11.8) \times (.143)$$
or
$$13.57 \times .143 = 1.94$$
or
2 science laboratories

Working backwards, you can check the calculations. If the two science classes were used seven periods a day, they could accommodate 14 sections of eighth grade science. With a total of 306 students, each class would have an average of 22 students—within the limit of 26 per class.

In planning a new school, the administrator must project future needs as well as existing needs. One relatively simple way to do this is to use the same formula but to adjust the total enrolled by a percent obtained from the enrollment projection. Imagine a district where enrollments at the middle school level are expected to increase from 800 to 1,000 in the next ten years. This is a 25 percent increase. If the current number of eighth grade students enrolling in science is 306 (as in the example presented), estimating future classroom needs can be done by increasing 306 by 25 percent. The resulting figure, 383, is then used in the formula. This method is simple and provides a relatively accurate projection of classroom needs for the future. In using this technique, the planner assumes that demand for a given subject will remain relatively constant.

## OTHER GENERAL CONSIDERATIONS

Providing an exhaustive list of considerations that should be made in planning a secondary school is virtually impossible. As noted here, middle, junior, and senior high schools are much more complex structures than are elementary schools; thus, listing standard features is less beneficial. There are, nevertheless, some factors that are quite important to all secondary schools and merit scrutiny.

## Site Development

The secondary school usually requires extensive site development. There is a need to create several outdoor athletic facilities (e.g., football field, tennis courts) and to provide sufficient parking (for faculty, staff, students, and visitors). High schools sponsor major spectator events. Athletic contests, musicals, plays, and graduation are times when thousands of persons may come to the site by automobile. Parking designs must take into account both the needs of customary usage (every day) and special events.

Because the site development is extensive and complex, security is a critical planning and design issue. Adequate lighting, fencing, and protected storage facilities exemplify issues that must be addressed. Access for automobiles, buses, and delivery trucks is both a security and a health/safety issue.

Site development at a secondary school also includes enhancing the aesthetic qualities of the school. Increasingly landscape architects are part of the facility planning team. Many principals recognize that a well-designed and maintained site has a positive psychological effect. Trees, shrubs, and lawns should be designed to enhance the physical appearance of the facility.

## Faculty Work Spaces

The vast majority of secondary schools operate in a departmentalized mode. The existence of separate departments (e.g., English, science) allows consideration for one alternative solution related to providing workspace—departmental offices. Some administrators, however, dislike this option and lobby for a single workroom for all teachers. Single workrooms are more prevalent in middle schools and small high schools. Teachers are more likely to use workrooms if these spaces are conveniently located to their classrooms and if the space is shared with faculty having similar assignments. For these reasons, the departmental office concept is usually preferred even though it is more costly (the total amount of space for departmental offices will naturally exceed the space for a single workroom for all teachers).

Typically, administrative areas have separate workrooms to accommodate secretarial staff. In planning a secondary school, it is critical to identify the anticipated work patterns of secretaries and aides. Knowing the specific work assignments facilitates structuring workrooms and determining their locations within the school. Additionally, consideration should be given to an instructional support area within the school similar to that described in the previous chapter on elementary schools (i.e., a place where aides and teachers can conduct individualized or small group instruction).

In addition to workrooms, faculty prefer to have separate lounge and dining facilities. In smaller schools, these two areas are frequently combined. Opting for a combined workroom/lounge simply to save money may prove to be a false economy. Given the diverse purposes of dining areas and workrooms, combining the two usually results in the area being used solely as a lounge/dining area.

## Support Services

Secondary schools require a number of support services. Among the more prominent are a health clinic and a counseling area. In larger high schools, a psychologist and a social worker may be part of the staff. The location of these functions within the school building varies depending upon the scope of services offered and the philosophy. In some high schools, for example, the counseling staff becomes involved in discipline, scheduling, and other administrative tasks. Thus, the desired location of the guidance offices is within the administrative complex. In other schools, counselors may wish to be detached from administration. Decisions regarding office locations are required for the following positions: guidance counselor, nurse, psychologist, athletic director, social worker, attendance officer, dean of boys, and dean of girls. In larger secondary schools, it is more common to disperse these offices rather than to have them all in the administrative suite. The goals and objectives of the specific services should be the factors determining location.

## Technology

The incorporation of technology into public school districts will be greatest at the high school level. Beyond the obvious needs such as computer laboratories, considerations must be given to fiber optics, coaxial cable, satellite dishes, electronic classrooms, and modern laboratories. The Dr. Phillips High School in Orlando, Florida is one excellent example of an attempt to design a high school incorporating the best of available technology (Arnett, 1987). The rapid deployment of technology in American society suggests that the greatest needs for modernization in secondary schools will come in this area. As with most issues of future planning, it is impossible to provide precise needs statements for a school that will be used 40–50 years into the future. Given this reality, flexibility and adaptability are attributes that should be assigned high priorities.

## Student Needs

Secondary schools typically provide lockers for students to store their personal belongings. The most common location for these lockers is along the hallways. In some schools, the lockers are placed in bays, areas off the hallways that are designed specifically to accommodate student lockers. Some principals dislike locker bays because they are frequently difficult to supervise. Regardless of location, the size, number, and type of lockers are important issues in planning a secondary school.

Interior recreation spaces are also essential for secondary schools. Unlike the elementary school where students simply use the gym during inclement weather, in secondary schools the gym is almost always occupied. A number of contemporary high schools have student lounges or common areas to provide interior space where students can relax and socialize in unscheduled periods (e.g., after lunch).

### Extended Uses

Secondary school buildings are experiencing extended usage for two reasons: (1) the scope of the program offered for pupils is broadening (i.e., the schoolhouse is being used more hours, more days), and (2) adult and community education are becoming more prevalent. State-mandated reform efforts during the 1980s, for example, have focused on intensification strategies. Thus, longer school days, longer school years, and required summer school for some students have increased facility usage. With a growing number of taxpayers no longer having children in school and with the growing acceptance of the concept of lifelong learning, many school districts are extending services to the general population. Ranging from recreational programs to adult computer literacy classes, the modern secondary school is apt to engage in a multitude of evening and week-end services. Extended usage should be a focal point in planning all schools, but it is especially cogent for secondary schools. Needs related to extended usage of a school building should be interfaced with security, health, and safety issues.

## SUMMARY

This chapter reviewed secondary school facilities. Compared to elementary schools, middle, junior, and senior high schools are larger, more complex, and more expensive. Planning for these schools is complicated by the fact that grade organizational patterns, size of schools, and total programming vary widely from one community to another. Frequently grade organization, especially for the schools in the middle, has been determined by economic and administrative considerations. If at all possible, this circumstance should be avoided. The more desirable justifications for grade organization are curriculum, instructional practices, and educational philosophy.

Typically, the secondary school is a showpiece for the school district. It is a facility that will house many community functions and spectator activities. It is also a building that must accommodate a wide range of educational needs. Instructional programs in secondary schools require many special facilities—and the design and location of these spaces are critical to the successful operation of a school.

## ISSUES FOR DISCUSSION

1. What were the issues driving the creation of junior high schools in the United States?
2. Discuss the varying concepts of a middle school—from both a standpoint of grade organization and instructional philosophy.
3. Identify key features of a middle school facility that would be different from a high school facility.
4. Identify the advantages and disadvantages of having departmental offices in a secondary school.
5. List the outdoor facilities you think should be provided for:
   a. a middle school, grades 6–8, with 550 students
   b. a junior high school, grades 7–9, with 1,300 students
   c. a high school, grades 9–12, with 2,500 students.
6. Discuss the advantages and disadvantages of locating the counseling offices in the administrative suite of a:
   a. middle school
   b. junior high school
   c. high school
7. List adult and community education programs that are currently occurring in your high school. How do these programs affect facility usage?
8. Identify the advantages and disadvantages of converting a high school to a middle school.
9. Discuss the advantages and disadvantages of providing a student lounge in a high school.
10. Identify the level of building utilization for the middle school (or junior high school) and high school in your community (or neighborhood).

# 7

# PROFESSIONAL
# ASSISTANCE

Perhaps the greatest contribution a school superintendent makes to a facility project is the creation of a planning team. This team becomes the root system—the foundation for all future decisions. If it is properly planted and nourished, the products that are visible to the community are likely to be relevant and aesthetically pleasing. This root system typically includes local participation (employees and citizens) and a number of highly specialized professionals. This chapter explores the range of professional assistance that can be used in a facility project by identifying possible services and selection procedures. If every facility project were the same, the task of determining who should be involved in planning would be quite simple. But this is far from the case. Each community, each school district, and each school project is unique. Thus, the creation of the planning team is a novel challenge.

## DESIGN AND CONSTRUCTION SPECIALISTS

If the average citizen were asked to name the professionals that need to be retained for erecting a new school, the most common answer would be an architect. This is true because taxpayers know that schools are special structures requiring sophisticated designs. A far fewer number of citizens would be familiar with other design and construction experts who typically play vital roles in educational facility planning. The growing complexity of school plants is necessitating the inclusion of additional specialists to augment the traditional responsibilities of the architect. What follows is a review of potential participants in the areas of design and construction planning.

### Architectural Services

The most critical decision about professional assistance usually is the selection of an architect or architectural firm. Most architects are part of a firm, although some practice individually (in this chapter, even architects practicing alone are referred to as firms). Firms vary in size with the larger ones having more than 100 professionals. The average size firm has about ten to twelve professionals. In examining potential firms, the school administrator should know the range of services available and the specific functions of the professional staff within the organization. This knowledge permits the school official to make more enlightened choices.

Larger firms possess many *in-house* specializations (i.e., they employ persons with specialized credentials in their firm). In addition to design architects the more common specializations found in larger firms include landscape architects, mechanical engineers, electrical engineers, structural engineers, interior designers, and acoustical engineers. Some firms even employ highly specialized consultants, such as educational and kitchen consultants. Firms that do not have a range of in-house specializations find it necessary to issue sub-contracts to meet the demands of larger and more complicated facility projects.

Frequently, clients possess a limited view of the role and responsibilities of architects. For instance, designing a facility is but one function they can serve. The American Institute of Architects (1987) identifies the following potentialities for services provided by its members:

### Predesign Phase

- predesign services (e.g., analysis of existing facilities)
- site analysis services

### Design Phase

- schematic design services
- design development services
- construction document services

### Construction Phase

- building or negotiations services (e.g., project administration)
- construction contract administration services (e.g., inspections, construction change directives)

### Post-Construction Phase

- post-construction services (e.g., warranty reviews)

**Supplemental Services**

• range of special services (e.g., life cycle cost analysis, computer applications, energy studies).

Perhaps the most prevalent predesign services include assistance with site acquisition, assessments of options (i.e., alternatives for meeting needs), and initial cost estimates (Davis & Loveless, 1981).

Architectural firms not only vary in size and in the types of services that can be provided, but also exhibit distinct differences in other key areas. Among the more important are total experience of the firm, amount of experience with educational facilities, percent of business that focuses upon educational facilities, past performances, philosophy, a willingness to listen to clients, and fees. Figure 7.1 illustrates a number of key variables that might receive consideration. These variables are grouped into four categories: (1) issues regarding the structure of the firm being considered, (2) the philosophy of that firm, (3) the firm's past performances, and (4) issues related to retaining the firm.

The total experience of a firm is important because it reveals the stability of the firm. Since educational facilities have a lifespan covering five or more decades, many school officials prefer firms that have been operational for a number of years—longevity is perceived as an indicator of stability. Previous experiences designing educational buildings are likewise relevant to selecting an architect. A firm, for example, may be quite established, yet possess little experience designing educational facilities. The current level of emphasis on designing schools

**Figure 7.1**
**Key Variables in Selecting an Architect**

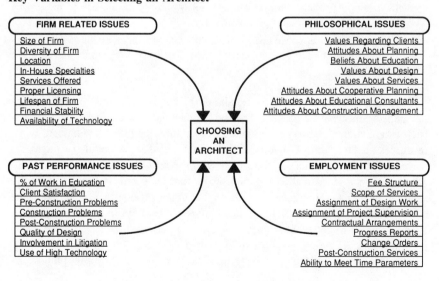

may also be important. A firm could be well-established and have a history of designing schools, but its current (or recent) work assignments may reflect a declining emphasis with educational structures. The quantity of experience is often far less important than quality. Many school superintendents are inclined to inquire with former educational clients about a firm's ability to communicate effectively with educators, the outcomes of design work, and so forth. Fees are another critical issue for most school districts. In fact, some school districts are prone to base the selection of a firm solely on this criterion.

One other factor is worth mentioning. The use of high technology in design is becoming increasingly important in architecture. CADD (as described in Chapter 2) may still be viewed as a futuristic concept by some school administrators, but in reality, it is a procedure already available in some firms (Skypeck, 1988). Likewise, school administrators should not assume that all architectural firms use more or less the same level of technology in serving clients. Whether or not a firm uses CADD, for instance, can become an issue in selecting an architect. Being fully aware of the potential benefits of CADD, both during design and after construction is completed, permits intelligent questions to be asked as various firms are being considered.

Architectural fees may be based upon one of several factors. The most common for educational projects are:

- a stipulated sum regardless of the cost of the project (e.g., the fee is $500,000.00 regardless of the cost of the entire project)
- a percentage of the construction cost (e.g., 6 percent fee on a $10,000,000.00 project is $600,000.00)
- actual costs for services based upon a prescribed rate without total fee parameters (e.g., specified hourly or daily rates which accumulate throughout the life of the project without established maximums or minimums)
- actual costs for services based upon a prescribed rate(s) with an established minimum and/or maximum fee (e.g., the accumulated fee must fall within agreed upon parameters)

Beyond the fees per se, the owner should be concerned about the schedule of payments. Since public monies are used for facility projects, many school districts establish intricate payment schedules to assure that billings will occur when resources are available. Obviously, it is beneficial if the schedule of payments demanded by the architect is congruent with the school system's revenue plan. Additionally, it is critical to separate those items covered by the fees (usually salaries, profit, and indirect costs) from other expenses that may be billed to the school district. Items not included in the fees are referred to as *reimbursables*. Reimbursables might include telecommunication charges, per diem, and transportation costs (Madden and Coughlin, 1985).

Educators frequently refer to the term, ''philosophy.'' Put simply, philosophy refers to values and beliefs. Just as teachers and administrators have values and beliefs about children and learning, architects have values and beliefs about serving clients, about designing educational facilities, and about planning procedures. For example, firms could vary markedly with regard to issues such as creativity, the use of technology, working with community groups, and working with other professional consultants. Effort should be made in questionnaires and in interviews to bring a firm's philosophy to the surface so that it can be evaluated.

One factor that receives considerable attention by many school districts is the geographic location of the firms. Since school systems are supported by local taxpayers, there is often pressure exerted to employ architects whose offices are in the school district—or nearby area. Castaldi (1987) points out that in this age of rapid travel, the argument for retaining *locals* is not as compelling as it once was.

Architect selection may be affected by planning decisions related to other professional assistance. For instance, a school district opting not to employ construction managers is likely to place emphasis on a firm's record of service during the construction phase of a project. Regardless of the scope of the planning team, the architect is expected to: (1) certify that various segments of the project have been completed properly. (2) keep the school officials apprised regarding the budgetary aspects of the project, (3) serve as the owner's agent if there are problems during construction, (4) do any necessary cost revisions, and (5) prepare and recommend change orders. These tasks, however, become even more crucial if the owner does not have a construction manager to assist with reviewing these responsibilities.

Finally, time is a paramount factor not to be overlooked. Can a firm meet your time requirements? Is a firm so busy that it is unlikely that they can meet your time requirements even though they say they can? School facility planning incorporates a multitude of tasks. If one party fails to meet deadlines, the entire process can be delayed. This is especially true of the architect's obligations. Unfortunately, since many facility projects are spawned by emergencies rather than by long-range planning, the time element is usually a weighty factor for school districts. A firm's use of technology is one factor to explore in this regard. The use of CADD and other high technology procedures can make a difference in the project's duration (Ashley, 1987).

Several other guidelines are useful when considering the employment of an architectural firm:

1. Knowledge of the laws in your state regarding the minimum qualifications for school architects (Castaldi, 1987).

2. A competitive selection process. The selection of an architect is time-consuming. Often it is best to start with a list of approximately ten to fifteen firms. These firms are invited to complete questionnaires addressing the needs and wants of the school corporation. That list is then whittled to a more manageable number for interviews. Some districts decide to interview all firms that respond to initial inquiries.

3. Determination of the scope of the project before selection of an architect begins (Madden and Coughlin, 1985). It is important to be able to articulate needs to prospective architects.

4. Recognition of what is considered the most important quality in an architectural firm. This information should be used to structure questionnaire/interviews (Smith, Stevenson, and Pellicer, 1984). Is experience more important than creativity? Is the geographic location of the firm important? Is the size of the firm a critical factor? Answering these types of questions in advance of considering firms makes the selection process more objective and precise.

5. Selection of the architectural firm as early as possible. Since so many services, including predesign services, may be available, early employment is usually beneficial to the school district.

6. Determination of the following roles: (1) the design architect (the person who actually designs the school); (2) the principal in the firm assigned overall responsibility for the project; and (3) the project architect (the one who will oversee construction once it commences).

7. Philosophy of the architectural firm. The degree to which the school board and administration desire to involve themselves in the design activities varies from one situation to another. In the interview, the architect should be asked what he or she believes to be a desirable architect/client relationship, especially with regard to client input. This question should only be asked, however, after the board and administration establish clearly what they would like the role to be. In this fashion, the interview allows the owners to determine if their desires are compatible with the philosophy of a given firm (Moore, 1989).

8. A contract or agreement for architectural services. This should not be taken for granted. Often the architect will suggest using the standard form prepared by the American Institute of Architects. The superintendent, in concert with the school district attorney, should check to be certain that any agreement details all the services and responsibilities expected from the architect. The standard form may not include these expectations (Uhler, 1988).

Figure 7.2 illustrates one suggested pathway for selecting architectural services. The actual process used by a school district should be based upon the unique wants and needs related to a specific project. Some administrators may wish to contact the American Institute of Architects in Washington, D.C. for materials and information regarding the selection of an architectural firm.

## Construction Management

Construction management (referred to as CM) is a concept growing in popularity (Kowalski, 1983). As school districts face increasing pressures to be accountable, administrators seek efficient alternatives to standard construction procedures. Much like architects, construction managers may be independent practitioners or function within firms. Often construction managers are en-

**Figure 7.2**
**One Pathway to Selecting an Architect**

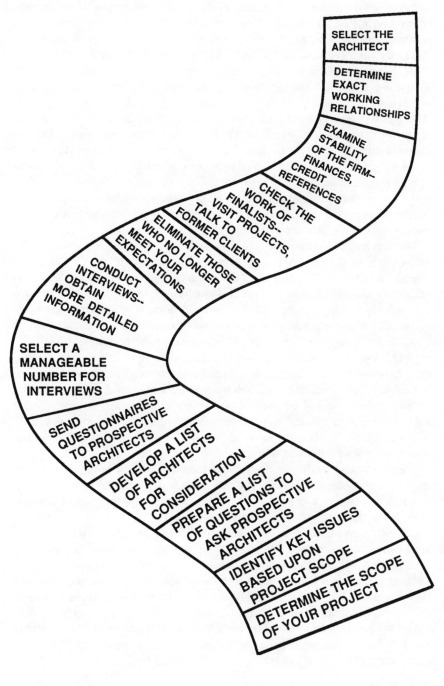

SELECT THE ARCHITECT

DETERMINE EXACT WORKING RELATIONSHIPS

EXAMINE STABILITY OF THE FIRM— FINANCES, CREDIT REFERENCES

CHECK THE WORK OF FINALISTS— VISIT PROJECTS, TALK TO FORMER CLIENTS

ELIMINATE THOSE WHO NO LONGER MEET YOUR EXPECTATIONS

CONDUCT INTERVIEWS— OBTAIN MORE DETAILED INFORMATION

SELECT A MANAGEABLE NUMBER FOR INTERVIEWS

SEND QUESTIONNAIRES TO PROSPECTIVE ARCHITECTS

DEVELOP A LIST OF ARCHITECTS FOR CONSIDERATION

PREPARE A LIST OF QUESTIONS TO ASK PROSPECTIVE ARCHITECTS

IDENTIFY KEY ISSUES BASED UPON PROJECT SCOPE

DETERMINE THE SCOPE OF YOUR PROJECT

gineers; others, however, are architects or possess training in business administration. The primary function of CM is to represent the owner (school district) throughout the building project; this is the leading alternative to the general contracting method for construction. The CM is expected to contribute to the planning process in terms of construction experience, knowledge of materials, knowledge of local work forces, and knowledge of construction practices.

Goldblatt and Wood (1985) identify the major functions of CM as material design and selection, cost estimates and budgets, schedules and coordination, supervision of actual construction, and certification of payments to contractors. Although the same types of contractors/workers are usually engaged in a building project regardless of whether CM or a general contractor is used, the real difference lies in the ways that these services are retained. CM attempts to break down the contracts into smaller units in hopes that quantity and competitiveness of bids will increase. Weinert (1987) identifies three types of projects where CM may be most useful: Projects that must be designed to budget and subsequently require close fiscal control; projects that are unusually complex; and projects that require completion in a timely manner.

The fees paid for CM may be based upon several criteria much as described for architectural fees. Since CM is often expensive, conservative school officials may reject it out-of-hand. The real cost of CM can only be determined by accurately examining two critical questions: (1) how much money is saved by added efficiency and more detailed bidding, and (2) how much is saved by reducing the amount of time that school officials must devote to the project? Only after deducting these from the fees paid can a school district really determine the costs of CM.

States vary markedly with regard to statutes governing CM. In most instances, the management of construction is not considered the practice of architecture or engineering, yet school administrators are advised to have legal counsel establish existing codes regarding the practice of CM in a specific state. In recent years, states have moved to more flexible approaches regarding the construction of school facilities. Increasingly, specific language about the use of CM is finding its way into these statutes (Goldblatt and Wood, 1985).

The selection of a CM firm follows guidelines similar to those presented for architects. Kluenker and Haltenhoff (1986) present a rather comprehensive guide to potential services and selection, and administrators seeking more detailed information on this topic are directed to their work.

One final benefit that deserves mention with regard to CM entails the use of local contractors. Utilizing local contractors can serve two positive outcomes: (1) it may be politically advantageous, and (2) it can reduce overall costs. Often CM makes the use of local contractors possible because the construction project is broken down into packages that allow and encourage smaller firms to participate. If local contractors are used, public monies are kept in the community, bids are apt to be lower because workers are already in the community, local workers are apt to take greater pride in the project, and local businesses are apt to be more supportive of the school system's efforts (Kluenker, 1987).

### Additional Design/Construction Personnel

In this age of modern technology, new needs are surfacing with regard to facility projects. These needs often require the inclusion of highly specialized individuals to assist with the design and construction phases. These specialists may include acoustical consultants, computer consultants, and telecommunication consultants. The integration of voice and video, for example, is having a profound impact upon educational programming. Consultants in highly technical areas often are not part of either architectural or CM firms. Their services must be obtained independently. The owner should establish at the time of entering into a contract with architects and/or CM: (1) the scope of specialized services that will be required (i.e., services not available in the respective firms) and (2) who will be responsible for retaining and paying for such services.

## OTHER SPECIALIZED ASSISTANCE

The completion of a facility project includes more than designing and constructing a school building. A number of special needs must also be addressed. The four primary categories of such needs are: (1) educational planning, (2) legal assistance, (3) fiscal planning, and (4) assistance from special agencies.

### Educational Consultant

The typical educational consultant is a college professor who possesses expertise and experience in the area of educational planning related to school facility projects. He or she may be retained directly by the school district or by the architectural firm (or in rare instances by the CM). When the educational consultant is retained by a party other than the school district, it is advisable for the superintendent (or designee) to recommend the consultant desired or at least to have a veto regarding this selection. Some large architectural firms employ an in-house educational consultant, and this individual may or may not be acceptable to school officials. The most common duties of the educational consultant are:

- conducting needs assessment studies which detail educational deficiencies—especially those related to facilities;
- developing educational specifications (discussed previously in this book);
- assisting with monitoring of the design phase (offering input about how educational specifications are being translated into actual design);
- evaluating the effectiveness of the entire planning procedure once the school is completed and occupied.

In some instances, the consultant is employed to assist with the selection of architects or CM. This is considered by some to be a dubious practice. Established educational consultants maintain professional contact with a number of firms and existing contractual agreements may prevent objectivity. Their inclusion in selection procedures may spawn legal or ethical questions. There is a dramatic difference between requesting consultants to help establish a review procedure and asking them to select firms.

The selection of an educational consultant should be based upon objective criteria and identified needs. School officials should not assume that all professors (or self-identified consultants) are capable of doing these tasks. There is no certification or board registration for educational consultants; thus, school officials must exercise great care in selecting one (Castaldi, 1987). The quantity and quality of previous consultant experience should be deemed critically important. In many states, public school projects require the approval of the state department of education. Where this is the case, it may be a good idea to review the reputation of a prospective consultant with state department officials. Just as with other professionals, it is advisable to enter into a contractual agreement for educational consultant services. This agreement should detail responsibilities, fee payments, and the like.

### Project Attorney

School facility projects include a number of legal issues. For this reason, an attorney needs to be retained to provide counsel with issues such as contracts, building codes, property acquisition, and labor disputes. Most often, school districts elect to name their regular school district attorney to this post. Since facility projects are not common occurrences for most school systems, attorneys are typically compensated separately for this service (i.e., an amount that is in addition to their regular fee/retainer for serving as school district attorney).

In a number of states, school districts may enter into lease/purchase agreements for new schools. Usually, public holding corporations (not-for-profit) are formed for this purpose; however, private holding corporations (for profit) may also be used if laws permit. The use of these holding corporations will be discussed in more detail in the chapter on finance; however, here it is important to note that a question regarding legal counsel can evolve when public holding corporations are used. Public holding corporations are ad hoc entities usually created by a group of local citizens. Since they will be entering into legal agreements, they also require the counsel of an attorney. Often the holding corporation will elect to use the same attorney that is retained by the school corporation. It is advisable to check relevant statutes and/or existing legal opinions (e.g., opinions of state attorneys general) to determine if this practice is permissible.

Fee structures for compensating project attorneys vary. They may be based upon a percent of the construction cost, a flat fee, or an hourly rate. There is one responsibility that is not given to the project attorney. This task entails a review of proposed bond sales to determine if the bonds are tax exempt. For this task, the school corporation should retain a highly specialized bond attorney.

### Bond Counsel

Tax-exempt bonds are often attractive investments for corporations and individuals. For this reason, public organizations issuing such bonds are able to obtain more favorable interest rates than private borrowers. One critical task in a facility project that includes the sale of bonds is the certification that an issue is indeed tax-exempt. This responsibility should be given to highly specialized bond attorneys. Since bonds are almost always sold by competitive bid on the open market (in some states negotiated sales are permitted), the reputation of the bond attorney can be quite important. The attorney should have a national or regional reputation and be someone (or a firm) acceptable to the seller and the buyer (Stollar, 1967).

The duties of a bond counsel can involve the following services:

- drafting the original bond resolution or ordinance
- developing a notice of bond election (if required by law)
- developing a ballot for the election
- reviewing the prospectus
- reviewing the notice of sale
- reviewing other financial advertisements
- reviewing all materials presented to underwriters
- reviewing the budget for the entire project
- rendering a legal opinion regarding the status of the bonds
- rendering a final opinion after the sale of the bonds.

It is advisable to discuss the scope of responsibilities expected of the bond attorney with the project attorney. The two attorneys need to work in harmony to provide the best services for the school district.

### Financial Consultant

Financial consultants are specialists who assist the school corporation with a variety of tasks related to financing capital outlay. These individuals may be education professors specializing in school finance, certified public accountants, or even attorneys. One misconception about the services of financial consultants is that their sole purpose is to help sell bonds. In reality, they can perform a number of functions as illustrated in the following list developed by Kowalski (1988):

- analyzing the existing financial status of the school district and determining the district's ability to incur further debt
- estimating the impact upon taxpayers of added debt
- creating/coordinating the planning calendar for the entire project (This task is important

since many decisions are governed by approvals required by law and related to financing.)

- helping in the development of a budget for the project
- assisting with securing special loans (e.g., some states have special loan programs available for school construction projects)
- serving as a resource for other specialists involved in the projects (e.g., conferring with attorneys, the architect)
- assisting with the sale of bonds
- appearing at hearings to help represent the school district (e.g., before state tax boards)
- helping with the structure of debt management.

Assistance with bond sales includes a number of separate tasks such as preparing the prospectus, writing ads for the bond sales, answering inquiries about the sale, distributing the prospectus, and offering advice about bids that are received. School districts are often tempted to cut corners to save several thousand dollars in a facility project. One such temptation emerges with regard to preparing the prospectus (the official statement for the sale of the bonds). Superintendents should realize that nonprofessional brochures are immediately apparent to purchasers, and such products tend to alienate sophisticated buyers (Guthrie, Garms, and Pierce, 1988). A good financial consultant is one who understands how school districts function—legally and politically.

### State Departments of Education

In most states, the state department of education maintains an active role in school construction projects. This involvement is so great and direct in some instances that a separate unit for schoolhouse planning exists. Before commencing a project, you should know what approvals are required from the department of education and what advisory services can be made available. Among the possible roles and services are:

- approving site selection
- regulating site size
- approving design plans
- approving finance plans
- providing approvals for tax increases
- stipulating design requirements
- granting loan approvals for special construction loans
- recommending persons to serve as consultants
- coordinating or assisting with approvals required of other state agencies.

The department of education officials can be especially helpful to administrators who have little or no previous experience with facility projects.

## Other Agencies

Specialized assistance may also be obtained from a myriad of federal, state, and local agencies. Examples include the Environmental Protection Agency, the state board of health, and the local planning commission. Contact with some of these agencies is mandated by law due to the fact that they must grant certain approvals (e.g., board of health approvals for sewage treatment systems). School administrators often overlook the fact that these agencies can be a rich source of advice. Typically, public agency consultation is provided without cost to the school system and can prove invaluable in latter stages of the project when specific approvals are required.

## SUMMARY

The planning team is the root system of a facility project. If the effort starts with a solid foundation, it is likely to blossom into a desirable product. A good root system requires the involvement of a number of special personnel. Architects are the most obvious because they design the structure. Others also play a critical role—even if these contributions are less conspicuous. They include construction managers, educational consultants, attorneys, financial consultants, and agency officials. Selecting the best individuals for your project can be a time-consuming task, yet if you base these selections on your specific needs, you are more likely to meet with success. A number of factors beyond cost need to be considered when retaining professional assistance, including experience, philosophy, accessibility, and communication skills.

In addition to professionals who charge a fee for their services, school officials can call upon the expertise and experiences of public agency officials. The most prevalent of these is the state department of education; however, a number of other federal, state, and local agencies can be of assistance as well.

## ISSUES FOR DISCUSSION

1. Determine what the law is in your state regarding the use of an architect or engineer for a public school project.
2. Discuss the differences between an architect and an engineer.
3. Obtain copies of the contracts for architectural services and construction management prepared by the American Institute of Architects (AIA) and review it.
4. Why would the size of an architectural firm be important to some school districts?

5. Compare construction management to the traditional method of using a general contractor. What are the advantages and disadvantages?

6. Establish a questionnaire that you would send to prospective architects for erecting a new school (elementary, middle, or high school). Provide a rationale for questions you include.

7. Would you consult your project attorney regarding the employment of a bond attorney? Why or why not?

8. Determine if your state department of education has a separate division for schoolhouse planning. What are the services provided?

9. Identify the characteristics you would expect in a financial consultant?

10. What qualifications would you look for in an educational consultant?

11. Develop a list of desired communication skills you would want in a project attorney. How would you assess whether these skills were present in a given individual?

12. Would you as a superintendent automatically recommend that the regular school attorney become the project attorney? Why or why not?

13. What questions would you ask an architect in an interview to ascertain his or her philosophy about working with educational clients?

# 8

# PROJECTING
# POPULATIONS

A total needs assessment has many facets and one of the most critical is the projection of future populations. Demography is the statistical study of human populations with special reference to size, density, distribution, and other related figures. Population projections can be global, national, state-wide, or local. For purposes of school facility planning, projections of school district enrollments are the most important, but certainly not the exclusive, demographic data of interest. Projections for the environment of a school district (i.e., the community, county, region, or state) are also valuable inputs for conducting a comprehensive needs assessment.

Skepticism often surrounds population projections. Some distrust any prediction of the future; others reject the outcomes simply because they are incongruent with popular perceptions or hopes. Too, critics are quick to react when forecasts are not absolutely precise. Despite these detractions, enrollment projections completed objectively and properly remain the best source of quantitative information relative to future facility needs.

Actual enrollment in public elementary and secondary schools are affected by a host of variables—many of which are well beyond the control of the school board and administration. The economy, local industrial development, energy costs, and housing loan interest rates are but a few. Enrollments are additionally affected by internal variables, that is, variables that the school district can control. Examples of internal variables include school boundaries, transportation decisions, and attendance policies. Given the complexity of demography, this chapter is divided into two parts. The first addresses environmental projections while the second examines methods for student population projections.

## ENVIRONMENTAL PROJECTIONS

Environmental projections refer to population estimates of existing units other than the school district. The most common are the state, the county, and the local community. They may also include neighborhoods or subdivisions. Environmental projections are designed to provide a picture of the past, current, and future trends in the general population of a given geographic location.

One widely used data source for studying environmental populations is the official United States Census. A national census is completed in the first year of each decade. Census data are especially useful for trend analysis (i.e., looking back over a 20- or 30-year period to assess what has occurred). These data are reported by states and by counties and contain a number of subcategories for analysis (e.g., male/female). Census data, per se, do not provide a projection but rather constitute a relatively accurate accounting of the past.

Virtually all states conduct state-wide population projections. In fact, some states have multiple projections completed independently by several different agencies. Likely resources for such projections are state boards of health, research bureaus in state universities, or specific state government agencies charged with demographic responsibilities. Agencies completing projections may also do population updates in years between the U.S. census. When using state-wide projections, it is important to note the source of the information used to make the projections. The source can be instrumental in determining if the projections are cogent to studies within the school district.

Local projections are usually more difficult to obtain, especially in rural counties. Utility companies sometimes complete population projections of local communities (i.e., cities, towns, townships) to facilitate their planning. Some counties maintain area planning commissions that likewise engage in demography and may be able to provide assistance with regard to estimates of future population.

Housing start data constitute yet another source of information regarding the general population. These data are maintained by county governmental units issuing building permits and are typically recorded by townships and cities (Glass, 1987). This information provides a profile of new housing and the data are especially useful if they include specificity regarding the cost and size of housing. In an area, for example, where census data indicate a growth pattern, housing start information may be used to help verify a trend. Given that housing activity may be spawned by a number of circumstances, these data should not be used as the sole basis for making projections of the general population.

## PROJECTIONS OF STUDENT POPULATIONS

Projections of student populations are usually completed on a school district basis meaning a projection is done grade by grade for the entire school system. It is also possible to do these calculations for individual schools. There are several options that can be used for forecasting enrollments but the use of retention ratios is the most common. In part, this is true because other methods are either time consuming and expensive or require data that are not available. The administrator should have a familiarity with the more basic options that may be used.

## School Census Method

The school census method utilizes two avenues for distributing surveys designed to collect information about future enrollments: (1) sending questionnaires home with students already enrolled in the schools, and (2) advertising in local media that parents with preschoolers (but without children currently enrolled in the school district) request a survey form from the district. Identification of potential students is done by ages. For example, a school district identifies how many three-year-old and four-year-old children are residing in the boundaries of the district. These data are then used by the school district administrators to estimate entry level (kindergarten) class size.

The school census technique can be accurate provided that the community population is relatively stable and that the school district receives a high percentage of completed surveys. If these conditions are present, the census method can be a contributing force in planning activities (Leu, 1965).

Surveys are not the only means of conducting a census. Actual interviews are also an effective tool. In small districts where a canvas of all homes in the community is not an impossibility, the interview method may prove to be the best alternative for collecting information. In rural communities, for instance, the school officials sometimes establish a cadre of volunteers to complete a district-wide house-to-house census (Stewart, 1987).

## Comparison Predictions

One rarely used technique for predicting future enrollments is the analogy method. This procedure requires the school district making the prediction (school district A) to identify a similar school district located in a similar community (school district B). In addition, conditions now prevalent in school district A are assumed to have existed in school district B in the past. By studying conditions and trends, the school district makes predictions based upon what has already occurred in school district B. In essence, the process becomes a form of case study. Because school districts and communities are so unique, it is extremely difficult to meet the test of identical or near-identical conditions. As a result, comparison predictions are rarely used by school systems (Brooks, Conrad, & Griffith, 1980).

## Cohort-Survival Method

The *cohort-survival method* (also referred to as the *percentage of survival technique*) is the simplest and most widely used process for estimating future enrollments (Kowalski, 1983). The procedure projects enrollments by computing the estimated size of each grade for the next immediate year from the size of the present year's next lower grade. That is, the enrollment pattern of third grade to fourth grade is used to predict future fourth grade enrollments. The process relies on the assumption that the future will be much like the past.

Table 8.1 contains retention data for an imaginary school district for a six-year period. The last row in the table contains the retention ratios. These ratios are mathematically determined by the number of students surviving, on average over the six-year period, from one grade level to the next (e.g., third grade to fourth grade). A ratio of 1.0 means that there is no change; a ratio greater than 1.0 indicates that over the past six years, enrollments increased; and, a ratio of less than 1.0 indicates a decline. The planner must decide on an historical base for developing retention ratios. Research indicates that the best projections are made from retention ratios based upon six to eight years of history (Alspaugh, 1981). That is, the previous six to eight years of actual enrollments are utilized to generate the ratios.

Once established, a retention ratio is utilized as a multiplier and applied to the current enrollment of a grade level to estimate what will be the next highest grade level enrollment for the following year. This is best explained by these two examples:

a. retention ratio from 3rd to 4th grade = 1.023; current 3rd grade enrollment = 325; projection for next year's 4th grade enrollment = (325 × 1.023) = 332

b. retention ratio from 9th to 10th grade = .987; current 9th grade enrollment = 980; projection for next year's 10th grade enrollment = (980 × .987) = 967

As these examples illustrate, a positive ratio (i.e., one greater than 1.0) produces an increase in anticipated enrollment. A negative ratio produces an expected decrease.

The procedure is applied to each grade level for each year that the planner is projecting into the future. Thus, each succeeding year in the projection is dependent upon the preceding year. The further into the future the enrollment is projected, the more the retention ratio either increases or decreases expected enrollments. Table 8.2 utilizes the data in Table 8.1 to project enrollments for a ten-year period.

Two categories of students deserve focused attention with regard to cohort survival projections: (1) kindergarten enrollments, and (2) special education enrollments. The most common method used to estimate kindergarten enrollments using retention ratios only is to establish the mean enrollment for the historical base and then to use this average as a constant in the projection. If a school district's average kindergarten enrollment for the past seven years was 1,000 (assuming the historical base is seven years), then in each of the years in which enrollments are projected the kindergarten enrollment is estimated to be 1,000. Obviously this technique is questionable, particularly in school systems

Table 8.1
Enrollment Data Providing a Six-Year Base

| YEAR | KNDG | 1ST | 2ND | 3RD | 4TH | 5TH | 6TH | 7TH | 8TH | 9TH | 10TH | 11TH | 12TH | SP ED | TOTAL |
|---|---|---|---|---|---|---|---|---|---|---|---|---|---|---|---|
| 83-84 | 234 | 250 | 267 | 301 | 300 | 306 | 321 | 320 | 333 | 350 | 351 | 336 | 321 | 90 | 4,080 |
| 84-85 | 345 | 267 | 289 | 302 | 301 | 305 | 343 | 321 | 322 | 342 | 353 | 344 | 302 | 91 | 4,227 |
| 85-86 | 326 | 234 | 299 | 303 | 304 | 322 | 324 | 324 | 334 | 345 | 354 | 355 | 333 | 92 | 4,249 |
| 86-87 | 321 | 233 | 300 | 304 | 309 | 321 | 325 | 355 | 335 | 346 | 356 | 322 | 311 | 93 | 4,231 |
| 87-88 | 212 | 233 | 288 | 305 | 310 | 311 | 326 | 324 | 336 | 347 | 342 | 343 | 312 | 94 | 4,083 |
| 88-89 | 345 | 256 | 299 | 306 | 311 | 312 | 329 | 345 | 337 | 348 | 342 | 354 | 313 | 95 | 4,292 |
| RATIOS | | 0.82613 | 1.18262 | 1.04535 | 1.00769 | 1.02289 | 1.04848 | 1.01067 | 1.00402 | 1.04056 | 1.00962 | 0.97902 | 0.92112 | | |

**Table 8.2**
**Enrollment Projection Using Data from Table 8.1**

| YEAR | KNDG | 1ST | 2ND | 3RD | 4TH | 5TH | 6TH | 7TH | 8TH | 9TH | 10TH | 11TH | 12TH | SP ED | TOTAL |
|------|------|-----|-----|-----|-----|-----|-----|-----|-----|-----|------|------|------|-------|-------|
| 83-84 | 234 | 250 | 267 | 301 | 300 | 306 | 321 | 320 | 333 | 350 | 351 | 336 | 321 | 90 | 4,080 |
| 84-85 | 345 | 267 | 289 | 302 | 301 | 305 | 343 | 321 | 322 | 342 | 353 | 344 | 302 | 91 | 4,227 |
| 85-86 | 326 | 234 | 299 | 303 | 304 | 322 | 324 | 324 | 334 | 345 | 354 | 355 | 333 | 92 | 4,249 |
| 86-87 | 321 | 233 | 300 | 304 | 309 | 321 | 325 | 355 | 335 | 346 | 356 | 322 | 311 | 93 | 4,231 |
| 87-88 | 212 | 233 | 288 | 305 | 310 | 311 | 326 | 324 | 336 | 347 | 342 | 343 | 312 | 94 | 4,083 |
| 88-89 | 345 | 256 | 299 | 306 | 311 | 312 | 329 | 345 | 337 | 348 | 342 | 354 | 313 | 95 | 4,292 |
| 89-90 | 297 | 285 | 303 | 313 | 308 | 318 | 327 | 333 | 346 | 351 | 351 | 335 | 326 | 0 | 4,193 |
| 90-91 | 297 | 246 | 337 | 316 | 315 | 315 | 334 | 331 | 334 | 360 | 354 | 344 | 308 | 0 | 4,191 |
| 91-92 | 297 | 246 | 290 | 352 | 319 | 322 | 331 | 337 | 332 | 347 | 364 | 347 | 317 | 0 | 4,201 |
| 92-93 | 297 | 246 | 290 | 304 | 355 | 326 | 338 | 334 | 338 | 345 | 351 | 356 | 319 | 0 | 4,200 |
| 93-94 | 297 | 246 | 290 | 304 | 306 | 363 | 342 | 341 | 336 | 352 | 349 | 343 | 328 | 0 | 4,197 |
| 94-95 | 297 | 246 | 290 | 304 | 306 | 313 | 381 | 346 | 343 | 349 | 356 | 341 | 316 | 0 | 4,187 |
| 95-96 | 297 | 246 | 290 | 304 | 306 | 313 | 328 | 385 | 347 | 351 | 353 | 348 | 314 | 0 | 4,181 |
| 96-97 | 297 | 246 | 290 | 304 | 306 | 313 | 328 | 332 | 386 | 361 | 354 | 345 | 321 | 0 | 4,182 |
| 97-98 | 297 | 246 | 290 | 304 | 306 | 313 | 328 | 332 | 333 | 402 | 365 | 347 | 318 | 0 | 4,179 |
| 98-99 | 297 | 246 | 290 | 304 | 306 | 313 | 328 | 332 | 333 | 346 | 406 | 357 | 319 | 0 | 4,176 |

Note: Special education students are spread across grade levels in the projections.

with fluctuations in the actual enrollments. The best method for overcoming this deficiency is to use birth data for estimating kindergarten enrollments.

The issue with special education enrollments is essentially the same as with kindergarten enrollments (i.e., for special education programs which are self-contained and not reported with grade level enrollments). The typical method used for projecting future enrollments in special education is to establish a mean for the base period and then to use this average as a constant in the projected years. One alternative which is mathematically more precise is to place the children in the grade levels where they would be enrolled if they were not in self-contained special education classes. This places the students with their actual cohort groups. If precise data for special education student ages are not available, the students could be dispersed evenly across the grade levels. If, for example, there were 122 students in the special education category which spanned K–12, this figure would be divided by 13 (the number of grade levels) and the product added to each existing grade level enrollment. These adjustments are especially recommended if the cohort-survival ratios are used to make projections beyond several years.

The cohort-survival method is extremely accurate in the short term (two to four years). Extension of projections based solely upon cohort-survival ratios beyond the short term become more susceptible to error (Alspaugh, 1981). This is especially true in locations where there is instability in the general population (e.g., a high level emigration).

## Retention Ratios and Birth Data

As mentioned, one concern about the use of retention ratios alone is the kindergarten population. One method that can be used to address this issue is the infusion of birth data into the mathematical calculations. First, these data must be available in some form that permits extrapolations. In states having all-county school systems (i.e., one school system for the entire county), the use of birth data is somewhat simplified if county birth data are available. But for the vast majority of school systems, this is not the case. What must be done then is to take county birth data and treat them mathematically to produce likely future enrollments in kindergarten.

The technique discussed here for using birth data is based upon the following assumptions:

1. Children enroll in kindergarten at age five.
2. Accurate birth data are available for counties.
3. The birth data are reported by the county of residence of the mother regardless of where the actual births occurred.
4. The school district has operated a kindergarten program for at least the previous six years.

5. There have not been any major policy changes, nor are such changes anticipated in the near future, which would affect kindergarten enrollments (e.g., changing transportation policies, moving from a half-day program to an all-day program).

If all of these assumptions can be met, the procedures are as follows:

*Step One.* Establish an historical base period (as was described in creating retention ratios). This base should be six to ten years.

*Step Two.* Take each year in the base and match it with the birth pool for the cohort group. Since children enroll in kindergarten at age five, this can be done by going back five years.

*Step Three.* Divide the actual kindergarten enrollment for a given year by its matched county birth pool. The product represents the percent of a given birth pool that actually enrolled in the school district.

*Step Four.* Do step three for each of the years in the base. Then calculate the average for the base years (the average percent draw from the birth pool).

Table 8.3 provides data for an imaginary school district.

Using the data in Table 8.3, the calculation for the years would be as follows:

$$320/760 = .4210 \text{ or } 42\%;$$
$$305/754 = .4045 \text{ or } 40\%;$$
$$310/781 = .3969 \text{ or } 40\%;$$
$$299/702 = .4259 \text{ or } 43\%;$$
$$289/689 = .4194 \text{ or } 42\%;$$
$$301/708 = .4251 \text{ or } 43\%;$$
$$279/691 = .4037 \text{ or } 40\%.$$

These data indicate a stable draw for the school district from the county birth pool. To obtain a multiplier for predicting future kindergarten enrollments, the planner simply calculates the mean (average) for the products of each year:

$$(.4210 + .4045 + .3969 + .4259 + .4194 + .4251 + .4037)/7 = .4138$$
or 41%.

Thus, the average draw for Star City Schools from the county birth pool for the past seven years was 41 percent. Now the planner can predict the future kindergarten enrollments for at least the next several years. The children born in 1985 will enroll in kindergarten five years later. Taking the birth figure for that year and multiplying it by the average draw, a projected kindergarten enrollment can be made. Assume that the birth pool for 1985 was 350. Multiplying that figure by .4138 produces an estimated kindergarten enrollment of 144.83 or 145 students. In school districts without kindergarten, this same technique works for calculating first grade enrollments. Simply use a birth pool six years prior to first grade enrollments (instead of five as used for kindergarten).

Obviously, this technique is limited to those years for which birth pools are already established. Yet, enrollment projections typically extend beyond three or

**Table 8.3**
**Birth Data and Kindergarten Enrollments for Star City Schools**

| Year | Kindergarten enrollment | County births 5 yrs. earlier |
|------|------------------------|------------------------------|
| 1983 | 320 | 760 |
| 1984 | 305 | 754 |
| 1985 | 310 | 781 |
| 1986 | 299 | 702 |
| 1987 | 289 | 689 |
| 1988 | 301 | 708 |
| 1989 | 279 | 691 |

four years. Predicting kindergarten enrollments beyond years for which birth pools are available can be done in several ways:

1. Using averages to predict future birth pools (taking the last six to ten years, calculating the average number of births for those years, and using the average to predict future birth pools).
2. Estimating future birth pools from larger demographic studies (e.g., state-wide population projections which include estimated future births).

Projections based upon retention ratios and birth data tend to be more reliable for projections extending beyond two or three years (Alspaugh, 1981).

### Special Considerations

In projecting student populations, the planner must be extremely careful to base projections on accurate assumptions and to analyze data frequently (Harris, Burrage, & Smith, 1986). Knowing whether a community has a stable general population, studying economic trends, and evaluating the impact of policy changes exemplify work that must be done in relation to assumptions. Since projections are not foolproof, they need to be updated periodically to adjust for changes in the environment and in the school district. Annual calculations are strongly recommended.

Since retention ratios are the dominant method for predicting school enrollments, two problems merit consideration. One, the cohort-survival method, assumes that grade level retentions do not change dramatically from year to year. In some school districts, this assumption may not be valid. Two, retention ratios are most often used for school district rather than for individual school projections. The results of school district projections based solely upon retention ratios may present a distorted picture for an individual school (Pullum, Graham, & Herting, 1986).

In using birth data, it is advisable to examine congruence between county birth data and school district enrollment trends. When these two factors are going in the same direction (i.e., they are both increasing or decreasing), the risk is decreased on the projections made from birth data. If the data are incongruous (i.e., one is increasing while the other is decreasing), the risk of error in projections made from birth data increases (Lows, 1987).

Finally, there is one general rule which is applicable to all planning situations where pupil population projections are used: *Multiple forms of input produce a more accurate projection.* The planner who relies on a single form of input is much more likely to err. A good demographic study of a school district should include information about the general population and the pupil population, and each of these should be the product of myriad sources of information.

## SUMMARY

This chapter reviewed the planning issues related to demography. Facility planning has both quantitative and qualitative needs to consider. The quantitative issue relates to the number of persons who must be served. Accordingly, estimating future populations is a vital element of comprehensive planning.

Studying the general population provides insight into trends that may affect the school district. A number of data bases are available for this task, including U.S. census data, state-wide statistics, and local planning studies. Pupil population projections can be done in several ways, but the most prevalent method involves the use of retention ratios. Facility planners are increasingly relying upon birth data to make more accurate long-term projections.

Enrollment projections are subject to error. They rely typically on techniques that assume the future will be much like the past. In many communities, this simply is untrue. Yet, demography is the best tool available for estimating quantitative needs. Updating such studies annually and basing projections on multiple forms of input reduce the margin of error.

## ISSUES FOR DISCUSSION

1. Differentiate between quantitative and qualitative needs as related to facility planning.
2. Develop a list of potential sources of demographic data in your community and assess the potential value of each to facility planning.
3. Why are projections based solely upon retention ratios likely to be more accurate in the short term than in the long term?
4. If a school district had negative retention ratios at each grade, a projection extending into the future indefinitely would produce an enrollment of zero. Is this true or untrue?
5. Discuss the potential value of national census data for facility planning.
6. Why is it better to use multiple forms of input in projecting future population?
7. Can you identify any projection techniques not covered in this chapter? Determine if these techniques have any relevance for school studies.

# 9

# FINANCING FACILITY
# PROJECTS

Financial planning for educational facility projects is a fundamental task for at least three reasons: (1) large sums of money are involved, (2) the monies come from public sources making accountability critical, and (3) financing plans must be in compliance with existing state statutes. Contemporary conditions also add to the importance of this responsibility. Fluctuating interest rates, changing laws governing tax-exempt bonds, changing tax laws affecting individual investors, and higher construction costs exemplify rather recent developments demanding comprehensive and precise fiscal planning.

Ever since the late 1960s when U.S. citizens began to challenge the constitutionality of long-standing school finance problems, e.g., *San Antonio Independent School District* vs. *Rodriguez* (1973), school finance experts, state legislatures, and school administrators have struggled with the issue of fiscal equality. Public education is a responsibility of state government, and in all states except Hawaii (where there is one state school system), the authority to operate public schools is delegated to local boards of education. Fiscal equality focuses upon the degree to which a student receives equal support for public education within a given state regardless of the local district in which he or she resides. Because most states require local districts to rely to some degree upon revenues from local property tax, and because most districts vary in wealth (assessed valuation), it is not surprising that, historically, districts have exhibited significant variance in both the ability to support educational initiatives and actual expenditures—including facility projects. Although great strides have been made in the last two decades to create fiscal equity for operating schools, school construction costs remain quite dependent upon local revenues in many states.

The battles over inequity of school funding formulas continue. In West Virginia, for example, a suit filed by the parents of five children in 1975 contended that the financing of public education in that state violated the constitutional provision requiring a "thorough and efficient" education. This case exemplifies how facilities are one factor affected by funding disparities of local school districts. After years of court battles, this case remains subject to judicial review. What is more important, the funding formula in West Virginia, the nucleus of this litigation, remains unchanged (Smith and Zirkel, 1988). The historical elements of this case, *Pauley vs. Kelly,* clearly exhibits how school financing, including financing of capital outlay, is a mixture of economics, law, and politics.

This chapter examines: (1) the sources of revenue for financing school facility projects, (2) potential financing plans, (3) recent changes in the tax laws, and (4) future issues related to financing capital outlay. Special attention is given to the topic of tax-free bonds, the most prevalent method used by school districts to pay for buildings.

## FUNDING SOURCES

Although the majority of funding for capital outlay is generated at the local and state levels, other sources of revenue have been used from time to time to help pay for school construction. These sources have received greater attention in recent years as a result of an awareness of the disparity that exists in formulas/statutes that require local property taxes to assume the major portion of the burden. Public funds can be generated from taxes from the federal, state, or local level. Following the lead of higher education, several school districts are experimenting with the potentialities of establishing tax-free foundations in an effort to generate additional funds for construction. These foundations, analogous to alumni operations in colleges, seek private gifts and donations.

### Federal Funding

Historically, the federal government has played a minor role in supporting school construction. Most federal dollars that have been designated for school plant financing have been directed not to the local district but rather to the state (i.e., state department of education). The state in turn channels the money to local districts via incentive programs designed to encourage and assist the development of "special" projects such as vocational education. In general, the total impact of federal dollars on school construction in recent decades has been minute.

Although past federal involvement in facility funding has been inconsequential, it has not been because of a lack of suggestions to institute change. A number of ideas have been advanced to increase federal participation in financing school construction costs. One justification for such increases rests with the realization that states themselves vary markedly in the ability to support public education. Thus, federal assistance could provide an avenue of equalization among the 50 states. Another reason proposed by advocates of a greater federal role is that such funding would, de facto, decrease reliance upon the property tax to fund school projects (Brooks, Conrad, and Griffith, 1980). The property tax, the major source of local revenue, has been unpopular with taxpayers and its limitations and inequities have been well-documented by school finance experts (Guthrie, 1988; Quindry, 1979).

One difficulty inherent in any discussion of a greater role for the federal government in financing capital outlay is the realization that federal aid to education is a perennially unpopular topic among most educators and taxpayers. There is, to be sure, a mindset that federal assistance always comes with "strings attached." This condition creates an approach-avoidance situation for most school districts. The lure of additional dollars is tempting, but the federal regulations (e.g., laws governing construction contracts) that are linked to those dollars are uninviting. One superintendent put it this way, "For 5 percent of the funding the federal government wants 100 percent of the control. It's just not worth it." The fear of losing local autonomy has resulted in many administrators, school board members, and taxpayers looking askance at federal assistance. This timidity about federal control, coupled with a conservative posture toward federal assistance to public elementary and secondary schools emanating from the three branches of government in Washington, D.C., suggests that increased federal support for school construction in the near future is unlikely.

## State Funding

The aftermath of landmark legal decisions regarding fiscal equality is a virtual smorgasbord of state school finance plans. Not surprisingly, these varying formulas include an assortment of plans for funding capital outlay. Some states have adopted plans for funding school construction that place a greater share of the burden on state revenues. Other states have maintained programs that require local districts to rely entirely upon local taxes. These differences are exemplified in the following three states:

*Hawaii.* Having the only statewide system of public education, it is not surprising that Hawaii maintains a program of 100 percent state funding for elementary and secondary facilities. There is no direct relationship between property taxes and school facilities. Funds for education are appropriated by the state legislature. There are no bond issues and local pressure groups find it virtually impossible to prevent or influence building initiatives (Thompson, 1988).

*Arizona.* Arizona's school finance formula is different from most states. Both capital outlay costs and debt service obligations are infused into the state's equalization formula. The effect is that less wealthy districts (i.e., those with below average assessed valuation per pupil) receive higher levels of state aid for school construction. The purpose is to equalize the effort (tax rates) that must be exerted at the local district level. The increased state assistance brings with it increased state control over the process of planning and executing facility projects. Thus, the plan is economically defensible but contrary to the political belief of total local control of schools (Jordan, 1988).

*Nebraska.* Nebraska is at the opposite end of the continuum from Hawaii. In this state, the financing of school construction is totally a local school district responsibility. The only role of state government is one of permissive legislation and regulation (Hudson, 1988).

These three examples verify the tremendous differences in funding practices among the 50 states. But providing funds for school construction is only one role state government can assume. The state also is responsible for establishing a myriad of laws that govern what local districts may or may not do—even with monies raised locally. In the early 1970s, the National School Finance Project (Future Directions for School Financing, 1971) uncovered some serious problems that existed with regard to funding capital outlay and what is more important, emphasized the responsibility of the state for these inequities. One difficulty associated with state mandates was imposed debt limitations. Many states impose debt restrictions upon governmental agencies, and in some instances, these limitations are unduly restrictive (e.g., in Indiana the restriction is 2 percent of assessed valuation). Because the debt ceilings are not adjusted periodically to account for inflation and other economic variables, they eventually become unduly circumscriptive.

Some states (e.g., Pennsylvania) have created grant-in-aid programs to help local districts pay for school construction. These programs may be developed according to an equalization concept (the example presented for Arizona exemplifies this approach), a percentage-matching concept (the state's contribution is based upon the total dollars raised locally), or a flat grant concept (a given amount per student or per project is made available regardless of other variables). The equalization concept comes closest to achieving the goal of *fiscal neutrality* (i.e., eradicating the effects of local district wealth upon required effort to raise revenues). Both matching and flat grant formulas are apt to penalize school districts with below average assessed valuations.

Loan programs are also used by some states to assist the funding of buildings. These loans typically are limited and provide a relatively small percent of the needed funds. The advantage of such programs is that they almost always offer interest rates lower than those available on the open market. Given the significant increase in construction costs since 1970, the overall effect of state loan programs has diminished—especially in those states where adjustments were not made to loan ceilings.

Several states experimented with full state funding for capital outlay only to determine that such a structure would be too costly for state government. Florida is one example. With a rapidly growing population and the need to erect new facilities, an attempt was made to pay school construction costs entirely out of state revenues. After seeing the impact of such a program, the Florida officials rescinded the full state funding program. In addition to Florida, California and

Maryland experimented with full state funding, but in these states, concerns emerged regarding the state taking control of all aspects of the project (Guthrie, Garms, and Pierce, 1988).

## Local Funding

The basic economics of generating local funds for education via the property tax is not as complicated as most believe. Two factors, property values and tax rates, combine to determine how much revenue is generated. Wealth of a school system is stated in terms of assessed valuation (the value of property to be taxed). However, total assessed valuation does not present a good measure for comparisons. A better measure is assessed valuation per pupil (i.e., the amount of taxable property for each student enrolled in the school district—determined by dividing the total assessed valuation by the number of pupils). The inequity between wealthy and poor school districts can be seen in the following example where two districts want to generate five million dollars for construction:

District A has an assessed valuation of $200,000,000.00 District B has an assessed valuation of $50,000,000.00. Assume that each district has identical enrollments of 3,000 pupils. District B will have to have a tax rate four times as high as district A to generate the needed $5,000,000.00.

In a state where local funding is used exclusively to support construction, this example illustrates the gross inequities of relying solely upon local school district wealth. The negative effects for the poorer district are exacerbated when it borrows money. Being poorer, the district is likely to have to pay higher interest rates on its debt obligations because of a poorer bond rating. In this regard, the inequity is compounded.

If local funding alone is so grossly unfair, why does it persist? The reasons are largely political. State legislators and governors often are not anxious to assume added fiscal burdens. Additionally, local school boards are usually protective of local control, and when they weigh the economic and political ramifications, they frequently opt for paying higher taxes. Finally, the argument can be made that decisions to erect new schools (or improve existing ones) is a local decision that benefits the local community—thus, local taxpayers ought to assume the financial burden. These positions favoring total local funding for capital outlay are being eroded by court decisions that bring political and economic issues face-to-face with the legal reality that public education is a state responsibility. A recent study in Kansas, for example, revealed that not only does wealth per pupil in that state vary widely, so does the quality of educational facilities (Thompson and Camp, 1988). Finally, Guthrie, Garms, and Pierce (1988) contend that little reform has taken place with debt financing simply because construction costs constitute such a small portion of the budget compared to operating costs.

### Other Options

As previously mentioned a small number of school districts are becoming active in a concept long employed in public higher education—fund raising. These districts have created tax-exempt subdivisions within their organizations that solicit donations and gifts from private citizens and from established foundations. Even though the interest in creating such unrestricted funds has escalated in the 1980s, there is little evidence that this effort is having a significant impact upon the funding of capital outlay. Nevertheless, most states permit private funds to be used to assist with school construction projects.

## FUNDING METHODS

Putting together a financing package for a contemporary facility project is a complicated task. New comprehensive high schools may have price tags that surpass 40 million dollars. Under these conditions, school officials not only need to know what the various sources of revenues are, they also need to understand alternative methods for generating these monies. Not infrequently, a financing package will be composed of several options.

### Pay-As-You-Go Financing

The pay-as-you-go method of financing schools historically has been a popular alternative for fiscal conservatives who embrace the notion that school districts ought not erect new facilities unless the money to pay for them has been accumulated. This is accomplished either by (1) savings in the operating/reserve funds or (2) tax levies which permit accumulation of funds for future building projects. Not all states permit the latter alternative. In simple terms, the pay-as-you-go method functions just like a personal savings account. To buy a new car, for example, two primary methods of payment are available. The first is to finance the car by securing a loan. This creates a debt obligation that must be repaid in a specific period of time. The second alternative is to pay cash. The first option is almost always more expensive in the long term (whether it is actually more expensive may depend upon economic conditions); however, the second alternative may be impossible for some individuals. A school district faced with facility needs essentially has the same alternatives. If paying for a school building with accumulated dollars is impossible, the district must borrow the money.

Advocates put forward three justifications for the pay-as-you-go method:

1. There is never any question as to whether the taxpayers can meet their obligation to pay for the building.
2. There is no chance of default on debt obligation.
3. No option is more economical because interest payments are avoided.

In modern times, these assertions have diminished in relevancy. The rising cost of buildings makes it impossible for most districts to accumulate enough money to pay for a project in advance. Additionally, the fear of default has been markedly reduced by the positive record of school districts paying their debt obligations. Perhaps most important is the fact that inflation has eroded the arguments that favor the pay-as-you-go method. Any savings accrued by waiting until money is available is apt to be counterbalanced by increased construction costs (Kowalski, 1983). In this era of collective bargaining and public scrutiny of budgets, it is difficult for public agencies to accumulate massive balances in their funds.

## Bonding

For the majority of public school districts, long-term borrowing is the forced choice for funding school construction. Critics may be quick to attack long-term obligations as being costly, yet the process is defended on the grounds that the debt is spread across generations (Guthrie, Garms, and Pierce, 1988). In this regard, those directly benefiting from the facility will share in the obligation of paying for it.

The sale of tax-free bonds constitutes the major vehicle for long-term borrowing. A bond (or note) is a security whereby the issuer agrees to pay a fixed principal sum on a specified date and at a specified rate of interest. The specified date is referred to as the maturity date. Most bonds are sold through a process of competitive bidding and come under the scrutiny of underwriters and investor analysts. Bonds issued by state or local governmental agencies such as school districts are called *municipal bonds*.

In some states *bond banks* have been established to aid the sale of tax-exempt bonds. This is done through a collective process (i.e., the bond bank takes four or five projects to the market at one time in hopes of receiving more favorable bids because the size of the issue is increased).

The majority of school construction is financed by *general obligation bonds* (called GO bonds). GO bonds are secured by a pledge of the issuer's taxing powers; thus, they are considered solid investments by many bond buyers. Some states establish a statutory limit on the amount of debt a school district can incur via GO bonds. This limitation is almost always established as a percentage of the governmental unit's assessed valuation.

In the vast majority of states, school districts are required to hold a referendum prior to a bond sale. Most states require a simple majority approval to go forward with the sale; however, about 25 percent of the states require more than a simple majority vote. Ever since the so-called "tax payers revolt" in California, referenda have been major hurdles for school systems pursuing facility projects. A study by Lows (1987) found that certain demographic variables are related to positive outcomes in referenda: voter turnout, preference for the Republican

Party among the electorate, percentage of housing occupied by whites, percentage of married couple families, and percentage of children under age 18. There may be other factors that have consequences for referenda since school districts and communities are unique entities with fluid economic and political conditions.

Once a school district has the authority to move forward with a bond sale, a strategy for marketing the debt needs to be established. Virtually all municipal bonds are sold on the open market in order to encourage competition. In select instances, it may be advantageous for a school district to pursue a negotiated sale (if permitted by state law). Negotiated sales should only be pursued after receiving professional counsel from the attorneys and the financial consultant.

There are several different classifications of bonds. Among the more prevalent are:

*Callable Bond.* This is a bond that can be recalled by the issuer and paid prior to maturity. The advantage of callable bonds is that the issuer (the school district) can take advantage of more favorable interest rates if they emerge after the initial bond sale. This process is commonly referred to as *advanced refunding*. Callable bonds constitute a disadvantage for the buyer in that they create uncertainty regarding long-term investments. Recent changes in federal tax laws place some restrictions on advance refunding.

*Coupon Bond.* Some bonds are sold with detachable coupons. These coupons provide evidence that interest is due. At the specified time, the coupon is detached and submitted to the issuer for payment of interest.

*Registered Bond.* The owner of this bond is registered with the issuing agent (or its bank or trustee agent), a registered bond cannot be sold or exchanged without a change of registration. Such a bond may be registered as to principal and interest or as to principal only.

*Serial Bond.* This is a bond where the principal is repaid in periodic installments over the life of the issue.

*Term Bond.* These bonds pay all of the principal at one specified time. Interest payments are made periodically during the life of the bond.

The primary purpose of selling bonds in a competitive market is to produce the most favorable interest rate possible. Interest rates are affected to some degree by five primary factors: the bond rating assigned to the issue, size of the bond issue (total dollar amount), length of the issue (duration of the debt obligation), types of bonds that are sold (e.g., callable, term), and economic conditions at the time of the sale (e.g., inflation rates, prime interest rates). One service the school district should expect from the financial consultant is an analysis of how each of these factors may affect a pending issue. The consultant also may be asked to recommend a time frame for selling the bonds to take advantage of market conditions.

*Bond ratings* are assigned by bond rating firms prior to public sales. These ratings can significantly affect buyer competition and, ultimately, interest rates. The two major rating firms are Moody's and Standard & Poor's. Each firm uses its own system for reviewing an issue, and each may rely upon different factors in making judgments. Basically, the ratings reflect economic and administrative qualities of the school district, the community environment, current debt obligations, debt structure, wealth, the quantity and quality of industry within the school district's taxing region, debt history, and the current condition of school properties. Tables 9.1 and 9.2 contain the ratings of these two major firms in the area of school construction bonds.

The *Tax Reform Act of 1986* was enacted in October in 1986. It replaced the Internal Revenue Code of 1954. Tax-exempt bonds were especially affected by this revision. The new codes require that bonds meet certain criteria to qualify as tax-exempt. Simply being issued by a governmental agency does not assure this advantage. Additionally, the new codes are more stringent with regard to invest-

**Table 9.1**
**Ratings Used by Moody's Investment Service**

| *Rating* | *Explanation* |
|----------|---------------|
| **Aaa** | These are bonds which are considered the best quality. They carry the smallest degree of investment risk and are generally referred to as "gilt edge." |
| **Aa** | These bonds are judged to be high quality by all standards. With bonds judged Aaa they are considered high grade bonds. The margin of protection is judged to be somewhat less than Aaa |
| **A** | These are considered upper medium grade obligations. Factors giving security to principal and interest are considered adequate but elements may be present which suggest susceptibility to impairment sometime in the future. |
| **Baa** | These are considered medium grade obligations. They are neither highly protected nor poorly secured. Interest and principal payments appear adequate for the present but certain protective elements may be lacking or may be characteristically unreliable over a long period. |
| **Ba** | These bonds are judged to have speculative elements. Their future cannot be considered as well assured. Often the protection of interest and principal payments may be moderate and thereby not well safeguarded during both good and bad times in the future. |
| **B** | These bonds lack the characteristics of a desirable investment. Assurance of interest and principal payments or other provisions of the contract over any long period of time may be small. |
| **Caa** | These are poor standing bonds. Such issues may be in default or there may be present elements of danger with respect to principal and interest. |
| **Ca** | These are obligations that are speculative in a high degree. Such issues are often in default or have other marked shortcomings. |
| **C** | These are the lowest rated bonds. These bonds are considered to have extremely poor prospects of ever attaining any real investment standing. |

Source: Moody's Industrial Manual, 1988, p. vi.

**Table 9.2**
**Ratings Used By Standard & Poor's**

| *Rating* | *Explanation* |
|---|---|
| AAA | This is the highest rating. Capacity to pay interest and repay principal is extremely strong. |
| AA | This rating differs from AAA only in small degree. The capacity to pay interest and repay principal is considered very strong. |
| A | A debt in this category has a strong capacity to pay interest and repay principal but is somewhat more susceptible to the adverse effects of changes in circumstances and economic conditions than the higher rated bonds. |
| BBB | This rating indicates an adequate capacity to pay interest and repay principal. Although adequate protection parameters are exhibited, adverse economic conditions or changing circumstances are more likely to lead to a weakened capacity for payment than higher rated categories. |
| BB,B, CCC, CC | These debts are considered on balance, as predominantly speculative with respect to paying interest and repaying principal in accordance with the terms of the obligation. BB is the lowest degree of speculation and CC is the highest degree of speculation. Although these debts are likely to have some quality and protective characteristics, these are outweighed by large uncertainties or major risk exposures to adverse conditions. |
| C | This rating is reserved for income bonds on which no interest is being paid. |
| D | A debt rated D is in default, and payment of interest and repayment of principal are in arrears. |

ments from bond proceeds (arbitrage). Arbitrage is the interest rate differential between the rate on a municipal bond and yield made with the investment of the bond proceeds. Imagine a school system that sells five million dollars worth of bonds for a new elementary school at an interest rate of 7 percent. Since the proceeds of the bonds are made available at the time of the sale, and since the school district will not need to expend all of those proceeds immediately, the proceeds are typically invested until they are needed to pay the bills. The rate of interest earned on the investment is usually higher than the one the school district had to pay to get the money in the first place. Assume that they could invest the money for one year at 8 percent. The difference between the rate on the issue and the rate on the investment is arbitrage. If a school district does not meet the criteria established in the 1986 Act, it may cause the bonds to become retroactively taxable. The 1986 revisions are complex and full discussion here is not feasible. Superintendents and other school officials working in leadership roles related to debt financing should seek consultation regarding the current parameters of tax-exempt bonds early in the planning process.

The sale of bonds involves a number of legal and economic decisions. Insurance, existing state statutes, and familiarity with the bond markets exemplify critical issues. Questions about advertisements, printing the bonds, delivery of the bonds, and the like are sure to arise. The school district's attorney (or project attorney), bond counsel, and the financial advisor have always been considered invaluable to this process; however, the recent revisions in the tax laws make their services even more essential.

### Lease/Purchase Agreements

As mentioned earlier, some states impose limitations on debt obligations for school districts. These limitations are typically stated as a ratio of debt to wealth (assessed valuation). The concept of lease/purchase emerged in states imposing debt limitations as one method of providing financing for needed schools without violating existing statutes. The process of lease/purchase entails a school being erected (or remodeled) by a legal entity other than the school district. The school district in turn pays the owner rental payments equal to the amount that is required to retire the debt obligation and the rental payments go toward an eventual purchase. The following example may prove helpful:

A school district is located in a state that imposes a debt limitation of 2 percent of assessed valuation. This district has a total assessed valuation of $100,000,000.00. The district needs to erect a new high school and the estimated cost is $15,000,000.00. This amount is well beyond the state's limitation (2 percent of the current assessed valuation is only $2,000,000.00). In order to meet its needs, the district enters into a contractual agreement with a separate corporation that will pay for the school to be constructed. This corporation then leases the school to the district and the annual rental payments are structured to retire the leasing corporation's debt obligation. If the leasing corporation has scheduled its debt retirement for 22 years, the school district would make the final payment in the twenty-second year and then assume ownership of the facility.

The corporations that enter into such agreements with school districts are commonly called holding corporations or holding authorities. These corporations may either be public (not-for-profit) or private (for profit). In the case of the public corporation, its single purpose is to sell first mortgage bonds in order to construct a school and lease/sell it to the school district. Private corporations, by contrast, provide the same service but do so as a business transaction to gain profit. The major advantage of the private holding corporation is that no bond sale is conducted. The corporation uses its own assets to construct the building. Avoiding a bond sale usually saves time and may also reduce the school district's need for special consultant services. By contrast, some school administrators dislike private financing because (1) it may result in higher interest rates compared to a public holding corporation, and/or (2) they believe that too much control of the project is assumed by the private finance company. School districts planning to use the lease/purchase method should carefully weigh the cost savings, time savings, and decision-making ramifications when contemplating using a public vs. private holding corporation. Individual circumstances dictate which option is best at any given time.

The laws vary among the 50 states regarding the use of the lease/purchase method of acquiring new schools. As noted previously, this practice is most prevalent in states maintaining highly restrictive debt limits that have not been adjusted as building costs have markedly increased over the past 40 to 50 years.

## DEBT MANAGEMENT

Regardless of whether a school district sells GO bonds or enters into a lease/purchase arrangement, a plan must be developed to retire the debt. This plan is based upon the sources of revenue for debt retirement and the conditions established for the debt retirement. With regard to acquiring such monies from local property taxes, the school district usually establishes a *sinking fund* or *debt*

**Table 9.3**
**Sample Amortization Schedule for a Bond Issue (term = 25 years, 9 months; interest rate = 8.5%)**

| bond year ending Jan.1 | principal balance (000) | principal payment (000) | interest payment (000) | total payment (000) |
|---|---|---|---|---|
| 1988 | $9,995 | ---- | $618,441 | $618,441 |
| 1989 | 9,995 | ---- | 824,588 | 824,588 |
| 1990 | 9,820 | $175 | 824,588 | 999,588 |
| 1991 | 9,635 | 185 | 810,150 | 995,150 |
| 1992 | 9,435 | 200 | 794,888 | 994,888 |
| 1993 | 9,225 | 210 | 778,387 | 988,387 |
| 1994 | 9,000 | 225 | 761,063 | 986,063 |
| 1995 | 8,760 | 240 | 742,500 | 982,500 |
| 1996 | 8,505 | 255 | 722,700 | 977,700 |
| / | / | / | / | / |
| / | / | / | / | / |
| / | / | / | / | / |
| 2011 | 1,580 | 715 | 189,337 | 904,337 |
| 2012 | 815 | 765 | 130,350 | 895,350 |
| 2013 | ---- | 815 | 67,238 | 882,238 |
| TOTALS | | $9,995 | $14,313,853 | $24,308,853 |

*service fund* (the two terms have the same meaning). A sinking fund is an account that includes monies accumulated for the specific purpose of making debt payments.

How does the school district know how much its debt payments will be in a given year? This information comes from schedules that are developed at the time the school district enters into debt obligations. These tables are called *amortization schedules*. They identify the amount of principal and interest to be paid each year for the duration of the debt obligation. If a school district has more than one outstanding debt, the required annual debt service payment is the sum of obligations noted on each amortization schedule. Table 9.3 illustrates an amortization schedule for an amount of $9,995,000.00. The data in Table 9.3 reveal how interest payments decline and principal payments increase throughout the life of this bond issue. The annual payments remain relatively stable. As this amortization schedule illustrates, a debt of just under ten million dollars will require a total payback of about two and one-half times that amount. The annual payment, listed in the last column of Table 9.3, is the amount that must be raised annually in the sinking fund (less any amount made available from sources other than local school taxes).

If the debt retirement is a mix of revenues from local property taxes and other sources (e.g., loans, state aid), the school district needs to create a debt management plan detailing all of these resources used for meeting debt obligations. This plan should include schedules pinpointing the dates on which financial transactions must occur. If state loans will also be used to retire a debt, the finance plan should include amortization tables for retiring those loans as well.

## OTHER RESPONSIBILITIES

The financial management portion of facility planning includes much more than debt management. Also requiring attention are such tasks as equipment and furniture acquisition, maintenance, and adequate budgeting for operations. Superintendents are apt to assume these responsibilities directly in smaller school systems or delegate them to the business affairs division in larger districts. The major reasons they are delegated to business affairs (as opposed to some other division such as instructional affairs) are: (1) that most school districts incorporate facility management under this division, and (2) that facility planning includes numerous tasks that are functions of business management. Preoccupation with the design and construction of the facility itself may cause school officials to neglect the less obvious responsibilities regarding equipment and maintenance, resulting in serious problems once the school is occupied.

Purchasing equipment and furniture can be a detailed task. In some projects, virtually all such items are included in the original specifications developed by the architect. In other situations, the movable equipment may be purchased directly by the school district through its normal business procedures (i.e., the items are acquired by using the regular funds of the school district). Regardless of the method used, the facility planner needs to account for equipment and furniture needs and to specify how these items will be obtained.

Budgeting adequately for operations is another fiscal responsibility for new, expanded, or renovated school buildings. The failure to study operating costs is one way to create a serious problem. One school district, for instance, erected a new high school that included 45 percent more space than the school it was replacing. The new school was designed to be an "all electric" facility—a utility that had higher rates than the utilities used in the existing facility. Despite these conditions, this school district failed to increase its operational budget the year the new high school opened. The result was a $1.5 million deficit in the first year of operation due entirely to higher operating costs. Cost analysis for operating new or renovated facilities is a frequently overlooked task.

Insurance is a responsibility that typically falls within the realm of business management in a school district. Schools should be protected against loss due to fire, tornadoes, and the like. Coverage also is needed for the contents of the school. Most administrators readily realize that property insurance is standard. Less obvious are special insurance policies related to construction, construction contracts, and debt financing. In concert with the architect and other professional resource personnel, a comprehensive insurance document should be completed for a facility project. This document details all the insurance policies obtained for various phases of the project.

Maintenance is another large responsibility that must be addressed. This topic is discussed in detail in three chapters later in this book. Managing a facility once it is opened is much more complex than it was 20 or 30 years ago. Modern school buildings reflect technological innovations, energy management decisions, and more sophisticated designs and equipment.

## SUMMARY

Facility planning includes a number of financial responsibilities. Foremost among these is debt financing. Since the statutes governing the financing of capital outlay vary markedly among the 50 states, there is no one method common to all school districts. The prevalent method remains the use of local revenues, either exclusively or in combination with other resources.

Reliance upon local revenues for debt financing typically necessitates the sale of bonds. Prior to changes in the tax laws in recent years, virtually all bonds issued by school districts were classified as municipal bonds (tax-exempt bonds). The new codes place specific qualification requirements for achieving a tax-exempt status. Thus, the task of debt financing has become even more intricate.

Financial management related to facility planning also includes tasks such as insurance, acquisition of furniture and equipment, and future planning for operational costs. Given that such a large portion of a facility project falls within the realm of business management, administrators in larger school systems specializing in fiscal administration are most apt to be a part of the facility planning team.

## ISSUES FOR DISCUSSION

1. Develop a position for full state funding for capital outlay related to elementary and secondary schools. Why are most states avoiding this option?

2. Identify the specific requirements for financing capital outlay in your state.

3. Describe circumstances that mitigate against using the pay-as-you-go method of financing capital outlay in your state.

4. Differentiate between serial bonds, general obligation bonds, and coupon bonds.

5. Make a list of the types of insurance that may be needed for a facility project. Compare your list to the actual insurance purchased by a school district in your area recently completing a project.

6. Why is the rating of a debt important?

7. Define the concept of *arbitrage*. Why should the government be concerned about it?

8. List the advantages and disadvantages of incorporating all equipment and furniture into the total cost of a project (thus including these items in the bidding process for the project).

9. Under what conditions would the pay-as-you-go method turn out to be more expensive than debt financing?

10. Develop an argument defending the position that school buildings should be financed entirely—or almost entirely—from local funds.

# 10

# PROJECTS INVOLVING EXISTING FACILITIES

Chapter 2 reviewed several issues that have emerged as high priorities within the realm of facility planning in the past 20 years. This chapter focuses on the ramifications of these issues especially as they relate to: (1) alternatives for retaining older buildings, (2) adding space without abandoning existing schools, and (3) disposing of excess school facilities. If one were to examine textbooks written about school facilities prior to 1970, it would be evident that these topics were given far less attention than the subject of new construction. This attention to new construction reflected prevailing practices during that era. Today, uncertainty about the economy, future enrollments, and needs of students in the twenty-first century have resulted in a cautious attitude toward the abandonment of existing school buildings.

## MODERNIZATION AND REMODELING

Major improvements to an existing school fall into one of two categories: *modernization* or *remodeling*. Modernization entails improvements to a facility without reshaping the spaces. For example, an older school may receive lowered ceilings, carpeting applied over existing floor surfaces, new paint on the walls, and so forth. This work will make the school more modern in appearance but the basic space configurations (classrooms, laboratories) within the school remain unchanged. By contrast, remodeling is more extensive. Not only are improvements made, but spaces are also reshaped to accommodate existing or anticipated instructional (and extracurricular) needs (Castaldi, 1987). Not infrequently, the term *renovation* is also used in conjunction with upgrading existing schools. Although this term commonly refers to renewal (modernization), some individuals use it interchangeably with remodeling. Therefore, it is advantageous to have a clear perspective of what is intended when any of these terms is used.

The growing interest in updating old schools as an alternative to new construction emerged with vigor in the 1970s. Several key factors were responsible. The economy was relatively unstable and inflation caused an upward spiral in construction costs, especially during the late 1970s and early 1980s (Council of Educational Facility Planners, 1985). Additionally, Americans were experiencing a change in philosophy about the "use and dispose" mentality that prevailed following World War II. The higher cost of automobiles and homes forced many citizens to consider whether it was feasible to restore costly items as an alternative to getting rid of them. This same form of economic scrutiny found its way into public decisions. Higher construction costs, coupled with concerns about the rising costs of governmental services, led taxpayers to look more carefully at how public funds were being expended. Still further, negative attitudes toward new construction were enhanced in many instances by a sentimentality for the historic and/or aesthetic value of older schools in a community.

No school superintendent should ever take for granted that either new construction or renovation is the obvious answer to a specific facility problem. In today's "fishbowl" mentality, the public demands to see evidence that potential solutions have been studied carefully and that cost comparisons have occurred. Obviously, individual circumstances determine the detail and extensiveness of such investigations. An examination of alternative solutions occurs within a feasibility study—a study that compares two or more possible solutions.

At times administrators and board members are quick to decide against new construction after looking only at cost or cost in combination with current educational needs. Such judgments are myopic because they ignore a host of other issues that emerge during the life of the school building. Additionally, political pressures sometimes direct school boards and superintendents to ignore facts in order to accommodate public sentiments. The average citizen often takes a position on remodeling or new construction solely from an emotional perspective. But the citizen will not be held accountable for the decision. The superintendent and school board are held to a higher standard. If they make decisions solely on the basis of emotions and if those decisions prove to be deficient, they will have to answer to the taxpayers.

There are numerous factors that can be included in the deliberations of new construction versus renovation. The uniqueness of each situation dictates that careful consideration be given to selecting those factors most cogent to specific wants and needs. As a starting point for making decisions, Figure 10.1 identifies ten criteria that are commonly used to make comparisons between the options of building a new school and renovating an existing facility.

The one factor that is rarely overlooked in determining the practicality of major improvements to existing schools is *cost*. An effective procedure for cost comparison is a feasibility study completed by the architect and other members of the planning team (e.g., educational consultant). Simply placing cost esti-

**Figure 10.1**
**Ten Criteria for Comparing the Options of New Construction and Remodeling**

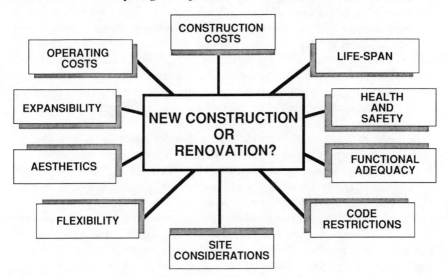

mates for remodeling and new construction side-by-side is insufficient. These figures become meaningful only when they are scrutinized vis-à-vis other criteria such as educational goals, curriculum, instructional methodologies, or extracurricular programs. Additionally, it is noteworthy that costs for construction projects vary significantly based upon geographic locations. Not only climate, but also labor conditions, economic growth, and property values are factors responsible for cost differences in various parts of the United States. While costs for new construction in rural southern communities may be as low as $60.00 to $70.00 per square foot, they may be as high as $150.00 per square foot in Alaska (Brubaker, 1988).

The *lifespan* of a building is an especially important consideration. New construction ought to last for at least 50 years. But how long will a renovated or remodeled school remain functional? This is a question that should be answered by the architect in completing the feasibility study. In conjunction with project cost estimates, lifespan data produce *cost per year data*. Costs per year (i.e., the cost of the project divided by the life expectancy of the building after construction) more accurately describe the actual financial obligations for a project.

*Health and safety* considerations include a host of factors—some more obvious than others. Clean air, security, and fire protection are readily recognized by school officials and taxpayers as important. But health and safety also include features such as access for handicapped individuals or adult usage of the facility outside the regular school day. Will a remodeled school be at least equal to a new facility in providing a healthful and safe environment? If not, how much difference exists between the two alternatives? Will the handicapped and adults be adversely affected by one of the alternatives?

The primary justification of a school building is to facilitate the educational process. To meet this goal a structure must be functional. *Functional adequacy* not only includes the degree to which instructional needs are sufficiently being served, but also includes usage of the school for noninstructional purposes (e.g., athletics, community usage). Are the two options equal with regard to functional adequacy? Simple remodeling often cannot remove serious concerns about the lack of special service spaces in an older school (e.g., the absence of an auxiliary gymnasium).

In many instances, state and local laws and codes affect decisions regarding major improvements to existing schools. *Code restrictions* emerge because older schools were designed at times when either specific codes did not exist or were quite lenient. The required size of classrooms, hallways, and special instructional spaces exemplify possible code issues that may impact negatively on the option of remodeling. In many older buildings, reshaping spaces is extremely costly due to original construction techniques (e.g., load-bearing walls between classrooms that make reconfigurations of classroom space difficult and expensive). Additionally, some states require that renovations or remodeling projects bring schools up to existing codes without exception. In these instances, school districts are usually forced to do an extensive amount of work beyond what is desired, such as placing elevators in two-story buildings.

One advantage of new construction is that a school district usually has flexibility in site selection. Thus, *site considerations* need to be weighed as well. The site should be studied from three perspectives. The first is a quantitative standard, i.e., the size of the site. The second is a qualitative standard, e.g., drainage, freedom from hazards. The third encompasses a separate criterion, the *location of the site*. The site of a current facility and the site selected for a possible new building might be equal in size and in quality, but are the locations equal with regard to meeting the needs of the school district? For instance, shifts in population within a school system may result in an existing building being located away from the majority of children who are enrolled in it. Renovation does not permit relocation of the building. By contrast, a new building can be placed in the center of the existing population (provided the necessary land can be acquired).

As mentioned earlier, decisions that are based only upon current educational needs are often myopic. They fail to look at potential futures. Given this incertitude, *flexibility* and *expansibility* are certainly important considerations. Can spaces within a school be readily changed if future instructional needs so dictate? Will it be possible to enlarge a facility if enrollments increase in the future? Older schools often cannot provide the long-term flexibility that can be designed into new buildings.

One criterion that school administrators find difficult to discuss with many patrons is *aesthetics*. When this term is used, cost-conscious citizens tend to become enraged. Why should schools be beautiful? Why should tax payers support "frills" in school buildings? These are the questions dubious taxpayers raise—especially where all or most of the revenues for capital outlay must come from local taxes. No matter how intense, this questioning should not diminish the importance of aesthetic considerations as they relate to designing a learning environment. The quality of a school building affects student learning directly and indirectly. Studies (e.g., Plumley, 1978; Garrett, 1981; Ledford, 1981) have exhibited that schools with different qualities such as lighting, color schemes, and carpeting affect learning. Indirectly, the environment produces consequences in the realm of student attitudes and feelings (Chan, 1988). School buildings project an image of the community—of the community's values and beliefs regarding the importance of education to future generations. As Eisner (1985) so astutely observes, the factory and assembly line mentality has had serious implications for public education in the United States. Schools should not look like factories, penal institutions, hospitals, or even orphanages. They should be warm, inviting, and unique.

The final criterion that deserves mention with respect to comparing the option of new construction with renewal of an existing school is *operating costs*. Even though remodeling may be less expensive initially, one must question if it will be less expensive in the long run. Older schools were erected when energy conservation was not a primary consideration. Cosmetic improvements to an older school may change the external appearance of the building but may do little to reduce utility bills. There can be hidden costs in remodeled schools that can go undetected for the first few years following improvements. The most common hidden cost is utility bills. As Ginsburg (1989) warns, the cost of day-to-day operations must be a major consideration in reaching facility decisions.

Deciding for or against new construction ought to be based on more than just one or two factors. The ten criteria presented here do not constitute an all-inclusive list, but do provide a comprehensive framework of the most common factors studied. Increasingly, educators are probing to determine if there are significant differences between new and older school environments with regard to learner outcomes (e.g., standardized test scores, discipline, self-image). These research efforts are still in their infancy; however, some studies are already suggesting that modern schools produce higher test scores and fewer discipline problems (e.g., Bowers and Burkett, 1989). The accumulation of knowledge through such comparative studies could have dramatic implications for making choices between new construction and renovation.

In deliberating between a new facility or the upgrading of a current school, the meticulous review of feasibilities should decrease the effect of emotions and heighten objectivity. The administration and school board should be prepared to defend the final decision not only on the basis of costs or personal feelings, but also on the grounds of educational needs, legalities, and political considerations.

A study of institutions of higher education revealed that a variety of methods can be utilized to determine building replacement costs. Among the methods identified were:

- the Engineering News Record (ENR) Index Method
- Boechke Index (American Appraisal Company)
- simple cost per square foot methods
- Handy Appraisal Chart (Markel Appraisal Company)
- Means Cost Per Square Foot and Historical Cost Index (Robert Snow Means Company)

Basically these methods fall into two broad categories: (1) building cost indices methods, and (2) cost per square foot methods. The former requires accurate historical data (e.g., original construction costs, specifications) and does not account for advances in building technology and materials. The latter does reflect advances in building trends and also requires specific data such as gross square footage, specifications, type of construction, and so forth (McClelland, 1985). School districts that maintain accurate records on facilities for insurance and other purposes are at a distinct advantage in completing cost comparisons between renovation and new construction.

Having a professional team complete a feasibility study incorporating the ten criteria listed here, supplemented by other issues unique to the needs and wants of a specific district, should result in a most adequate study. Incorporated into this study should be *life-cycle cost estimates* for the alternatives. Life-cycle estimates should include costs related to design, research and development, investments, operations, and maintenance (Hentschke, 1986). This factor will provide a more objective means of comparison.

## ADDING SPACE

One of the most difficult tasks a school administrator may face is recommending additional space for a school district with a declining enrollment. Yet this is exactly what is being done by many school officials. The public usually does not understand that the need for additional space can stem from a number of conditions. Increased enrollment is the most obvious—and the easiest to explain and defend to the taxpayers. But as mentioned, some districts that are shrinking in size also have space needs. How is this possible? Take for example a superintendent who decides that it is necessary to close an elementary school due to declining enrollments. That decision does not occur in isolation; rather, it is an organizational decision that has ramifications for other parts of the school system. The students attending the school to be closed must be assigned to other elementary schools. This may necessitate changing school boundaries—and ultimately an addition built onto one or more of the elementary schools to accommodate the displaced students.

Two of the most likely reasons for needing more space while experiencing a declining enrollment are: (1) the expansion of curriculum and (2) changes in instructional techniques. The presence of the computer in the school environment is an excellent example of how the latter factor results in environmental needs. Many schools have created separate spaces for computer laboratories, especially in buildings designed prior to 1980 (because computer laboratories were extremely rare at that time). Additions to the curriculum evolve in several ways. Mandates imposed by state government are among the most prevalent. Requiring all-day kindergartens or restricting the size of classes are specific examples (Sylvester, 1988). In Indiana, for instance, state reforms in the early 1980s included directives regarding maximum class sizes for early elementary grades (18 in kindergarten and first grade and 20 in second and third grade). Since most schools in that state had classes that exceeded these maximums, the mandate generated a need for more classroom space. In larger school systems, the total number of additional classrooms needed to meet this mandate was substantial.

The customary response to the need for more space is to place an addition on an existing school by using conventional construction. Today, many schools are purposefully designed to accommodate additions (this attribute is referred to as *expansibility*). Additions on existing buildings may be either vertical (e.g., adding a level) or horizontal (adding a new wing); however, not all buildings can accommodate both options. Additions should be designed by an architect; if large enough, they deserve the same level of planning as does a totally new school or a major remodeling project. Most states require that an architect or engineer be involved in major additions to schools. It is common for additions to be designed in conjunction with a remodeling program for the existing facility, i.e., both remodeling and expansion work occur simultaneously.

Often school officials are unable to pinpoint the duration of conditions that result in the need for additional instructional space. If the need is caused by enrollment increases, superintendents sometimes are unable to determine accurately how long the present trend(s) will last. Districts with fluid demographic patterns, for instance, are particularly difficult situations. Migration patterns may be driven by relatively unstable conditions such as interest rates on housing loans or the cost of gasoline. Under such uncertain conditions the *portable classroom* (also called *relocatables* or *modular classrooms*) is considered an alternative to permanent construction. But incertitude is not the only reason for opting for portable classrooms. Time limitations can also compel school administrators to use them (Allison, 1988). In some school districts, the increases in school enrollment are so rapid that they generate needs that must be met immediately. The time is not available to plan and execute conventional construction.

Manufacturers of portable classrooms promote their products by noting: (1) the low cost of such units compared to permanent construction, (2) the variety of sizes of the product, (3) the ability of the product to meet varying needs, (4) the good resale value of portable classrooms (the demand for them is quite high in certain parts of the country), and (5) the low level of maintenance required

(Sylvester, 1988). One major drawback associated with portable classrooms is that they are almost always prefabricated and not custom built to meet the specific needs of the purchasing school district. Other concerns voiced by superintendents are associated with aesthetics, health, and safety.

## ALTERNATIVE USES FOR SCHOOLS

When a district no longer needs to keep a school open, it is faced with some choices regarding the disposition of the property. The alternatives available to the superintendent and board basically fall into two categories: (1) alternative uses where the school district retains ownership, and (2) disposal of the property. Preceding the decision of what to do with a building, however, is the more difficult decision of actually closing a school. School closings are explosive issues requiring special care. As far back as 1974, the American Association of School Administrators created a list of critical questions relative to this topic:

In closing a school, can the administration:

1. Keep students relatively close to their neighborhoods?
2. Keep students from crossing major physical barriers?
3. Maintain a similar socioeconomic, racial and ethnic mix?
4. Close the school with the lowest enrollment?
5. Close a school with a weak academic performance record?
6. Close the least educationally flexible building?
7. Close the "high cost" maintenance/capital outlay building?
8. Close the building that can be recycled?
9. Close the building that requires the least additional cost of district-wide transportation?
10. Close the building most in keeping with the recommendation of a special task force (if one were used)?

If the answer to a majority of these questions is "yes," then the school probably should be closed (American Association of School Administrators, 1974).

Once a building ceases to be used for its original purpose, disposal alternatives must be considered. Local school systems have the authority to lease or sell properties; however, any such transactions must be in compliance with state statutes (Baldwin, 1988). As with most matters pertaining to school facility planning, differences in laws addressing school properties exist among the 50 states. In some states, statutes dictate the options available for the disposal of property. In North Carolina, for instance, the school district may (1) lease the property to eligible clients, (2) sell the property to eligible clients, (3) exchange the property for other property with another governing body, and (4) demolish the structure and sell the site at public auction (Graves, 1985).

Schools often establish a special identity. In essence, they belong to the community in which they exist and the citizens develop an emotional attachment to them. Because of this attachment it is not surprising that many schools end up becoming community service structures, such as community centers or recreational centers. In 1978 (during the period of rapid declines in student enrollment), the Council of Educational Facility Planners published a booklet entitled *Surplus School Space—The Problem and the Possibilities,* specifically encouraging community participation in decisions about surplus schools. Particularly noteworthy among the efforts to retain surplus schools for use for other public services is the work of Kirk Noyes, one of the pioneers in renovating schools into housing for the elderly (Noyes, 1987). His efforts are significant because they simultaneously address two societal needs: (1) finding uses for surplus school, and (2) providing housing for a growing population of senior citizens.

In pondering what to do with excess school facilities, the administrator should raise the following questions: Is excess space needed for other purposes? The space may not be needed as a school, but could it be used as a warehouse, an office building, or for some other existing need in the school district? Will future enrollments require additional space? Does the possibility exist that enrollments will increase in the next five to fifteen years? What will it cost to maintain the space if it is no longer used as a school? Can the space be used to serve other public interests (e.g., community needs)? Will changes in curricula, instructional methods, or state mandates necessitate additional space? What restrictions exist regarding the use of a building (e.g., zoning laws)? These basic questions generate creative thinking and ultimately produce information useful in making final decisions.

Frequently, school districts decide to retain surplus school space to use for special programs. Among the more common uses in this regard are an administrative building, an adult education center, a community education center, a pre-school center, an office building providing space for teachers and support staff, a vocational education center, a media production center, and a research and development center.

If the school district decides not to retain the property, five basic alternatives may be pursued. First, the property can be *deeded to another governmental agency* (assuming state law permits) such as parks and recreational departments which may be willing to assume ownership of unused schools provided they are in reasonable condition. Second, the school district may be able to *lease the property* (again, if laws permit). Such leases may be either for a short or long-term. One advantage of the lease arrangement is that the school retains ownership. This may be advantageous when (1) the facility in question is in excellent to good condition, and (2) there exists a possibility that the district will once again need the space. Often the most appealing option is to *sell the property* (building and site). A number of conditions affect the feasibility of this alternative including the condition of the building, the site, and the demand for space in the category in which the vacated school would fall. The sale of property will necessitate direction from the school attorney, as all states have laws governing the disposal of public properties. Another option is commonly referred to as *mothballing*. Here the school district retains the building but ceases to use it for any purpose. This action may be expedient if increases in enrollments are quite possible within five years or so. Mothballing has a certain degree of risk associated with it. Maintenance can be costly and time-consuming, insurance rates can be high, and vandals can prey on an unoccupied building. Finally, the school district can *raze the building but maintain the property* on which it is located. This option is especially attractive if the building is in poor condition but located on a highly desirable site. Uncertainty regarding enrollments may be a factor urging the administrators to retain a site should another school be needed. Another possible reason for retaining a site after the building is demolished is that the land on which the school sits may be high in value. If this is true and state laws are accommodating, the school district may choose to lease the land as a long-term investment.

## SUMMARY

New schools are not the only facility projects requiring extensive prearrangements. Modernization and remodeling also require planning and management. Since schools develop special identities in communities, citizens are often reluctant to close old buildings. In weighing new construction against renovation, school officials are often swayed by politics, sentimentality, initial costs, and present needs. The more enlightened administrator will examine a broader range of criteria. In addition to those mentioned, the suitability of site, operating costs, potential future needs, and aesthetics are incorporated into the planning process.

Adding space to schools is also a facility planning issue. This can be accomplished either by standard construction or by the use of relocatable classrooms. Deciding which option is best for a given school system depends upon a number of factors, not the least of which are time, uncertainty about the future, and cost.

During the late 1970s and early 1980s, surplus space emerged as an issue for many districts. In some instances, surplus schools were converted to serve a non-instructional purpose within the school system. In these cases, the school district retained ownership and utilized an existing resource to bolster support services. In addition to using surplus schools to serve some need of the district, the options for excess space include leasing, deeding the property to some other governmental agency, razing the facility and retaining the site, mothballing, and outright sale of the property.

## ISSUES FOR DISCUSSION

1. Develop a list of reasons why taxpayers often view renovation as more economical than new construction.

2. Identify a school project where either remodeling or modernization recently occurred. Determine from the district's administrator's to what degree the life of the building was extended.

3. Contact architectural firms to determine if their fees are higher for remodeling than for new construction.

4. Develop of list of advantages and disadvantages regarding portable classrooms. Do you know anyone who teaches in one? If yes, ask them how they like teaching in this environment.

5. Determine what your state laws are regarding the disposal of surplus property by public school districts.

6. Why might some schools be unable to accommodate vertical expansion?

7. To what extent should the community-at-large be involved in the decision of what to do with surplus schools?

8. Should public school districts lease empty buildings to churches or other groups who operate private schools?

9. Determine if laws in your state permit school districts to lease land as a form of investment.

10. Are some school properties more desirable than others to private investors? Why or why not?

# 11

# SCHOOL DISTRICT MAINTENANCE

As the title of this book suggests, the administration of school facilities can be divided into two broad topics: planning facilities and managing them. Historically, the former subject received the bulk of the attention in professional writings, especially in school administration textbooks. Caring for school buildings was essentially a chore thought to require little more than common sense and basic custodial skills. Superintendents and principals are now acknowledging that facilities management has taken on greater importance. In large measure, the additional attention accorded facilities management stems from two realities: (1) modern school buildings represent substantial investments which the public scrutinize, and (2) modern schools contain sophisticated equipment that require operators who have more than basic custodial skills. Both factors make the maintenance task increasingly complex and visible. But the increased emphasis upon facility management is also related to nearly two decades of neglect (referred to as deferred maintenance) (Chick, Smith, and Yeabower, 1987). The inflation spiral in the 1970s and 1980s, coupled with demographic fears of declining enrollments, created uncertainty; this incertitude disrupted the flow of resources dedicated to equipment and facility repair and replacement. This neglect for educational facilities has created a capital renewal crisis that extends from primary schools through our colleges and universities (Harris and Byer, 1989).

Exactly what is a school district maintenance program? What are the organizational options available for implementing such a program? What responsibilities are associated with the function? These are the questions that are examined in this chapter.

## DEFINING SCHOOL DISTRICT MAINTENANCE

Two distinctions need to be made relative to school district maintenance. The first is the difference between maintenance services and custodial services; the second is the difference between school district programs and individual school programs. *Maintenance* generally refers to the overall responsibilities related to the upkeep of buildings, building sites, and equipment housed in the buildings. Included are responsibilities associated with repair and replacement. *Custodial services,* on the other hand, generally refer to duties necessary to keep a specific building clean and functional. Included are such tasks as sweeping, emptying trash, waxing floors, cleaning windows, and the like. Custodial services are but one part of the overall maintenance program.

The management of facilities can be viewed from two perspectives. The first is a school district program, i.e., a program that includes all schools and other facilities owned and operated by the school district. A *school district maintenance program* includes all aspects of repair, replacement, and day-to-day upkeep from a perspective of centralized administration (i.e., from the perspective of the school district as an entire organization). In some school systems, school principals are required to have separate maintenance plans addressing the specifics of a single facility. An *individual school maintenance program* ought to be congruent with the overall plan for the school district but should include more specificity. The remainder of this chapter is devoted to the topic of school district maintenance programs. The building specific elements of maintenance are presented in the next chapter.

The topics of facility planning and facility management are not as mutually exclusive as they may appear. In practice, school administrators often make key decisions as if these two were unrelated. That is, they plan new facilities with virtually no consideration for the resources that will be required to keep the schools operational once they are constructed. Infusing maintenance considerations into the design of a new facility can make the task of developing a maintenance plan less cumbersome. This occurs because design decisions are weighed against the life-cycle costs (e.g., selecting a floor surface by comparing initial cost to the maintenance expenses and anticipated life span of the product). A good example of a dysfunction between design and maintenance is the school district that elects to build an inexpensive school. The board and administration may boast to taxpayers about the low level of initial costs. Years later, however, the patrons are confronted with maintenance costs that are well above average.

Virtually all school systems function with some form of a maintenance program—even if it is a relatively informal or unstructured component of the organization. But the mere presence of maintenance services does not suffice in today's entangled world of administration. In addition to personnel and budgets, progressive school systems rely upon a comprehensive plan that gives meaning and direction to the responsibility of protecting capital investments. Unfortunately, far too many school district officials overlook the importance of comprehensive planning and subject themselves to serendipity. It is in these districts that emergency situations usually create a cycle of crisis spending.

## COMPONENTS OF A DISTRICT PLAN

A basic assumption in planning is that no matter how threatening the circumstances, it is better to anticipate change than to simply experience it. Unless this assumption is accepted, there can be no meaningful future planning in school facility management (Millett, 1980). Regrettably, there is no universal format for creating a school district maintenance plan. The actual content of such a document depends upon the philosophy, resources, and needs of individual school systems. One generic option suggested here is profiled in Figure 11.1. The first element in this plan is the *philosophy and mission statements*. The philosophy relates the values and beliefs that give meaning to the plan. The mission statements outline the general purpose of school district maintenance. As Glass (1984) so aptly points out, a good maintenance program requires commitment from the board and the superintendent. The commitment should be manifested in the philosophy and mission statements; if this occurs, these documents then provide a framework for the entire plan.

The second component identifies the *goals and objectives*. This portion of the plan is usually more specific than the philosophy and mission statements. Additionally, mission statements are not frequently changed (perhaps every five years), whereas goals usually have a shorter life span. Typically, the time table

**Figure 11.1**
**A Plan for School District Maintenance**

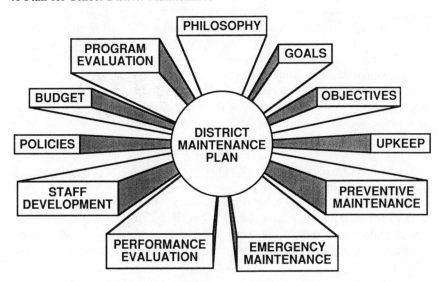

for goal statements is determined by the evaluation cycle (e.g., a calendar year or a school year).

The third element pertains to the *identification of responsibilities*. Who will be responsible for school district maintenance often varies markedly depending upon such variables as school district size and philosophy. Thus, it is important to detail in the plan lines of authority so that those who are guided by the document have a clear understanding of work assignments.

The fourth component in the maintenance plan is a statement identifying the specific functions covered by the document. Although some portions of facility management will clearly fall within the realm of a school district maintenance plan (e.g., custodial services), others, such as insurance programs, may not. Again, what is covered by the document depends largely upon the size of the school district, human resources, and philosophy.

In general, the responsibilities for a district maintenance program can be categorized as follows: (1) *preventive maintenance,* (2) *upkeep,* and (3) *emergency (or unplanned) maintenance.* A comprehensive program addresses all three components. Clear statements defining each of these functions and outlining how they are to be managed are provided. Included in these statements are definitions, procedural policies and directives, emergency telephone numbers, timetables, and the like. An employee in the school district should be able to determine how and when to proceed with a given situation based upon the document's content. For example, the section on preventive maintenance includes schedules for replacing equipment components such as air filters. The upkeep section provides schedules for minimum custodial services.

An effective maintenance plan is never complete without a section on evaluation. Two elements need to be assessed on a regular basis. The first is the outcome(s) of the maintenance program. Is the program meeting its goals? Is the program congruent with the philosophy and mission statements? This part of the evaluation task is referred to as *program evaluation.* The other area requiring assessment is human performance—the supervisory function of determining the effectiveness of individual employees. This component is referred to as *performance evaluation.* Evaluation, either of programs or personnel, may serve two functions: (1) to provide information necessary to improve programs or performance, and (2) to provide information necessary to determine if goals were met or if employees should be retained (or given merit increases). The former is referred to as *formative evaluation* and the latter as *summative evaluation.*

Staff development in maintenance services is more important today than it has ever been. In some geographic locations, job applicants may be scarce and training is necessary in the early stages of employment to compensate for new employee skill deficiencies. Additionally, the needs of new employees, the rapid deployment of technology, and the advances in construction materials require that all maintenance staff receive periodic training. Accordingly, staff development deserves a proper level of importance in the district's maintenance plan.

Evaluation outcomes are an excellent source of data for structuring inservice programs.

Finally, the paradigm suggested here recommends that two resource documents, the budget and relevant policy statements, be attached as appendices to the district's maintenance plan. The budget provides information relative to fiscal resources earmarked for maintenance services. The policies provide a convenient and useful reference.

Planning is often ignored because it is expensive, time-consuming, and difficult. But as Tougaw (1987) points out, the key to protecting the investment of billions of dollars committed to educational facilities each year is proper planning today and a commitment to sound maintenance well into the future. Without a comprehensive district plan, the superintendent and director of maintenance are inclined to become "crisis managers." Some state departments of education have taken the initiative to develop guides for formulating policies and regulations, offering standards for equipment and materials, and guidelines for maintenance procedures. One excellent example is the handbook entitled *Administration of Maintenance and Operations in California School Districts: A Handbook for School Administrators and Governing Boards* (1986), prepared by the California State Department of Education.

## ORGANIZATIONAL OPTIONS

The locus of control for facility management varies widely among school systems. To a great extent, the differences are attributable to the size of the district (i.e., number of facilities, size of facilities, enrollments). In a small school system, the superintendent may take a direct and active role in managing this function. By contrast, a large district may have a full-time director of buildings and grounds (also referred to occasionally as superintendent of buildings and grounds). A study in the early 1980s revealed that while almost all large districts employ an administrator to specifically manage the maintenance program, 60 percent of the small districts (below 1,200 students) do not do so (Abramson, 1981). How does a superintendent determine the structure that is best for his/her given situation? Available resources (human and material), existing problems and needs, and past practices are key determinants of organizational format. But more often than not, it is the superintendent's (or school board's) values and beliefs about administration and organization that determine how maintenance services will be structured.

Basically, maintenance programs can be arranged as:

- a separate division of the organization
- a subdivision of a major division in the organization
- a function that does not have any formal status in the organization.

Separate divisions for buildings and grounds are most prevalent in large school systems. The division is generally under the supervision of an assistant superintendent (e.g., assistant superintendent for buildings and grounds) who reports directly to the superintendent or to one of the chief deputy superintendents. The second classification, subdivision, is the most common in the United States. Subdivisions function as part of a larger organizational division (e.g., business affairs). In such situations, a director of facilities is likely to report to the division's highest ranking administrator (e.g., assistant superintendent for business). In small districts, there may be a person assigned supervisory responsibilities for district-wide maintenance, but that individual does not have a separate budget or is not considered a member of the district's administrative team. Usually in these situations, that person reports directly to the superintendent. Figure 11.2 provides two school district line and staff charts exemplifying organizational options.

The role and status of directors of buildings and grounds are directly related to school district size. The larger the district, the higher the position and status within the organization. This is explained in part by the proclivity of larger school systems to have divisions of authority and responsibility. The differences related to district size occur around enrollment levels of 6,000 pupils. That is, the status of directors is higher in school systems with more than 6,000 students (Abramson, 1981). A survey conducted of administrative salaries for the 1988–89 school year indicates that the average salary for a superintendent of buildings and grounds for that year was $35,500.00. The figure increased from an average of about $32,500 the previous year—a finding that indirectly supports the notion that the job is growing in stature and importance (Carter and Rosenbloom, 1989).

School districts are organizations sharing many common features with private businesses. Yet, school systems are unique in that they are publicly owned, human intensive, and non-profit entities engaged in the delivery of services. But like all organizations, schools possess a culture and face the inevitability of conflict. Maintenance directors, for example, often find themselves in the middle of territorial disputes regarding authority and the use of resources. The following situation explicates this point:

John is principal of the high school. He reports to the assistant superintendent for instruction. Mike is the director of building and grounds. He reports to the assistant superintendent for business. John is unhappy because he does not believe Mike is giving enough attention to his building. But since the two report to different administrators, they seldom talk to each other. Rather, they share their concerns with their respective supervisors. Thus the conflict that permeates both of their jobs is unresolved, and in fact is intensified as both assistant superintendents become increasingly protective of their subordinates (and also protective of the "turf" included in their respective divisions).

Territorial disputes are most likely in districts with highly bureaucratic structures (i.e., districts where authority lies with divisions and division heads engage in

**Figure 11.2**
**Illustrations of Two Organizational Options for Providing Maintenance Services**

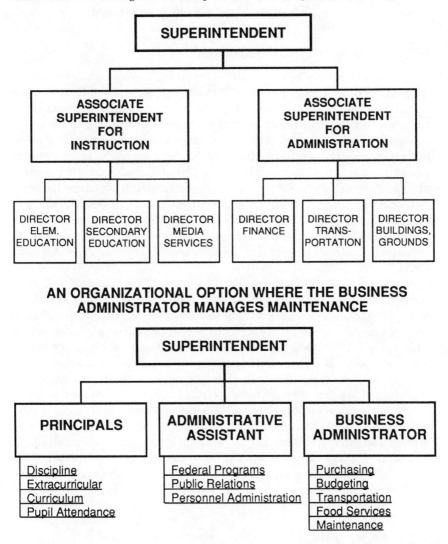

AN ORGANIZATIONAL OPTION WHERE THE BUSINESS
ADMINISTRATOR MANAGES MAINTENANCE

territorial disputes) or in highly unstructured school systems (i.e., districts where virtually no policies or regulations exist to give direction to the maintenance program) (Kowalski, 1982). If the district's maintenance plan includes specific clarifications regarding authority, lines of communication, and line and staff relationships, it should prove to be a potent tool for diminishing conflict.

Even in the smallest school systems, it is a management error to ignore the necessity of facility management programs. The exact role of this service within the organization needs to be clearly articulated and understood—not only by the employees, but by the school board and the community as well.

## STAFFING THE DISTRICT PROGRAM

The quantity and quality of the staff of the district's maintenance program are the products of a number of circumstances. Among the more influential are the size of the school district, the district's philosophy regarding maintenance (e.g., how important is this function in relation to other operations), the available resources (both financial and human), and the present condition of school facilities and grounds. The district staff usually includes everyone in the maintenance program not assigned directly to individual buildings (custodians). Besides a director, the maintenance staff may include specialists such as plumbers, carpenters, or electricians. Some larger school systems even have a separate facility to house these individuals, e.g., a carpenter's shop. Increased awareness of employee health and safety issues is causing a number of superintendents to consider moving maintenance operations out of basements an other unsuitable locations.

A survey in the early 1980s revealed that just over 67 percent of all directors of buildings and grounds did not have a college education (Abramson, 1981). More recent job specifications for maintenance specialists suggest that expectations and requirements are rising. Two factors appear to be responsible: (1) school buildings are simply more sophisticated, necessitating higher levels of knowledge and skills, and (2) superintendents are increasingly recognizing the importance of good maintenance to overall management effectiveness. Historically, maintenance directors were apt to be individuals who "worked their way up" through the ranks of the school system. That is, they started in some lower level position and, based upon excellent performance (or some other criterion), were promoted to the top position in this division. But facility management today requires more than technical skills. The individual in charge needs to understand policy development and interpretation, have the ability to supervise and evaluate employees, and possess requisite skills for formulating and administering a divisional budget. A superintendent has four choices in selecting such an individual:

1. employ a person who has both the management and technical skills;
2. provide the technical skills to someone who possesses the management skills (e.g., promoting a principal or other individual with management training to this position and, via staff development, providing technical skills as necessary);
3. provide the management skills to someone who possesses the technical skills (e.g., promoting a maintenance worker who then receives management training as necessary through staff development); or
4. employ an individual without considering qualifications (e.g., a politically motivated appointment).

Obviously, the last option is the non-administrative approach to the issue and the option most likely to create serious problems.

Superintendents are confronted with a myriad of considerations in selecting a maintenance department head. For example, should a person be promoted from within or should someone outside the district be hired? This question has a way of surfacing when there is a vacancy. The issues related to internal promotions should not be taken lightly. Sound arguments are presented on both sides. Not offering internal promotions may cause career-minded individuals to leave the organization. Conversely, reliance upon internal promotions can result in inbreeding and stagnation (Castetter, 1981). In any event, the inclination to employ managers from outside the organization is no excuse for disregarding the obligations of staff development. Employees deserve the opportunity to improve themselves; in the long term, such improvements benefit the school district as well as the individual worker.

The lack of certification/licensing requirements is responsible for a situation where persons with a multitude of backgrounds occupy the top position in the buildings and grounds division. Large school systems may employ an architect or engineer. Some school systems have turned to "executive types" (e.g., individuals who possess M.B.A. degrees). It appears likely that the continued infusion of technology into modern school buildings will fuel the trend toward higher job qualifications. Correspondingly, increases in salaries and organizational prestige can also be expected.

## ADMINISTERING THE MAINTENANCE PROGRAM

The administration of a maintenance program may include any number of responsibilities. It is preferable for a school system to decide which responsibilities are to be included before employing someone. This encourages a selection procedure based upon objective criteria. In reality, the opposite often occurs. That is, a person is hired and allowed to establish the scope of responsibilities based upon personal skills and interests.

Among the more important functions related to administering a maintenance program are:

*Recommending Policy*. Generally, the superintendent makes policy recommendations to the school board. The board has the choice of either supporting or rejecting these recommendations. The superintendent frequently calls upon staff to assist with the formulation of policy proposals. The director of buildings and grounds is one individual who is often expected to contribute to this process.

*Carrying Out Policy*. Indeed, the chief purpose of the administration is to carry out the policies established by the school board. Routinely, this requires the formulation of administrative regulations. Regulations are administrative initiatives designed to assure compliance with policy (Kowalski, 1983). The development of regulations requires certain skills (e.g., communication skills).

*Long-Range Planning*. As discussed previously in the chapter, the maintenance administrator should be familiar with long-range planning techniques—at least to the extent necessary to develop a district plan on an annual basis. Even if the director is not required to complete this task alone, a participatory role is expected.

*Employment Practices.* Developing job descriptions, announcing vacancies, soliciting applications, interviewing job applicants, and evaluating job performance are but a few of the responsibilities that may be assigned to the maintenance director.

*On-the-Job Supervision.* The day-to-day operations in maintenance require supervision. Employee supervision serves two purposes: (1) to improve performance, and (2) to identify whether individuals are doing their job properly. Both require a certain amount of technical skill as well as knowledge about performance evaluation.

*Processing Work Orders.* Like all segments of the organization, the maintenance department is apt to become inundated with paper work. Work orders, requisition forms, and other similar documents typically become a part of the director's work life. Managing this process is a common expectation.

*Developing and Administering Budgets.* In larger systems, maintenance is apt to have a separate budget. The director, just like a principal or assistant superintendent, is expected to understand enough about finances to participate in budget development and to manage the budget once it is adopted.

In addition to the tasks outlined here, there are a multitude of other possible responsibilities related to administering a maintenance program. The essential message is that the job is certainly one requiring a range of knowledge, skills, and experiences. As mentioned earlier, the need to employ better educated and more highly qualified individuals is illuminated by a number of current conditions. But as public schools spend increasing dollars on managerial and other employee salaries, new concerns emerge for school superintendents and boards of education. Most notably, how can school districts keep up with the rising costs of maintenance programs?

## THE OPTION OF CONTRACTING

Recently, several leading figures in school administration have urged school systems to move toward private contracting to supply maintenance services. They believe school systems should enter into an agreement to receive full maintenance services from private, for-profit agencies. Foremost among the advocates for "contracting out" is Lieberman (1986). He cites a number of reasons to support his position, but the two most visible are that:

1. Public school systems have been plagued by unionism which has attenuated the ability of administrators to manage the school system. Collective bargaining in the public sector has not worked and will not work. Accordingly, the judicious choice is to free the organization of the burdens created by myopic attempts to emulate labor practices

in the private sector. Private contracting is viewed as one means to accomplish this initiative.

2. Thrift, economy, and the "bottom line" are more important in profit-motivated organizations than in public institutions. Using profit-seeking, private agents in the public sector will have a circuitous effect upon the school district. In other words, the advantageous elements of business decisions in the private sector will "spill over" into the school system.

Not everyone shares Lieberman's enthusiasm for private contracting in the public sector. Many superintendents are quick to point out that such agreements diminish school board and administrative control. For example, what happens to a school district when the private contractor's employees go on strike? The school system suffers the consequences of the strike, yet school districts frequently are not in a position to resolve the conflict. Political ramifications are another concern leveled against private contracting. Many maintenance employees are taxpayers (residents) in the school system. They do not look favorably upon losing their jobs even if such a decision may be economically beneficial for taxpayers. Fears regarding private contracting, however, are diminishing as a number of success stories emerge. Private service agreements have been far more prevalent in transportation and food services than in maintenance. Nevertheless, superintendents are observing that the concept of contracting out can work in certain situations.

One should not view the use of service contracts as an "either or" proposition. New York, for example, has a statute requiring all public works contracts involving expenditures of more the $7,000.00 and all purchase contracts of more than $5,000.00 to be awarded through a specified competitive bidding procedure. Routine and emergency maintenance often does not exceed the statutory amount; thus, New York school districts can avoid the law by structuring work packages. In the Albany school district, however, the school board did just the opposite. They established a policy in 1974 to consider the total cost of each maintenance area (e.g., roofing, plumbing, and so forth) for the full school year as a biddable item under the statute. In this district, using private contractors, whose services for labor and materials are obtainable at a fixed priced via competitive bidding, has proven to be highly successful (Venter, 1985). The Albany situation is one example of a school district that still retains a maintenance staff for summer work and other minor types of projects, but relies on private contractors for the bulk of their larger projects. This represents an option between traditional staffing and contracting out.

## SUMMARY

The management of school facilities has traditionally been a neglected area of school administration. Rising costs and high technology buildings are changing this situation. Today, progressive school districts develop comprehensive maintenance plans, employ highly skilled individuals for maintenance management, and explore a range of options before making management decisions. Administrators are gradually accepting reality—sound maintenance programs require increased staff development, creative management, and more fiscal resources.

The administration of school district maintenance has evolved as a managerial task requiring both technical skills and leadership knowledge. The person in charge of this operation may hold a variety of titles. Likewise, the scope of maintenance services evolves in different ways based upon different factors in school districts. Organizationally, maintenance operations may range from a major division in a large school district to a subdivision under business affairs in a moderately sized district to a virtual nonentity in a small district. The value placed on maintenance services is largely the product of the philosophy of the school board and the superintendent.

## ISSUES FOR DISCUSSION

1. Identify factors that may have been responsible for maintenance being a low priority in many school districts.

2. Develop an outline for an annual maintenance plan for your school district (either the one in which you reside or in which you are employed).

3. Discuss the differences between technical skills and administrative knowledge.

4. Identify some reasons why maintenance supervisors often become involved in conflicts.

5. Create a job description for the position of director of maintenance for a school district with which you are familiar.

6. Discuss the differences between: (a) formative and summative evaluation, and (b) program and performance evaluation.

7. In what ways can maintenance considerations contribute to effective school design?

8. Take a position for or against contracting out for maintenance services. Identify the key points to defend your position.

9. Does the administration of maintenance services entail more or less political considerations than the administration of instructional programs?

10. What are the advantages and disadvantages of having a policy that requires internal promotions in a maintenance department?

# 12

# MANAGING THE INDIVIDUAL SCHOOL

Facility management does not always occur as a function of central administration. Rather, it takes place in the individual school facility. This is the level at which the day-to-day housekeeping tasks must be carried out to assure that the instructional programs can continue. At the district level, it is the superintendent (or his/her subordinates) who oversees maintenance programs. Within the individual school, the responsibility for maintaining the environment is shouldered by the principal. For this reason, it is critical that one understands the relationships among: (1) the director of maintenance for the school district, (2) the custodians, and (3) the building principals (Drake and Roe, 1986).

Basically, the principal is accountable for the security, health, and safety aspects of the facility. More specifically, the building level administrator is the person who knows and understands the curriculum and instructional strategies and must interface these factors with available support services. This means not only seeing that teachers have the equipment, materials, and services they require, but also means keeping the building clean and functional.

In managing the school facility, the principal should be cognizant of five basic purposes of custodial services: (1) protecting the facility and its equipment, (2) maintaining a healthful and safe environment, (3) keeping the building functional for instructional purposes, (4) maintaining good community relations (the public's contact with custodians and the building should be positive), and (5) maintaining the provisions that permit a clean environment (Jordan et al., 1985).

In relation to these broad purposes, this chapter provides an overview of staffing, building level responsibilities, the required knowledge base for the principal, and the creation of the individual building maintenance plan.

## STAFFING

The topic of staffing for maintenance services raises a number of questions. How many custodians are needed? What will be their work relationship with the principal and with the teachers? How will they be evaluated? To whom shall they report? These questions deserve consideration prior to exploring the various tasks associated with building level maintenance.

### Size of Custodial Staff

The optimum number of custodians required for a school depends upon: (1) the size of the facility (square feet), (2) the size of the student body (enrollment), (3) the age of the building, (4) the condition of the building, (5) the duties assigned to the custodial staff, (6) the size of the site, and (7) the range of programs offered in the facility. Some facility planning experts have advanced formulas for making staffing decisions. Greenhalgh (1978), for example, indicates that it is reasonable to have one custodian for every 15,000 square feet of space, for every 11 classrooms, for every 8 teachers, and for each 250 pupils. But such rules of thumb are far from infallible in a world where school buildings exhibit an increasing level of differences. These guidelines do, however, provide a starting point for examining issues related to staff size.

Consider the following items that could alter the number of custodians needed to staff an individual school:

- the number and type of special instructional areas in the school (e.g., laboratories)
- the amount of sophisticated equipment used in the school (e.g., computerized climate control systems, telecommunication systems) (Rondeau 1989).
- the extent to which the community uses the school for various functions in the evenings and on week-ends
- the quality of materials that were used in the original construction of the building (e.g., a floor surface that may require high levels of maintenance)
- the degree to which the site has developed athletic fields or other designated areas (this factor determines how much site care is necessary)
- the level of building occupancy in relation to its intended capacity (e.g., a school with a utilization level of 98 percent may require more maintenance than a school of equal size that has a utilization level of 55 percent)
- the present condition of equipment within the building

One other factor worth mentioning with regard to staffing is the scope of the custodian's duties. In some schools, custodians are expected to do more than just housekeeping chores (e.g., make minor repairs). In other situations, the custodians may be restricted to cleaning. Not infrequently, the scope of work assignments is a matter established and governed by collective bargaining agreements. These agreements may even dictate the number of custodians to be assigned to a given school. In schools where there are multiple custodians, one is usually designated as head custodian to assist the principal with the overall supervision of this function. The degree to which principals delegate supervisory authorities to head custodians varies markedly.

Unfortunately, there is no magic formula for staffing that has universal effectiveness. Rather than hoping for such an equation, principals ought to concentrate on refining the quantitative and qualitative statements that express the custodial needs of a given school. Superintendents, in turn, should make staffing decisions based upon needs assessments—not simply on the basis of numbers. The range of functions found in schools makes it critical to base decisions on real needs and not generalizations.

## Determining the Work Schedule

Well-organized schools maintain work schedules for the custodial staff. These schedules outline what is expected at given times on given dates. At the start of each school year, the principal should meet with the custodial staff to outline expectations and goals for the school year (Hughes and Ubben, 1984). During this meeting, the work schedules should be distributed and discussed.

It has become common practice for larger schools to have both day and night shifts for custodians. Night custodians are not hindered by occupants in the building, permitting them to do some tasks that would be virtually impossible during the school day (e.g., cleaning classrooms). Having evening custodians also serves at least two other functions: (1) it is accommodating for community use of the building, and (2) it is a deterent to vandalism.

An example of a daily schedule for a custodian working from 4:00 P.M. to 12:00 A.M. is detailed here:

4:00    check messages and/or instruction provided by supervisor

4:10    start cleaning classrooms in assigned area of the building
(empty trash; sweep floors; clean chalk boards; arrange desks; clean walls if necessary)

5:45    coffee break

6:00    clean restrooms in assigned area of the building
(empty trash; clean lavatories and other fixtures, mop floors; clean walls if necessary; check if all systems are functional)

7:15    dinner

8:00    clean corridors in assigned area of the building

9:00    clean teachers' lounge

9:30    clean media center
(sweep floors, empty trash, dust tables and cabinets; clean window surfaces)

10:30 coffee break

10:45 check areas after evening use and clean up if necessary

11:30  check alarm systems, heating/ventilation systems, turn off lights in area, put away
       materials, lock doors where appropriate.

Several documents have been developed to assist principals with assigning
custodial tasks (Hughes and Ubben, 1984; DeRoche and Kaiser, 1980; Greenhalgh, 1978). These documents identify primary maintenance tasks and provide
time estimates for completing tasks. As schools become less uniform in design
and more advanced construction materials and equipment are used, these types
off aids diminish in utility for the principal. Larger school systems often attempt
to incorporate work standards for custodians into their district maintenance man-
uals and expect principals to generate individual school schedules based on these
guidelines. For those desiring greater detail, a rather comprehensive listing of
custodial standards was prepared by the Association of School Business Officials
(1981) in a publication entitled *Custodial Methods and Procedures Manual.*

The principal may delegate the responsibility for establishing work schedules
to the head custodian or to an assistant principal. Doing so does not diminish the
principal's accountability for preserving a healthful, clean, and safe learning
environment. Even if the principal does not personally develop work schedules,
he or she should approve the schedules and periodically review their effectiveness. Those in the school environment will readily detect the importance the
principal places on custodial functions.

### Establishing Positive Communications

In visiting various schools, one can often encounter unsolicited comments,
both positive and negative, about the custodial staff. The fact that the comments
are made is evidence of the important role these individuals assume in the total
operation of a school. In large measure, it is the principal who must create a
positive work climate in which the custodial staff feel important and wanted.
Here are several initiatives that will help achieve this goal:

- The principal should educate the occupants of the school building about the value of
  good custodial services. Students and parents rarely question the importance of teachers, yet they often view custodians as relatively unessential. If this myopic perception
  exists, the principal is in the best position to change public attitudes.

- The principal should educate the occupants of the school building about personal
  responsibilities for maintaining a healthful and safe environment. The principal often
  does this by example. How often can a principal be seen picking up candy wrappers in
  the hallway? If the school leader doesn't care about the building, it is likely that the
  other occupants will behave the same way. By example and by expectation, the principal lets everyone know that keeping the school clean and functional is a shared
  responsibility.

- The principal teaches others to respect the custodians as human beings by treating them
  as fellow workers and showing appreciation for their contributions to the school.

- The principal sets goals, schedules, and other work-related documents for the custodians. The custodians are evaluated at least annually and the evaluation data are used to
  seek improvements.

- The principal periodically points out positive achievements made by the custodial staff
  to the total school community.

- The principal includes custodians in school functions (e.g., Christmas parties).

- The principal periodically seeks advice and input from the custodians. Their thoughts,
  feelings, and suggestions are not ignored.

- The principal resolves conflict between custodians and teachers in a fair and impartial
  manner.

- The principal does not allow any custodian to run the school—to make decisions that
  are inappropriate for a custodian.

## Selecting Custodial Staff

Even though custodians are technically part of the overall maintenance program of a school district, most often they report directly to the school principal
(or designee). This usually means that principals are responsible for employment
decisions related to these positions. Over the years, there have been attempts to
profile the ideal custodian by developing lists of desired attributes and traits.
Such lists are far less relevant today for at least three reasons: (1) various
legislation and court decisions (e.g., for the handicapped) cast a legal shadow on
generic job restrictions, (2) needs and operational procedures are far less standardized among school districts today than was the case 30 years ago, and (3) the
criteria that appeared on such lists were often the products of the author's bias,
not empirical data.

Filling a vacancy for a custodial position is no different than employing an
individual for any other position. Enlightened administrators complete the task
by objectively using criteria that are clearly job related (i.e., they are directly
associated with specific tasks required by the position). For example, whether or
not an applicant needs to have basic carpentry skills depends upon the scope of
job responsibilities for a specific vacancy. Overall, however, there are several
factors that are important in virtually all custodial positions: a sense of cooperation, an ability to work with others (human relations), and respect for the role of
schools in our society, including a respect for teachers and children. The final job
specifications for custodial positions should be approved by either the personnel
department or the superintendent of schools. As mentioned in the last chapter,
the existence of a district-wide maintenance plan could prove helpful to the
principal in deliberating the needed qualifications for custodial staff.

In some communities, custodial positions are treated as patronage jobs to be
handed out by influential board members or administrators to friends and rela-
tives. These situations, needless to say, are less than desirable. The custodian
who believes his job is safe because a relative or friend is protecting him can

become a troublesome employee. Again, the best way for a principal to avoid these situations is to develop defensible job requirements and expectations prior to employment and to engage in both program and performance evaluation once individuals are hired. Additionally, many school systems now have nepotism policies aimed at reducing problems associated with favoritism in employment practices.

## CUSTODIAL RESPONSIBILITIES

Highly organized school systems clearly differentiate tasks that are to be performed by school district maintenance staff and those to be performed by building custodians. As noted before, union contracts are often a key factor in establishing boundaries for work assignments. The principal's potential contribution to differentiating job expectations should not be overlooked. For instance, the principal could work with the director of building and grounds to develop a list of job responsibilities that specifically address the needs of a given school. Flexibility in assignments (i.e., not requiring all custodians to perform the same tasks regardless of the school to which they are assigned) may prove to be an asset. One of the first initiatives of the principal in this regard is the collection and organization of data pertaining to facility maintenance (Davis, 1973). Building materials, programs, and usage are examples of criteria that may contribute to the acceptance of differing work assignments.

The tasks most commonly performed by custodial staff include:

- maintaining floor surfaces
- removing trash
- cleaning windows, mirrors, and wall surfaces
- cleaning light fixtures
- sanitizing appropriate areas
- reporting malfunctioning equipment
- keeping fixtures operational (e.g., filling soap dispensers, replacing toilet paper, cleaning of drains)
- regulating climate control
- maintaining the grounds (e.g., mowing)
- inventorying custodial supplies in the building
- overseeing alarm systems and control systems
- being partially responsible for building security (e.g., locking doors)
- providing clean-up services after community functions, athletics, and so forth
- cleaning up after emergencies (e.g., sick child, wet floors)

Tasks that may be assigned under certain conditions to custodial staff include:

- minor electrical repairs
- minor carpentry tasks

- painting (both interior and exterior)
- minor plumbing repairs
- replacement of broken windows.

Whether custodians should be expected to assume assignments in this latter listing depends upon their qualifications as well as on organizational issues such as the separation of maintenance and custodial duties. Job requirements that reflect realities regarding local labor markets (e.g., availability of skills, competitiveness of the school district with other employees in the community) generate the best applicant pools. It does little good to require custodians to be "jacks-of-all-trades" when neither the local labor pool nor the salary for the positions are congruent with such expectancies.

## WHAT THE PRINCIPAL SHOULD KNOW

Maintenance management requires the principal to know a great deal about the physical environment in which he or she works. The principal also needs to know the policies, procedures, and plans that give structure to maintenance work throughout the school district. With regard to the custodial staff, the principals should have at school and at home the following information:

- the names, telephone numbers, and addresses of all custodians
- the names, telephone numbers, and addresses of persons to contact in the event of an emergency involving a custodian
- a list of special skills possessed by each of the custodians
- a list of the work assignments for each custodian (in the event there is a problem, the principal can identify whose assignment(s) is involved)
- a list of potential substitute custodians.

Lane and Betz (1987) developed a list of items with which the principal should be familiar in the school:

- the location of the heating and air conditioning controls (in case of an emergency)
- the location of circuit breakers
- the location and operational aspects of all alarm systems
- the location of water controls (including automatic sprinkler systems)
- the location and operational aspects of security lighting systems
- the operational dimension of the clock and public address systems
- the established fire and disaster drill formats
- the location of blueprints for the school
- the location of master and spare keys for the building
- the nature of cleaning agents used and the location of their storage
- the functional aspects of the telephone system and who to contact if there are problems

- the policies and regulations governing community use of the facility
- the policies and regulations pertaining to communications with the district's maintenance staff.

Beyond these specific pieces of information, the principal needs to remain well-informed about the effectiveness of the custodial and maintenance efforts. The best way to do this is to conduct periodic assessments of the environment. Some principals prefer to do this alone; others conduct the appraisal with the custodial staff present. Regardless of how such activities are completed, written documentation of periodic assessments is advisable. These assessments need to be injected into the principal's daily schedule. If they are not, more than likely this responsibility will be eclipsed by other demands upon the principal's time.

## DEVELOPING A BUILDING MAINTENANCE PLAN

The existence of a school district maintenance plan does not reduce the necessity to create a similar document for individual schools. A building plan:

- should be an extension of the district plan. The two documents should be congruent.
- should provide a priority listing of tasks to be accomplished.
- should have both short-term (one year) and long-term (five year) foci.
- should address both upkeep and renewal.
- should provide more specificity than does the district plan.

In some school systems, the physical plant department and the school principals work in concert to simultaneously develop the district plan and individual building plans.

Individual school plans are only valuable if they reflect the specific needs of a given school. Mutter and Nichols (1987) suggest a seven-step approach to conducting audits of existing facilities as a method of establishing priorities for maintenance work. Their outline exhibits how building level and systemwide efforts can complement each other:

Step 1: Select an instrument for conducting building audits (addressing both physical structure and general appearance).

Step 2: Involve the building users in the survey.

Step 3: Involve the physical plant specialists in the survey.

Step 4: Reconcile differences that emerge in the evaluations (e.g., differences between the faculty's perceptions and the maintenance department perceptions).

Step 5: Establish maintenance priorities school-by-school.

Step 6: Establish systemwide priorities.

Step 7: Create a five-year renewal plan.

Establishing priorities has become a critical issue for most school principals and maintenance supervisors. The period of high inflation from 1974 to 1982 created for many schools a "maintenance gap" (Dale, 1986). That is, the cost of replacing components in buildings exceeded the fiscal resources available in maintenance budgets. This created a cycle which has not subsided even though inflation has become less of a concern. Thus, a building plan often needs to address some method for setting maintenance priorities. Many administrators must face the reality that they will have insufficient budgets.

Increasingly, school districts are adopting policies concerning the use of facilities by community agencies. Superintendents today are recognizing the need to make schools "community centers" of activity (Kowalski and Weaver, 1988). Doing so has a positive affect upon public support for schools. As the principal develops the school maintenance plan, consideration should be given to using the building for such purposes. Given that community groups will occupy the facility outside the regular school day and, given that the added use of the facility increases demands for custodial services, a comprehensive plan should address the manner in which the policies governing community use of facilities will be implemented.

The building maintenance plan also needs to address staff development activities for custodians (Rondeau, 1984). In larger school systems, the physical plant department, in conjunction with the personnel department, arranges such activities on a systemwide basis. Some staff development is most effective, however, if it is carried out at the building level. This permits the employee to improve skills in the real work setting.

Finally, the building plan should include an evaluation component. Just like the systemwide plan, it should address both program and performance evaluations. This should occur even if the district policies do not require such evaluations. Program improvement is unlikely unless periodic assessments provide data giving direction to structured improvement efforts.

## SUMMARY

Managing school facilities includes a specific role for the school principal. This role largely involves the supervision of a custodial staff to assure the environment remains clean and functional. Often the principal is the key decision-maker employing, supervising, and evaluating the custodians. Thus, there is an extremely important personnel dimension to building level facility management. The way custodians are treated within the school is often a product of the climate that the principal establishes. If the school leader views the task of maintaining a clean and healthful environment as essential, others are prone to share the perception.

The effective administrator at the building level develops a site-specific maintenance plan. This plan is an extension of the district-wide plan and should include high levels of specificity. Rarely does a principal have adequate resources to meet all facility up-keep needs; thus, the building plan also serves as a reference document for establishing priorities.

## ISSUES FOR DISCUSSION

1. If you were a principal, would you prefer to hire the custodians or would you rather someone else have this responsibility (e.g., personnel director)?
2. List some reasons why custodians often do not receive much respect from employees and students.
3. Should custodians be able to set regulations regarding bringing food into classrooms? Why or why not?
4. Develop a form for conducting an audit of a school in which you work or one to which you have access.
5. Discuss the effects of inflation in the late 1970s and early 1980s upon school maintenance budgets.
6. Discuss the advantages and disadvantages of having a day shift and night shift for custodians (in an elementary school; in a middle school; and in a high school).
7. Find out if your state department of education has a manual or handbook for custodial services that is made available to school districts. Find out if the school district in which you work or reside has such a document.
8. List some reasons why custodians today require inservice programs.
9. Assume you are a principal and you are given two choices:
   a. your custodians report directly to you, or
   b. your custodians report to the school system's director of building and grounds. Which option would you select? Defend your choice.

# 13

# FOCUSED MANAGEMENT ISSUES

In the past two decades, Americans have advanced some rather dramatic changes in values. Many of these alterations are spawned by the realization that our natural resources are not inexhaustible. For example, concerns for clean air and energy now permeate legislative and industrial decisions, resulting in a greater balance of consideration between the economy and the environment. Americans are gradually changing their views about "using and discarding" costly items such as homes and automobiles. These new beliefs about our physical and social worlds affect all public institutions—including the public schools. In particular, they are influencing the way we manage our school buildings.

The growing deployment of technology is one ramification of the desire to preserve resources. Sophisticated maintenance equipment, although initially expensive, is being utilized in new school construction to protect large public investments, assuring that they do not become obsolete prematurely. In this respect, scientific advancements are being used in a timely manner to protect dwindling assets found in our natural surroundings.

This chapter examines six key issues in contemporary facility management. Each of these issues has touched virtually every school district in the United States. As such, they constitute major concerns in the work settings of school superintendents, principals, and directors of buildings and grounds.

## PREVENTIVE MAINTENANCE

The most desirable level of maintenance is preventive maintenance. This has become abundantly clear to experts in facility management after observing the problems created by years of practicing deferred maintenance. Preventive maintenance involves an ongoing process of inspections as well as services. The goal is to assure that components of the facility remain totally operational and functional according to manufacturer specifications. Problems are avoided either through regular servicing and/or the replacement of components prior to their being taxed to their tolerance limits. Emergency repairs and equipment "down time" are not only expensive (e.g., cost of materials, overtime pay), but also often inhibit instructional programs. Not infrequently, radio and television stations carry early morning announcements that a particular school is closed because of a boiler malfunctioning or water pipes bursting.

Most school districts have found it fiscally difficult to employ a comprehensive preventive program. Some would argue that the problem has been one of priorities rather than one of dollars. In any event, school officials and school board members are beginning to perceive maintenance as an investment rather than as a necessary evil. Instead of looking at maintenance costs in a given year, they are projecting such costs over the life of a facility. When this is done with some degree of accuracy, the costs of a preventive program do not appear excessive.

Simko (1987) offers a proactive approach to maintenance which he contends can save money. Included are the following stages:

*Stage 1.* Develop a strategic plan charting the school district's course for the next two decades. Use lifecycle inventories to set realistic goals and priorities.

*Stage 2.* Conduct an assessment of existing facilities. Give focused attention to deferred maintenance. Establish the remaining useful life of key components.

*Stage 3.* Create an effective plan of action which permits necessary work within reasonable annual expenditures. By integrating the anticipated lifecycle data with the actual assessment data, priorities for a given year are established.

*Stage 4.* Obtain approval for the budget and execute the work.

In part, school administrators have avoided preventive maintenance due to the fact that such programs require extensive data and qualified individuals to collect and interpret these data (Morris, 1981). The computer has contributed to a change in this condition. Even a microcomputer can be an effective tool for operationalizing a preventive program. The computer permits the creation of an extensive data base that facilitates the necessary planning and management tasks (Borowski, 1984). Computer inventory systems are even used to create data bases for individual schools (Stronge, 1987). Given that such inventories were rarely developed in the past because they required extensive manual labor, the availability of the microcomputer is certainly an advantage for maintenance management. Technology is helping to change the perception that preventive programs are too expensive. Today, prevention is seen as a method to reduce long-term maintenance costs.

## A HEALTHFUL SCHOOL ENVIRONMENT

One of the planning attributes for school facilities is a healthful and safe environment. Individuals readily identify physical hazards (e.g., broken stair railings), but they are less likely to be aware of invisible problems (e.g., air quality). Some decisions related to a healthful environment are rather permanent. Take, for example, site selection. A site may be noisy, subject to air pollution, and contain otherwise hazardous conditions. It is difficult to remedy these problems. But many other environmental concerns can be corrected and controlled through an effective maintenance program.

Air quality is one important aspect of the interior of a school building. Problems may be created by biological factors such as bacteria, molds, parasites, viruses, and other similar agents. These biological hazards are not due entirely to unclean conditions as some would surmise. Schools often contain animal, plant, and microbiological specimens that require proper storage and ventilation designs (Rowe, 1987). The biological contaminates can be affected by existing air quality in the building (e.g., a human environment may induce the growth of mildew). In this regard, poor air quality can be made worse by biological elements in the environment.

A rather recent addition to the list of concerns regarding interior air quality is *radon*. This chemically inert, radioactive gaseous element is produced by the disintegration of radium. Since 1986, radon has become a well-publicized health hazard. In late April of 1989, national television networks carried a news story regarding the vulnerability of schools to radon. The presence of radon is especially likely in schools that are erected on concrete slabs.

Virtually all secondary schools contain chemicals that are used for science instruction (as do many elementary schools). These elements may also produce gases and odors that negatively affect the air. Proper storage of chemicals is not only a safety measure with regard to fire and/or explosions, but should also provide security from theft. Appropriate ventilation in chemical storage areas is essential.

Improper ventilation for the entire building is another common cause of air quality problems. Frequently several factors interact to create what Reecer (1988) refers to as a "sick building syndrome"—a tightly sealed, poorly ventilated facility with airborne pollutants. Custodians can reduce airborne pollutants, especially biological ones, by using effective hygiene procedures. Ventilation is a far more complex concern. Some common causes of poor ventilation in schools are: (1) a poorly designed or poorly installed ventilation system, (2) reduction of the operations of the ventilation system below recommended levels (e.g., reducing the time the system runs to conserve energy), (3) the use of the facility by numbers of people surpassing specifications, (4) airborne elements produced by programs that were not anticipated when the building was designed, and (5) a poorly maintained ventilation system (Reecer, 1988). Certain areas of a school building require special considerations with regard to ventilation. Science laboratories, art rooms, industrial/technical shops, foods laboratories, and any other spaces that produce strong fumes or odors fall into this category. State codes usually establish air standards related to ventilation systems and school officials should be aware of those regulations. Experts indicate that a minimum of ten to fifteen cubic feet of fresh air per minute is adequate for the normal classroom (Hawkins and Lilley, 1986). The practice of reducing recommended or legally required operating levels of ventilation units to conserve energy not only can be detrimental to the building's occupants but can also result in fines or law suites.

Finding problems is the first step to correcting them. An audit of air quality is highly recommended for all public buildings. School officials can consult with local health department or state health department officials regarding such audits. The recent concerns surrounding the possible presence of asbestos and radon have heightened public awareness regarding the need for the periodic testing of air quality.

By far the most publicized interior health hazard in schools is asbestos. A number of facility experts have issued warnings about the potential dangers of this substance (e.g., Yeager and Bilbo, 1983). The Environmental Protection Agency determined that 30,830 schools in the United States harbor such products and that it would take between $300 million and $2 billion just to remove all asbestos-laden school ceilings. Asbestos is a mineral which has been demonstrated to be a carcinogen, linked to lung cancer and other pulmonary diseases (Rublin, 1985). The EPA has targeted schools in an effort to protect children who occupy these facilities for prolonged periods at early ages (Hawkins and Lilley, 1986). The real danger exists with asbestos dust. The dust is created when the material crumbles and is allowed to enter the air freely (referred to as the *friable* nature of asbestos). For this reason, the removal of asbestos from a school is a highly dangerous and controlled activity. School districts must retain the services of an asbestos abatement contractor if they have this problem.

A district suspecting that they may have a problem should take steps to address the potential hazard. The most recent legislation, passed in October 1987, increases the likelihood that schools will have to take action. The 1987 law classifies any material with more than 1 percent by volume of asbestos as an asbestos material (McGovern, 1989). The measures school administrators need to pursue include: (1) designating an in-house asbestos manager, (2) securing a competent consultant, and (3) involving the school district attorney in actions that may be necessary (Simoter, 1987). If actual removal becomes necessary, the attorney can be helpful in drafting necessary contracts and securing permits that may be required for the work.

Toll (1988) offers eight suggestions for retaining an asbestos contractor:

1. Check the qualifications of any firm you might consider. Make sure it is properly licensed.

2. Request competitive bids.

3. Check a firm's experience and quality standards (work standards and practices).

4. Make sure a firm will provide proper on-site supervision.

5. Inquire if a firm has a safety training program for its employees that complies with local, state, and federal agency specifications.

6. Check to see if the firm uses subcontractors for any of its work and investigate the subcontractors.

7. Insist on obtaining information regarding a firm's bonding and insurance.

8. Investigate a firm's history with regard to maintaining documentation of work completed (e.g., job-site logs, air sampling records, personnel monitoring reports).

Although arguments continue regarding the hazardous nature of asbestos in public buildings, school officials ought to take positive steps to assure that their districts are in compliance with laws and that the individuals who occupy the buildings are not forced to work in dangerous conditions. At the very least, the asbestos issue should be addressed in school district policy and this policy should be included in the school district's maintenance plan.

## ENERGY CONSERVATION

In schools that were erected in 1970 or earlier, the absence of energy saving designs is apparent. Because energy costs at the time were so low, it was considered unnecessary to use higher priced, energy efficient components in construction. Thus, single-pane windows and the absence of vestibules at entrances are found in many older schools. The energy shortages that have occurred since 1970 have escalated the cost of energy significantly—and have raised consciousness about conservation. Given these conditions, it is not surprising that the need to monitor and control energy usage is now widely recognized in educational circles (Clark, 1984).

Energy performance in a school is an integral part of architectural design. The creation of an energy-conscious environment requires the purposeful infusion of energy needs and potential operating costs into the planning process. In all likelihood, 80 percent of the decisions that affect energy conservation are made in the first 10 percent of the design process (Lawrence, 1984). Yet, energy conservation does not relate entirely to design. Maintenance and operation also play critical roles in determining usage levels in schools.

Among the energy conservation measures that can be taken by a school district is the energy audit. This first facet of a comprehensive response provides a data base for determining actual consumption. Energy expenditures can be viewed from two perspectives: (1) cost per square foot of space, and (2) cost per occupant. Once established, these figures are compared to average costs in the same geographic area, creating a relative indicator of consumption. In studying energy usage, it is advisable to rely on a sample of at least three years. This reduces the possibility of drawing erroneous conclusions from a restricted data base. Suppose, for example, the energy consumption was studied for only one school year. Suppose further that during that year there was an unusually harsh winter. These data may produce a distorted picture of actual energy consumption. A three year sample will reduce this risk. The computer is an asset in energy audits for two reasons: (1) it simplifies data collection, and (2) it facilitates data analysis (e.g., via simulations). Thus, it is easier to conduct multi-year assessments with aid of technology.

Once a school system has determined it has energy problems, the administration should identify possible cost saving solutions. Typically, this will require the assistance of consultants (e.g., engineers, architects). Solutions will fall into one of three broad categories: solutions that require alterations in operations, solutions that require alterations in maintenance (especially preventive maintenance schedules), and solutions that require design changes (major renovation). One example of a school district that addressed energy conservation is Norwalk, Connecticut. At the time the program was initiated, the school district operated 23 schools, each with different conditions related to heating. The following steps were taken to address the concern:

1. Setback time clocks were replaced with optimiser systems (an optimiser system calculates the exact start and stop times for the heating system based upon outside temperatures).
2. Old rotary oil burners were replaced with air-atomized oil burners.
3. Temperature recorders were used to monitor the override actions.
4. A staff development program was initiated to train teachers and custodians about the system and its use (Soupon, 1985).

The issue of staff development deserves special emphasis. Installing expensive new equipment may prove fruitless unless the custodial staff is trained to operate these devices properly. The updating of maintenance and custodial staff knowledge about energy usage should be a long-term commitment by the school district. Periodic workshops and seminars are needed to keep these employees aware of ways they can contribute to energy conservation in their work environments. These experiences are most meaningful when they are sequenced and extend over several years.

Consumption studies in schools conclude that districts face unique energy-related problems. As such, individualized conservation plans for school districts are recommended. Worner (1981) summed it up this way:

In general, each school district has its own characteristic energy problem. Structures are made of different building materials. Numerous types of heating, cooling, and ventilation systems are used with varying degrees of automatic and manual control. Operating efficiency varies from poor to excellent. Use patterns, programs offered, and climatic conditions differ over a wide range. Therefore, each district must develop its own unique approach to addressing local energy problems. (pp. 306–307)

A good conservation plan begins with enlightened construction designs and is subjected to periodic adjustments throughout the life of the building.

## ROOF MAINTENANCE

A school board member once asked an architect, "Why can't you design a roof for a school that won't leak?" "I can," responded the architect, "but I don't think you can afford it." Perhaps this is an oversimplification; however, there is some truth in the answer. Roofs are perennial problems for schools. They consume a major portion of the maintenance budget and are the leading source of litigation between school districts and architects/engineers (Nimtz, 1988). Roof problems often stem from pressures to accept low bids in original construction. The problems may also stem from faulty design or improper installation.

Since the 1973 energy crisis, the single-membrane roofing industry has evolved as the major supplier for schools. Prior to that time, built-up roof systems were standard. Basically, there are three types of single-membrane systems: modified bitumen or rubberized asphalt, EPDM (ethylene propylene diene monomer—a rubber polymer compound), and PVC (polyvinyl chloride) (Mullin, 1985). The roof material gaining in popularity is the standing seam metal roof. This system is a response to complaints about leaky roofs. Nimtz (1988) describes the system as follows:

The concealed fastening system is the key weathertight feature of the standing seam roof. The metal panels are attached to the building structural members—called purlins—with a series of movable clips inside the panel's raised seam. The seam stands two to three inches above the roof plane in a typical system. With fewer exposed fasteners than in the traditional through-fastened metal roof or conventional roofing systems, the areas for potential leaks is reduced.(p. 51)

Advocates of the standing seam metal roof argue that that product is the most cost-effective alternative when data are produced from life-span comparisons.

Young (1987) advises a three-step approach to roof management: (1) establishing roofing information files (e.g., design, installation, warranty, and inspection information), (2) developing a roof inspection program, and (3) developing a maintenance schedule. The information file is essentially a data base and may already be available in school districts with comprehensive information systems. Periodic assessments are designed to identify potential malfunctions prior to actual emergencies. Waldron (1988) suggests the following components for such a survey:

- readings to determine subsurface moisture (e.g., nucleur scan, capacitance meter readings)
- visual observations of the general appearance, surface conditions, and membrane conditions
- visual observations of edge conditions and around equipment (e.g., flashing, caulking)
- visual observations of pitch pans, vents, drains, and other roof penetrations

- interviews with custodial and maintenance staff to determine if problems have occurred and the nature of problems.

Galvanic moisture probing and roof cores also provide valuable data but these techniques should not be used if the roof is still under warranty. Finally, a critical element of roofing maintenance is a schedule for performing necessary work. Preferably, this schedule should be integrated into the overall preventive maintenance program.

Most schools are designed with flat (or relatively flat roofs). These roofs are plaqued by pooling water, especially if the roofs do not have adequate drains or drains that are not functioning properly. On most roof surfaces, standing water will eventually create failures permitting the moisture to penetrate the roofing surface. Faced with roofing problems, the maintenance department must make a choice between two alternatives: (1) repair, and (2) replacement. The choice should be made with the assistance of qualified engineers and/or architects. Remedial work is advised where it is determined to be most cost effective when viewed from a remaining life-span perspective (i.e., cost comparisons that take into life expectancies of the alternatives).

Energy conservation measures often include the addition of insulation to schools. Insulation can reduce life-cycle costs for a roof, but it can also create problems. The outcome depends upon the type of roof existing on the school. Added insulation, for example, has created some unanticipated problems with built-up roof systems. Insulation can trap heat in the roof causing tar to vaporize. This in turn dries out roofing felts, resulting in "tar bubbles" that eventually rupture (Nimtz, 1988).

There are some basic principles that can be followed when considering roof design and maintenance:

- Select an architect/engineer in whom you have confidence to assist with major decisions.
- Make sure the top surface of a roof is sun and fire-resistant.
- Insist on assurances of positive surface drainage.
- Never take for granted that the roof will be installed properly—insist on inspections.
- Study costs from a life-cycle perspective. Don't let initial costs be the only guide to making a decision.
- Take the time to study the most recent technological developments and designs.
- Consider geographic location (climate) when making roofing decisions.

## VANDALISM AND SECURITY

Some argue that vandalism is not a maintenance problem but rather an administrative problem. Regardless of how it is viewed, these destructive acts require facility management. In large measure, the degree of vandalism may be a reflection of economic and social conditions of a given school's environment. That is, inner-city schools may be more prone to suffering vandalism than schools in small communities. School districts with over 5,000 students tend to have higher crime problems; the larger the district, the higher the perceived crime problem (Lindbloom and Summerhays, 1988). Yet, all schools face vandalism issues to some extent. The problems may result from criminal acts (e.g., burglaries), acts of retribution (e.g., angry students retaliating against the school), or senseless destructive behavior (e.g., individuals who obtain gratification from destroying another's property).

Preventing vandalism is no simple task. Policies, regulations, and rules are important, but standing alone, they do not eradicate the problem. Also important is the maintenance of the building. Schools that allow the work of vandals to go unrepaired are inviting more destructive acts. Principals often comment that once a school takes on a messy or deteriorating appearance, students are less apt to care about the environment. Students are more likely to write on the restroom walls, lockers, and desks if these surfaces already are marred by graffiti.

Security is perhaps the most important element in preventing vandalism. The total security of a building, however, addresses much more than destructive acts. Fire, disasters, and other such concerns need to be integrated into security plan. Security seems to be of greatest concern for the school districts at the extremes of the size continuum, i.e., the smallest and the largest school systems tend to express the greatest concerns for security. Unfortunately administrative initiatives in this area are less than encouraging. Only about 40 percent of the school districts in the United States report using electronic security systems to alert police and fire departments (Lindbloom and Summerhays, 1988). Given the potential for problems and the availability of such systems, this figure is quite low.

It is doubtful that any school district can totally eradicate vandalism. But positive steps, including steps in the maintenance program can be taken to reduce incidence. In this age of modern technology and sophisticated planning models, educational leaders are expected to institute preventive measures.

## PLAYGROUNDS AND SITE SAFETY

As schools are increasingly used for a variety of community activities, the school site and playgrounds emerge as higher maintenance concerns. Elementary school playgrounds, in particular, become quasi-recreational areas in the neighborhoods. Given that accidental injury is the leading cause of death for American children over age one, the importance of safety on a playground cannot be overemphasized, especially in periods when there is no adult supervision.

Most litigation brought against school districts with regard to playgrounds and outdoor accidents focus on the responsibility to properly maintain equipment and conditions or negligence in supervision. Recently the courts have initiated a new standard in such cases—*the duty to warn* standard. The person filing suit against a school district must show in court that: (1) a duty to warn existed, (2) no warning was given or inadequate warnings were given, and (3) the injury was caused by a lack of inadequacy to warn (Davis, 1988).

Improper maintenance of the site may also be the focal point of litigation. Cracked sidewalks and dangerous conditions such as uncovered holes on the site can result in expensive law suits. One positive action to reduce the probability of these and similar problems is to interface the school district's maintenance plan with insurance coverage. Know what liabilities exist. Take corrective action where it is warranted. The linkage of school district policy, insurance coverage, and maintenance procedures is likely to improve playground safety.

## SUMMARY

This chapter explored six issues that are pervasive in contemporary facility management. Preventive maintenance is a concept that has come of age. Forward-thinking school administrators are trying to avoid another decade of deferred maintenance problems by incorporating comprehensive planning models and technology into the maintenance process.

Air quality has emerged as a growing concern in the area of health and safety. Energy conservation remains a goal even though the effects of the energy crises have temporarily subsided. Both the desire to improve the environment and the desire to conserve fossil fuels are conditions resulting, at least in part, from changing values and beliefs among Americans about the environment and the future.

Roof maintenance continues to consume a large portion of the maintenance budget in many school districts. Recent improvements in design and materials offer promise that this condition will improve.

Vandalism is a troublesome act for school buildings. Even though this is the case, over one-half of the school districts in America continue to operate without a modern security system.

Finally, increased utilization of school facilities and playgrounds is illuminating the potential for accidents and litigation. Proper maintenance of outdoor equipment and the site coupled with intrusive planning that interfaces potential liability with insurance coverage are two measures that are suggested.

## ISSUES FOR DISCUSSION

1. List the circumstances that contributed to the period of deferred maintenance between 1975 and 1985.
2. Does your local health department or state health department provide services for monitoring air quality in schools?
3. Why do some schools decide to curtail the operation of ventilation systems?

4. Discuss the problems associated with selecting a type of roof in new construction solely on the basis of cost.

5. To what degree do environmental conditions (climate) dictate the type of roof you might select for a school?

6. What are the advantages and disadvantages of retaining an architectural firm to do roof assessments?

7. Discuss the advantages and disadvantages of your school district's policies concerning vandalism.

8. Should school districts prohibit persons from using their playgrounds during non-school hours? Can the school district prohibit such use?

9. How would you go about finding out the extent of existing insurance coverage for playground and site accidents?

10. What issues do you believe are emerging for maintenance management that were not addressed in this chapter?

# 14

# THE FUTURE

When we think about the future, we often concentrate solely on those factors largely beyond our control. The economy, scientific discoveries, and social conditions are prime examples. There is little doubt that these universal conditions will play a major role in shaping the future, but they are not the only determinants for the twenty-first century. Two other elements merit scrutiny: (1) past practices, and (2) administrative behaviors.

To a great extent, planning in education, including facility planning, has been a reaction to existing conditions (Peterson, 1986); that is, most decisions are developed out of necessity. This behavior is an exemplification of crisis management, putting out one "brush fire" after another. Underlying such practices is the belief that we are helpless beings of our surroundings. In some measure, there is psychological comfort in concluding that we are unable to control (or at least partially direct) the future. After all, acceptance of this view tends to diminish the expectations we hold for our public leaders. Management experts, however, favor the hypothesis that purposeful intervention can influence tomorrow's agenda. And as social scientists continue to reinforce the relationships between strategic planning and the future, the public too will adopt this position. In so doing, they will demand more comprehensive planning from those given the responsibility to operate our public schools.

The issue of planning was discussed earlier in this book. Comprehensive systems planning requires monitoring, recording, and analysis of pertinent data. These activities extend beyond the organizational level (i.e., the school system) and must include the environmental field (i.e., the community, society). This chapter explores two critical sources of information relative to strategic planning: (1) the current status of school facilities, and (2) potential influences in the future.

## THE CURRENT STATE OF SCHOOL FACILITIES

In looking ahead, we should be aware of where we were and where we are. Past decisions partially explicate our current state of affairs. This point is most cogent given that the status quo is certainly not acceptable. America presently faces a school facility dilemma, and the problem extends from higher education to pre-school programs. Not only are many school buildings in need of repair or replacement, but this long overdue recognition comes at a most inopportune time. Consider some of the conditions that mitigate against a comprehensive solution:

• an increasing number of the public no longer has children in school;

• a climate of taxpayer revolt still prevails in many parts of the United States;

• many states still rely heavily upon local taxes to fund school construction, and in many of these states local taxpayers can prevent school construction (imagine what would happen to defense spending if the budget had to be put to a public referendum);

• the costs for repair and replacement of school buildings have escalated faster than the general economy; and

• an increasing number of taxpayers have a low level of confidence in governmental agencies—including public schools.

Just how bad is the current state of educational facilities? Some label the situation a crisis. This judgment is supported by a recent study conducted by the Education Writers Association (Lewis, 1989). That effort culminated in the assessment that at least 25 percent of the nation's public school buildings are in poor physical condition and make shoddy places for learning. Additionally this study revealed that:

• only 6 percent of the nation's public schools have been built since 1980;

• at least 50 percent of the current facilities were erected during the 1950s and 1960s to accommodate the "baby boomers";

• many schools built in the 1950s and 1960s were erected with cheap materials and utilized fast construction techniques—giving many of these buildings a reasonable life-span of only 30 years;

• maintenance and repair budgets are usually the first items to get reduced in austerity programs;

• 43 percent of the nation's schools are obsolete;

• 42 percent have environmental hazards;

• 25 percent are overcrowded; and

• 13 percent are structurally unsound (Lewis, 1989).

Boyer (1989) astutely noted that educational buildings reflect our priorities as a society. In this respect, these findings are especially troublesome. The results of this research also reveal the burdens that are being relegated to the next generation of taxpayers.

Underlying past, present, and future facility planning decisions are two critical questions: Who should pay for school facilities? How good do school facilities need to be? In addressing the first query, two dimensions should be recognized. The first relates to levels of government. Although public education is a state responsibility, many states continue to require local districts, via local taxes, to pay for all, or most of school construction costs. The negative effects of this practice upon the current condition of school facilities has been repeatedly chronicled in the professional literature (Thompson and Camp, 1988).The second dimension of the economic burden inquiry involves a popular belief that those who benefit from education ought to pay the majority of the costs for the service. Accordingly, it is usually tempting for taxpayers to opt for low-cost facilities even though such buildings tend to have short life spans and to expect future generations to be responsible for their own educational needs. This contention is flawed by the myopic assumption that only students currently enrolled and their parents are the beneficiaries of public education. In truth, a free public school system is a foundational component of a democratic society. The economic benefits of an effective educational system reach most segments of American life.

Both dimensions of the fiscal responsibility question are inextricably related to the second query, that of quality. As long as state officials refuse to accept all or a major portion of the burden of school facility funding, and as long as taxpayers embrace a most narrow view regarding the beneficiaries of public education, it will be difficult to escape a repetition of past mistakes. Another decade of poor decisions will only further compound the present deplorable condition.

If the current generation of taxpayers did not have to address the issue of poor facilities, it is possible that adequate resources could now be directed to instructional initiatives. If one accepts the conclusion that public education is, in general, underfunded, then it can be argued that past facility funding decisions are a contributing factor to this condition. Poor planning decisions continually force fiscal resources to be expended for maintenance, operations, or replacements. The current school facility problems are also exacerbated by the reality that little has been done to equalize the fiscal burden of financing capital outlay since the last boom of school construction that occurred in the 1950s and 1960s (Lewis, 1989). The cost for school facility construction still relies heavily upon local property taxes in many states.

In focusing on the future, it appears that school administrators, other educators, and school board members should work to accomplish the following:

1. There should be a greater distribution of fiscal responsibility for capital development between states and local school districts. This may be accomplished by developing more persuasive arguments related to the state's responsibility for assuring *equality*.
2. The public needs to be better informed about the ways in which *all* citizens benefit

from public education and the mutual dependency between a democratic society and a system of public education.

3. The life-cycle costs of school facilities need to be put in the context of overall costs for supporting public education. The prospect that the 1990s will be another decade of deferred maintenance and referenda defeats is real. Even in the absence of other considerations, eradicating the problems that already exist constitutes a massive chore for school administrators over the next two decades. Yet we know that new challenges, scientific discoveries, social changes, and disasters will emerge—and they too will require expenditures of limited funds. And in addition to eradicating existing problems and coping with new developments, administrators face the reality that education will suffer if tomorrow's schools are not better than what we now have (Collins, 1987).

## NEW CHALLENGES

The prime interest rate, the family structure, advances in medicine, nuclear fusion, and environmental changes are only a few of the conditions that could seriously alter the direction of facility planning. Items considered luxuries just ten years ago (e.g., carpeting, coaxial cable) are now deemed to be necessities (Coley, 1988). Our best hope for anticipating tomorrow's needs is to monitor, sequence, and analyze what is occurring in our world. It is not an easy task. No single plan is likely to emerge, but it is hoped that on a community-to-community basis, effective administrators and citizens will work together to improve upon the past practices (Graves, 1985).

Earlier in the book, conditions currently affecting facility planning were reviewed. Several of these variables are repeated here, but in this instance, the focus is the future, not the present. Energy, for example, is a factor affecting current decisions, but it is also likely to remain an issue for the next 20 to 30 years. What follows are the more commonly identified factors attracting the attention of facility planners.

### The Economy

With regard to future planning, the state of the national economy is apt to play an increasing role in local school district decisions. The economy not only has tangible influences upon capital development (e.g., interest rates), it also affects taxpayers, legislators, and school board members psychologically. In the period 1988 to 1990, it is projected that $22 billion will be spent on school construction projects, from kindergarten through grade twelve. This is almost three times as much spent during the period of 1986–88 (Ficklen, 1988).

In the past, some well-informed school administrators have worked collaboratively with financial advisors to time bond sales to take advantage of favorable market conditions. In years to come, similar strategies need to be identified and integrated into facility planning. Planners who are able to keep abreast of economic developments and who utilize this information to formulate visions of the future can inject a vital ingredient into strategic planning. Economic planning is becoming a more precise administrative function.

### New Building Concepts

Virtually all architects agree that new concepts will emerge with regard to designing schools. Ideas such as air-supported schools or underground schools are distinct possibilities in the next decade (Brubaker, 1988). These concepts are no longer thought of as science fiction or idle dreams. They are design ideas spawned by real geographic and ecological concerns. In the past, for example, the restricted availability of land in urban areas resulted in high-rise buildings. It is not possible that this same condition, coupled with the ever increasing concern for energy conservation, will result in future structures being erected in the opposite direction?

Earlier in the book the factors of creativity and technology were discussed in relation to architects. Effective systemic planning requires up-to-date information about what is occurring in school design. This information can be monitored by reviewing professional journals, research studies conducted at architectural colleges, professional conferences, and materials made available by the American Institute of Architects.

### Scientific Discoveries

Perhaps no category of potential influences is more potent to school design than scientific discoveries. Even as this book is being written, scientists appear to be on the verge of unraveling the mysteries of nuclear fusion. If successful, this single event would supply a cheap, clean, and inexhaustible source of energy that could markedly alter all of education. Just imagine the impact on school design if energy were no longer a concern. Global reliance on fossil fuels would subside, creating significant alterations in the world economy—and in the priorities of American education. School buildings might be designed without restriction regarding exterior glass. The possibilities are unlimited.

During the 1980s, school administrators learned well the potential implications of science and its application, technology (Hill, 1989). Fiber optics, microcomputers, and satellites have already created new delivery systems for concepts such as distance learning. There is no doubt that science and technology will continue to broaden the options available to planners. New building materials, instructional equipment, and climate control are but three examples.

The issues related to science and technology are having a dramatic effect on facility planners because: (1) development is occurring at an accelerated rate, and (2) deployment is occurring at an accelerated rate. For example, a school building may have a life span of 40 to 50 years, but new microcomputer generations are occurring about every five years (Kauffman and Lamkin, 1985). School environments must be sufficiently flexible to adapt to a host of technological innovations that will become available in the next two to three decades (Christopher, 1989). Architects and school administrators should recognize that the most sophisticated technology available today may be outdated in less than a decade.

### Environmental Research

As frequently stated, school buildings exist to accommodate the teaching/learning process. Despite the universal acceptance of this notion, we know amazingly little about the ways that environmental conditions affect certain students. Much of what has been done in this area can be classified as descriptive research (i.e., a recording of what is observed in various school situations). And although this information is helpful, it in no way constitutes an acceptable theoretical framework for the future.

Data that can contribute to our school environment knowledge base are generated in many different disciplines and with a myriad of foci (e.g., educational psychology, learning styles). Unfortunately, the results often remain fragmented. A first step to improving the study of the effects of the physical environment on children and learning would be to increase funding for such efforts. Earthman (1986) offers two additional suggestions:

1. Methodological problems associated with isolating and controlling the vast number of variables associated with student achievement and behavior need to be addressed.
2. More effort needs to be made in synthesizing the results of research efforts on isolated topics associated with designing school environments (e.g., lighting, color schema).

This latter suggestion entails *meta-analysis*—an approach that permits a characterization of the tendencies of the research as well as confirmation of the magnitude of any differences among conditions. When more data are made available through controlled studies, both architects and school administrators will be in a more enlightened position to make critical decisions about educational environments.

### Expanding Mission

Predictions about public education almost always suggest that the standard school day and the standard school year are going to become extinct. Additionally, school systems are going to be required to provide a growing number of services in such areas as day care, youth organizations, and adult education (Christopher, 1989). Adult and community education are already emerging as key issues for many public schools (Kowalski and Fallon, 1986). It is not beyond the realm of possibility that schools will evolve as a major provider of certain services for all citizens. Given that in many communities the schools already operate the largest food service program and given the demographic projections for the next century, is it not possible that school cafeterias will be supplying meals to senior citizens and public preschool centers?

The space requirements associated with an expanding mission will obviously vary from one community to the next. It is unrealistic to assume, however, that a declining number of school-age children will offset the demands associated with increased services (Coley, 1988). Not only are new clients likely to be served directly by public school systems (clients outside the traditional age range of 5 to 18), but traditional students are apt to receive a greater number of services as well (tutoring, health care).

### Political Outcomes

Facility planning is already a highly regulated activity in many states. Laws, codes, and state regulations stipulate what must be done. Political decisions do not have to relate directly to facility planning in order to have a significant impact. For instance, several concepts have emerged in the past two decades that could force public schools into a competitive mode. First, *educational vouchers* and then parental *choice* emerged as concepts allowing parents to select the schools their children attend. Minnesota already has enacted a Choice Law and several other states, such as Arkansas and Iowa, are well on their way to doing so. Competition for students could markedly increase the attention that is accorded educational facilities. Schools with electronic classrooms, computer laboratories, and interactive television studios may have a distinct advantage over outdated and drab buildings.

Home schooling is another future potentiality. At present, this practice is largely the product of religious motivators. But what will be the impact upon school systems if technology permits private contractors to offer schooling directly into student homes via television and computers? And will this form of home schooling be encouraged or discouraged by state governmental officials?

### Population Patterns

The migration pattern away from farms to urban areas and then to suburbs is well understood in America. But what does the future portend in this regard? Experts often disagree as to whether there will be a resurgence of urban living. In large measure, this will depend upon solving social and energy-related problems. Fortunately, demographic analysis is one planning component that is readily accepted by practicing school administrators. Beyond the traditional enrollment projections, however, school officials tend to do very little. There is a need to monitor and map societal conditions that may affect future migration patterns. This lesson is quickly learned in locations experiencing radical shifts in population. In the Orlando, Florida area, for example, school districts have adopted strategic planning to aid demographic studies.

Birth rates also impact upon the future. Currently, an interesting trend is occurring in the United States. Birth rates for white females are declining while the rates for minorities, especially Blacks and Hispanics are increasing (Hodgkinson, 1985). Since minority populations tend to be highly concentrated in certain geographic areas, the actual population growth generated by higher birth levels is possible to project. But will this shift in national population affect basic societal values and beliefs relative to schooling? Multicultural education is already a component of curricula in many schools. Could continued growth in Hispanic and other minority populations affect school designs in the future?

### Social Issues

The American public school system developed during a period when the family structure was relatively stable. In the earlier parts of the twentieth century, divorce was far less common than it is today. Moreover, an increasing number of unmarried women are having babies—many of these mothers are teen-agers (Hodgkinson, 1985). The result is an ever-growing group of children who come from single-parent households. This one social issue alone is already having a profound affect upon some school facilities. Take, for instance, the following two examples:

1. Students from one-parent families often have no one at home during the school day because the parent is working. If they become ill during school, they may have to remain there. This problem is so acute in certain schools that bigger and differently designed health rooms have become a necessity.
2. The need for special services is often greater in schools having high concentrations of single-parent students, especially if the school serves lower-income neighborhoods. Space for counselors, social workers, and psychologists becomes necessary.

There are many other social issues that could affect school systems and, ultimately, school buildings. The connection between societal needs and the public schools is clearly visible in our past. The social legislation passed during the Kennedy and Johnson administrations during the 1960s exemplifies federal intervention into social issues that in turn result in new programs and additional facility requirements for local school districts (e.g., free lunch programs, remedial instruction for disadvantaged children).

Changes in societal needs, wants, and values are largely responsible for the content of the curriculum in grades kindergarten through twelve. Most often these influences make their way to state legislatures where they are either rejected or accepted and added to the state's list of required study. Needs, wants, and values may also play an important part in local school district policy decisions. The addition of a music program or Spanish in the elementary schools could result from public pressures. Given that changes in society are occurring at an ever more rapid pace, it is essential that comprehensive planning include the monitoring of local, state, and national trends. Demands for curricular expansion typically evolve over a period of years.

### Reform Efforts

Ever since the early 1980s, American education has been in the spotlight as various reform efforts culminated in reports such as *A Nation at Risk* (The National Commission on Excellence in Education, 1983) and *A Nation Prepared*, a Carnegie Forum Report (1986). Analysts are now linking the various aspects of reform with school facilities. Piccigallo (1989) notes, for example, how the deplorable condition of the New York City public school facilities constitutes a major barrier to instructional improvement. It is estimated that it will take $4.2 billion in the next decade to renovate the schools in that district alone. Many of the current New York City schools were erected prior to World War II. Piccigallo asks, "Should anyone realistically be expected to work, creatively and productively, under such wretched conditions?"

It is within the inner cities, where reform is most needed, that schools are in the worst condition. But the problem of outdated or unacceptable facilities is not restricted to urban areas. The suburbs and small cities also face this problem. As measures are taken to improve schooling in the next two decades, school facility renovation and replacement will emerge as critical issue. Instructional planners will be unable to escape the reality that environmental conditions affect learning.

### Teacher Empowerment

One trend often overlooked in the literature on school administration involves the consequences that result from a movement known as *teacher empowerment*. This movement is striving to create more autonomy and authority for teachers. If successful, teachers will demand to participate in school facility planning to a greater extent than has been true in many school districts in the past.

Educational planners and architects who philosophically accept the concept of participatory planning and who, by experience, can evidence success with this mode of decision-making are apt to have a distinct advantage in the future. Additionally, those who respect the right of teachers as professionals to participate in the process and who recognize their potential contributions to quality facility design are likely to be tomorrow's trend setters. Teacher participation may generate conflict during planning, but it is likely to produce more effective learning spaces.

## MANAGING THE FUTURE

The influences listed in this chapter characterize the range of factors that could influence school facility planning and management in the future. Administrators often conclude that tomorrow is so uncertain that the best facility planning alternative is simply to design flexible and adaptable schools. While flexibility, expansibility, and other such attributes are certainly advisable, they constitute a generic and limited approach to the future. Industrious leaders can do more than make generalizations.

This book emphasizes a systems analysis approach to planning. To a great extent this paradigm is preferred because it is inclusive. A planning format that attempts to integrate the environment, the school system, and the learners will produce the most comprehensive information. Figure 14.1 illustrates some factors in each of these components that could influence the administration of school facilities.

Strategic planning requires effort and expertise. Some excellent examples of this process can be observed in private industry (Holloway, 1986). As information about planning becomes more readily available, forward-thinking executives are abandoning planning models that rely on the following traditional assumptions:

1. We know where we want to be in 20 years.
2. We know the steps we have to take to get there.
3. Our environment is relatively stable so it should not present a problem.

Replacing this traditional format is a range of *vision-driven* planning paradigms. In these models the assumptions are substantially different:

1. The environment is ever-changing.
2. We are somewhat unsure as to where we want to be in 20 years.
3. We are somewhat unsure about the steps we need to take to achieve our goals.

Vision-driven means that instead of a single target 20 years ahead, there are multiple targets—each the product of visions emanating from the integration of inputs (and specific needs and wants) gathered via systems analysis. Take, for example, an attempt to measure the impact of microcomputers in the year 2010. One possible vision is that in 2010 all students will have computers in their homes. Another vision is that students will no longer be using microcomputers at that time because they will already be obsolete. And yet another vision is that microcomputers will be so advanced that students will carry them in their pockets. Strategic planning is a process of periodically updating data. Thus, as new information about microcomputers is collected, filtered, and infused into the planning process, one or more of the visions may become obsolete well before the targeted date of 2010.

Of more importance is the continuous addition of data which permits the planners to adjust the steps that are specified for each of the potential futures. Staying with the example of microcomputers, assume that one vision is that each child will have a computer at his/her workstation in every class by the year 2010.

**Figure 14.1**
**Potential Influences on the Future Administration of School Facilities**

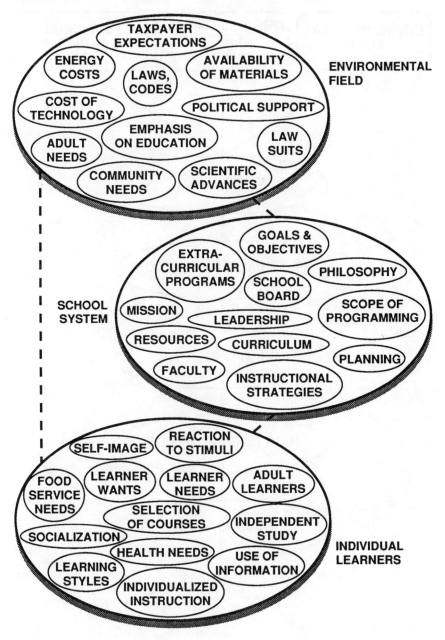

**Figure 14.2**
**A Five Step Approach for Structuring Visions of the Future**

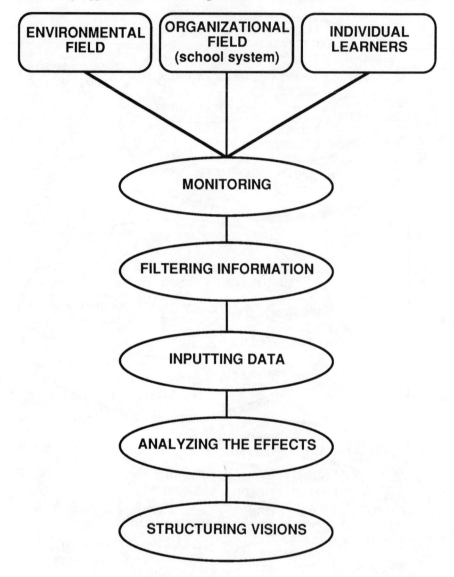

What steps will be required to achieve this vision? As data are made available, and if the vision is retained, the steps to achieve this vision may be adjusted periodically (possibly every one or two years). The visions are, in essence, goals; the steps are objectives. The objectives are subject to short-term review (every one or two years) and the goals are reviewed in more lengthy cycles (four to six years).

When the process used for scanning technology is duplicated for all the other factors (e.g., energy, environment, economy), the school district leaders are engaging in a vision-driven systems model for planning. The interrelationship of factors is the same as presented earlier in the book in Chapter 3. The difference is that the discussion here addresses management of the future rather than planning related to specific decisions about a single building program.

Keeping abreast of environmental, organizational, and individual learner needs and wants is an extensive task. It essentially requires a five-step process: monitoring, filtering, inputting, analyzing, and structuring visions (or restructuring visions). The relationship among these factors is presented in Figure 14.2.

Monitoring relates to active scanning procedures designed to collect information. Filtering is a procedure designed to screen information that is collected in order to decide which information is especially cogent to the planning process. Inputting entails actually infusing the relevant data into the planning information bank. Analyzing is a process of interfacing new information with other inputs and data already in the information bank. Finally, analysis is used to create or alter existing visions.

The process of strategic planning is not perfect. But when compared to the alternatives, it is overwhelmingly the best option for managing the future. The application of this administrative tool to facility planning should produce a wealth of information that will improve both planning and managing school buildings. It is far superior to crystal ball gazing and random guessing.

## SUMMARY

The future of school facility planning and management is indeed uncertain. The future is affected by a number of factors including past decisions and present practices. These two influences alone have created a serious facility problem that must be addressed by the next generation of taxpayers. Past practices of relying exclusively, or nearly so, on local property taxes to construct school buildings has been a major contributor to current difficulties.

It is virtually impossible to list all the factors that could give direction to school design in the future. The economy, new design concepts, an expanding mission for schools, environmental research, political considerations, scientific developments, social issues, political issues, and demographics are some of the more obvious ones.

The best available tool for managing the future is a comprehensive planning process that melds systems analysis with visions. Vision-driven models rely on a continuous five-part process of scanning, filtering, inputting, analyzing, and vision structuring. Although not foolproof, this effort will result in a comprehensive data bank that can be utilized in making critical decisions.

## ISSUES FOR DISCUSSION

1. Identify the possible reasons for the serious problems that currently exist nationwide with regard to school facilities.
2. Identify the current status of school facilities in your community. How many buildings are antiquated, unsafe?
3. In what ways could advancements in school building design affect the future of school facilities? Do you know of any examples of air-supported structures in your state?
4. Attempt to develop alternative visions with regard to the effects of interactive television upon the design of school buildings in the year 2010.
5. Identify factors that are likely to impact the future of school facility management that were not covered in this chapter.
6. Describe what you believe to be the strengths and weaknesses of using a vision-driven planning model to project future needs.
7. Are there differences between strategic planning and futurism? If so, what are they?

# APPENDIX A

## GLOSSARY OF SCHOOL FACILITY TERMS

*acoustics*  the science that deals with the production, control, transmission, reception, and effects of sound

*AIA*  American Institute of Architects

*alcove*  a recess or small opening off a larger room; in schools, a nook for study or counseling

*alternate bid*  a proposal to use a different method, material, or quantity than is specified in the bidding documents (e.g., bidding a tile floor when carpeting is specified)

*amortization schedule*  a schedule of payments needed to retire an outstanding debt (both principal and interest)

*arbitrage*  the simultaneous purchase and sale of the same or equivalent security in order to profit from price discrepancies; a school district investing proceeds from a bond sale at a higher interest rate than is being paid on the bonds

*asbestos*  a soft, fibrous, incombustible material formerly used in many building materials; considered to be a health hazard if not properly contained

*backfill*  earth used to fill in the cavity created during the construction of exterior foundation walls

*back up heating system*  a secondary source of producing heat for a building in case the primary system cannot function (e.g., using fuel oil as a back up system for natural gas)

*barrier-free environment*  with relation to schools, a facility that is free of barriers that would prevent normal and customary usage by a handicapped person

*baseboard*  the finish board covering the plaster (or other wall material) where it meets the floor

| | |
|---|---|
| *base molding* | a molding used to trim the upper edge of interior baseboards |
| *bid bond* | a surety submitted by a bidder that assures that the bidder will meet obligations stated in the bid |
| *bond* | a written promise, generally under seal, to pay a specified sum of money (called a face value) at a fixed time in the future (called the maturity date) and carrying a specified rate of interest |
| *bond attorney* | an attorney who specializes in rendering opinions regarding bond issues; in relation to schools, an attorney who certifies that the bonds qualify as tax-exempt investments |
| *Bond Buyer* | a newspaper with wide circulation advertising the sale of bonds |
| *bond election* | a referendum asking voter approval for the sale of bonds |
| *bond rating* | a judgement made by a rating agency identifying the relative level of risk involved with purchasing specific bonds |
| *breach of contract* | when one or both parties to a contract fail to meet stated obligations |
| *BTUs* | units of heat; used in measurements (British Thermal Unit) |
| *cafetorium* | a room in a school that is designed to serve the dual purpose of cafeteria and auditorium |
| *callable bond* | a bond that may be redeemed by the owner prior to maturity |
| *capital outlay* | an expenditure that results in the acquisition of fixed assets or additions to fixed assets that are presumed to have benefits for more than one year; an expenditure for land or buildings |
| *casement* | a glass frame that is made to open by turning on hinges affixed to its vertical edges |
| *casing* | a metal or wooden member around door and window openings to give a finished appearance |
| *catch basin* | a cast iron, cement, or wooden receptacle into which the water from the roof, floor, and so on will drain; it is connected to the sewer or drain tile |
| *ceramic tile* | a clay product with an impervious, glazed surface designed for easy maintenance |
| *change order* | an order issued by the architect upon approval of the owner directing a change (in materials, methods, or quantity) in the building contracts (e.g., deciding to increase the number of rooms that are to be carpeted after contracts are awarded) |
| *circuit* | a path over which electrical current may pass |
| *clerk-of-the-works* | an individual representing the owner who completes clerical and supervisory tasks during the construction phase of a project in addition to those assigned to the architect |
| *column* | a round vertical shaft or pillar that can be either load bearing or non-load bearing |

| | |
|---|---|
| *commons area* | an area in a building designed as a gathering place (e.g., a place where students could socialize after lunch) |
| *construction manager* | a person or firm employed by the owner throughout the design and construction activities |
| *contingency fund* | a specific amount set aside in a project budget to pay for unanticipated costs (e.g., emergencies or change orders) |
| *contractor* | a person offering to do work for a specified amount of money (e.g., an electrical contractor) |
| *convector* | a heat transfer surface designed to emit its heat to surrounding air largely or entirely by convention currents |
| *cornice* | the part of the roof that projects from the wall |
| *CPM* | Critical Path Method; a scheduling program requiring a listing of tasks, sequencing of tasks, and estimated times for completing tasks |
| *curb cuts* | used in relation to barrier-free environments; a gentle slope in curbs allowing persons in wheelchairs to cross the curb |
| *damper* | a movable plate that regulates the draft of a stove, a fireplace, or a furnace |
| *debt service fund* | a fund used to finance and account for payment of interest and principal on debts (e.g., retirement of bond obligations) |
| *design architect* | the architect(s) actually doing the design work |
| *double-hung window* | a window designed with two sashes, one made to raise and the other to lower |
| *drain* | a means for carrying off waste water; a sewer or other pipe used to convey ground, surface, or water; a conveyor of waste water |
| *dry well* | a pit located on porous ground walled up with rock allowing water to seep through the pit; used for disposal of rain water or effluent from a septic tank |
| *eave* | the part of the roof that extends beyond the wall line |
| *educational consultant* | a planning specialist who identifies educational needs for a school facility project; usually a professor specializing in school facility planning |
| *educational specifications* | a document containing information about the intended uses of a school building (e.g., how instruction will occur, the scope of the curriculum, and so on); used by architects to design the school; also called *educational program statement* |
| *egress* | the act, place, or means of exiting |
| *elevation drawings* | drawings of the front, sides, and rear faces of a building |
| *eminent domain* | the right of a governmental agency to obtain private property either by a negotiated sale or by court action |

| | |
|---|---|
| *enamel* | paint comprised of a considerable portion of varnish; produces a hard, glossy surface |
| *enrollment projection* | a mathematical estimate of future school enrollments; used to produce quantitative data used in facility planning |
| *erosion* | a gradual wearing away of a substance such as soil by water |
| *excavation* | a pit or hole formed by digging |
| *expansion joints* | a designed break in walls, floors, or ceilings that permits expansions and contractions to occur without unduly damaging the structural integrity of the facility |
| *face brick* | a brick used on the exterior of a building |
| *fascia* | a vertical board nailed on the ends of rafters; part of a cornice |
| *fenestration* | the arrangement, design, and proportioning of windows and doors within a building |
| *financial consultant* | a specialist who assists school districts in creating a plan to finance a long-term debt and assists in the sale of bonds; usually a professor specializing in school finance or a certified public accountant |
| *fire brick* | a brick designed to be especially hard and tolerant of heat; used in fireplaces |
| *fire door* | a door that is designed to remain intact in fires |
| *fire stop* | a projection of brickwork on the walls between the joists to prevent the spread of fire |
| *fixed assets* | land, buildings, machinery, furniture, and other equipment that the school system intends to hold or continue to use over long periods of time |
| *fixture* | a receptacle attached to a plumbing system in which water or other waste may be collected until it is discharged into the plumbing system |
| *flashing* | sheet metal work over windows and doors and around chimneys installed to prevent water from seeping into the structure |
| *floor plan* | a horizontal cut through a building showing rooms, partitions, windows, doors, and stairs |
| *flue* | an aperture in a chimney permitting the passage of smoke |
| *foot candle* | a measurement of light equal to that emitted by a candle at a distance of one foot; a common reference point for lighting standards and codes |
| *footings* | that part of a building that is placed on soil of sufficient quality to bear the weight of the building |
| *foundation* | the base or lowest part of the structure |
| *foyer* | an entrance hallway or lobby |
| *friable* | easily crumbled; used in relation to asbestos |
| *general obligation bonds* | debts supported by the full faith and credit of the school district; some states limit the debt level that can be achieved by using general obligation bonds |

| | |
|---|---|
| *grade* | the level of the ground around the building |
| *graphics* | pictures, drawings, or other designs usually placed on interior walls of schools |
| *hip roof* | a roof sloping up from four walls of the building |
| *HVAC* | used in construction planning to refer to heating, ventilation, and air conditioning |
| *insulation* | a specially prepared material placed between floors and walls to reduce the conductivity of heat and sound |
| *internal heat gain* | uncontrolled gain in heat caused by sunlight or by humans occupying a building |
| *joist* | a small timber that supports the floor |
| *lavatory* | a restroom or a fixture used to wash hands and face; a small sink |
| *liability insurance* | expenditures for insurance coverage of the school system or its officers against losses resulting from judgements awarded against the system |
| *load bearing* | a vertical structure member (e.g., a wall) supporting ceilings and/or roofs |
| *locker bays* | alcoves created to place student lockers in a specified area as opposed to placing them along the walls in hallways |
| *lowest and best bid* | a concept often included in statutes regarding the awarding of contracts for public construction projects; allows the school administrators and school board some level of discretion in reviewing bids |
| *masonry* | a material such as brick, stone, or concrete block used in construction |
| *multi-purpose room* | an area in a school that serves several different functions (e.g., an area in an elementary school that serves as a gym, cafeteria, and auditorium) |
| *municipal bonds* | bonds issued by state and local governmental units (e.g., school districts) |
| *natatorium* | an indoor swimming pool |
| *non-collusion affadavit* | a sworn written statement indicating that a bidder did not conspire with others to fix bid amounts |
| *nonferrous* | not containing iron (e.g., copper or brass) |
| *nosing* | the rounded edge of a stair tread |
| *open space concept* | a term used in relation to a school that does not put walls between rooms, especially classrooms |
| *OSHA* | Occupational Safety and Health Act |
| *outdoor learning laboratory* | outdoor areas utilized for teaching (e.g., a wooded area used to teach some science units) |
| *panic bars* | a mechanism placed on doors that releases the hatch when pushed |
| *penalty clause* | a provision in a contract stipulating a penalty if the conditions of the contract are not met (e.g., a contractor agrees to reduce his fee by a |

specified amount for each day his work is not completed beyond the agreed upon date

*percolation tests*
soil tests designed to determine the soil's ability to absorb liquids; used in relation to building projects to determine site ability to dispose of roof water and/or effluent

*performance bond*
a surety submitted by a contractor proving insurance that the work will be done as specified

*PERT*
Performance Evaluation and Review Techniques; a scheduling program requiring a listing of tasks, sequencing of tasks, and estimated times for completing tasks

*phased construction*
a building project that is completed in distinct phases; often used in renovation/additions when part of the school must remain operational while construction is occurring

*preliminary drawings*
the first architectural drawings of a project completed after schematic drawings; the first drawings to provide more than spatial relationships

*preventive maintenance*
a program designed to replace and service facilities, equipment, and so forth in a timely manner to prevent malfunctions from occurring

*project architect*
an architect assigned to be in charge of a specific project

*property insurance*
expenditures for all forms of insurance covering damage or loss of property related to fire, theft, storms, or any other cause

*prospectus*
a document containing all pertinent data concerning a bond issue; also called an *official statement*

*punch list*
a list of items yet to be completed on a project; a list periodically produced toward the completion of a project identifying specific elements still requiring attention

*radon*
a heavy radioactive gaseous element of the group of inert gases formed by disintegrating radium; recently identified as a health hazard for some homes and schools

*recessed doors*
doors opening into hallways designed so as to not extend into the flow of traffic

*referendum*
a vote on a measure submitted (e.g., a public vote on whether to allow a school district to sell bonds)

*remonstrance*
a concept used in some state laws that permits a segment of the taxpayers to file an official objection to a planned facility program

*safety glass*
glass with plastic or wire laminated within to prevent splintering when damaged

*satellite food services*
a program where food is prepared at one site and delivered to and served at another site

*schematic drawings*
the very first drawings prepared by architects; drawings concentrating on total space, space allocations for specific areas, and spatial relationships

*school site*
land and all improvements on the land other than structures; includes parking areas, sidewalks, playgrounds, athletic fields, and so forth

| | |
|---|---|
| *security zoning* | creating zones in a building that permit one area to be used without compromising the security of the remainder of the building (e.g., zoning the gymnasium to permit evening use without allowing users to enter the remainder of the building) |
| *serial bonds* | issues redeemable by installments, each of which is to be paid in full, ordinarily out of revenues of the fiscal year in which it matures, or out of revenues from the preceding year |
| *sinking fund* | synonymous with *debt service fund;* used to retire debt obligations |
| *site survey* | a geographic survey of a parcel of land designed to determine the boundaries of the property, the existing gradients of the various slopes, and the identification of obstructions |
| *soffitt* | the underside of a part or member of a building |
| *solar heat* | heat transferring devise that relies on sunlight as a source of energy |
| *specifications* | the written descriptions of materials, methods, and quantity that accompanies a set of drawings |
| *subcontractors* | individuals or firms who are retained to do portions of a contract (e.g., a painting firm employed to compete portions of a general contract) |
| *superintendent of buildings and grounds* | a title used in some school districts for the administrator in charge of buildings and grounds programs; now less common than *director of buildings and grounds* |
| *surety bond* | a written promise to pay damages or to indemnify against losses caused by the party or parties named in the document, through nonperformance or through defalcation (e.g., a bond given by a contractor) |
| *teaching station* | a space in a school where teaching occurs; a classroom, a laboratory |
| *terrazo* | a floor surface commonly found in schools (especially hallways) composed of marble chips and cement that is ground and polished; a durable surface that is easily maintained |
| *test borings* | a soil test designed to produce information about the subsoil and its load bearing qualities |
| *topography* | the distinctive features of the land (used in reference to school sites) |
| *visual barrier* | solid materials that impede a line of sight |
| *visual contact* | designing areas so that a person in one room can see into another (e.g., creating a visual contact between a coaching office and the locker room |
| *wainscot* | the lower part of a wall when finished with a material different from the remainder of the wall |
| *working drawings* | technical drawings used to guide workers in the construction of a building (or renovation) |
| *zoned heating* | a system allowing heating to be controlled in specific areas (called zones) of a building |

# APPENDIX B

# COMMON BARRIERS IN SCHOOL ENVIRONMENTS

I. External Barriers

A. *Parking Lots.* Parking lots are a source of problems for many handicapped individuals. The most common concerns are:

1. Parking spaces that are too narrow do not allow a non-ambulatory or semi-ambulatory person to move from an automobile to a wheelchair or crutches (or visa versa).

2. Placing a curb or step between the parking space and the paved walkway can be a barrier for the non-ambulatory or semi-ambulatory.

**Figure B.1**
**Parking Space for Handicapped**

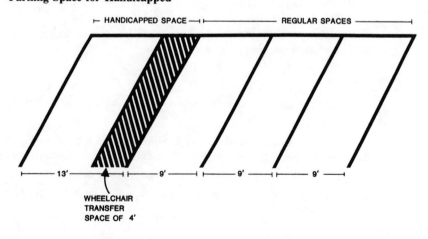

3. Designing parking places parallel to curbs is another common barrier for persons using a wheelchair or crutches.

4. Parking spaces designed on sloping terrain are a potential hazard.

5. Parking spaces which are excessively far from the entrances of the building constitute an often overlooked barrier.

B. *Approaches.* Approaches to a building constitute a second external source for concern. The most common barriers in this category include:

1. Parking lots that are located across the street from the school building present a danger, particularly when the street has heavy traffic.

2. Not having at least one entrance specifically designed to accommodate the handicapped is a common problem.

3. Where a special entrance is provided, it is not always coordinated with other environmental provisions for the handicapped person (e.g., close proximity to parking places provided for the handicapped).

4. Doormats that are not recessed or placing grating in front of doorways are problems for the handicapped person in a wheelchair or using crutches.

5. Providing curb cuts or other forms of ramping to allow access from parking lots to sidewalks is often overlooked.

6. Narrow and/or elevated walkways can be hazardous to persons in a wheelchair (e.g., wheel slips off pavement and turns over).

C. *Entrances.* Another external barrier includes the actual entrances to the building. The common barriers in this category include:

1. Doors that are too narrow to accommodate devices such as wheelchairs are the most common barriers relating to building entrances.

2. The height of a threshold (piece of metal placed below the door) above the floor level is a problem if it exceeds one inch.

3. Inadequate spacing where double doors are used in entry ways is a problem.

4. Doors that require excessive pressure to open can deny access to certain handicapped individuals.

5. Improper doorknobs, handles, and so forth, and the absence of "kickplate" on the lower half of the door are potential dangers.

II. Interior Barriers

A. *Hallways.* The interior of a school building may contain a high number of barriers. Hallways often present problems:

1. With increasing frequency, schools are using carpeting as a floorcovering. If the pile of the carpeting is too deep, it prohibits effective use of wheelchairs.

2. Items protruding from the walls into the hallways can be dangerous.

3. Lockers that are not designed and/or installed for use by the handicapped are common barriers.

4. Water fountains installed without an alcove large enough to accommodate a wheelchair or those with controls placed too high are inaccessible to certain handicapped persons.

5. Coin-operated telephones installed without an alcove large enough to accommodate a wheelchair or those with controls placed too high are barriers.

6. Floors that change levels without adequate ramping are dangerous or restrictive to many handicapped persons.

7. Floor treatments that leave hallways slippery under any conditions constitute a hazard.

B. *Stairways and Elevators.* A second category of interior barriers involves stairways and elevators. The common problems found in these areas include:

1. Stairs that are constructed with open risers are dangerous for non-ambulatory or semi-ambulatory persons.

2. Stairs constructed with projecting "noses" are dangerous.

3. Risers that are spaced more than 7 inches apart present a limitation for access for certain handicapped persons.

4. Handrails placed too high (or too low) cannot be properly used by some persons.

5. The shape of the handrail does not always allow proper gripping, particularly by certain handicapped persons.

6. Entrances to elevators are often too narrow to accommodate wheelchairs.

7. Controls for an elevator are not always placed at the proper height to allow all persons to use them.

8. Elevator operation buttons commonly do not utilize raised lettering, numbers, and so forth, to accommodate persons with vision problems.

9. Improper calibrating of elevators can cause the floor levels (between hallway and elevator) to be uneven.

10. Elevators not equipped with audible floor signals (bells or tones) prevent the person with severe visual problems from using the service.

11. The lack of an elevator providing access to upper and/or lower levels is a very common barrier, particularly in older schools.

C. *Classrooms and Laboratories.* Instructional areas such as classroom and laboratories often possess internal barriers. The most common include:

1. Seating arrangements in classrooms and lecture halls do not always accommodate handicapped persons.

2. Instructional areas utilizing fixed equipment (e.g., lab tables, sewing machines) often lack adequate provisions for proper use by certain handicapped persons.

3. Physical education programs do not always provide adequate locker facilities, shower facilities, and so forth, to accommodate all types of handicapped persons.

Figure B.2
Common Barriers on Stairways

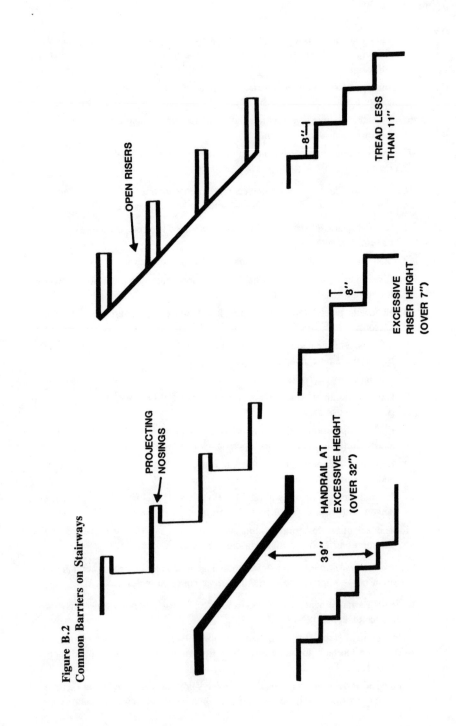

OPEN RISERS

TREAD LESS
THAN 11"

8"

EXCESSIVE
RISER HEIGHT
(OVER 7")

8"

PROJECTING
NOSINGS

HANDRAIL AT
EXCESSIVE HEIGHT
(OVER 32")

39"

4. Lecture halls, auditoriums, or similar facilities often have sloped floors and/or narrow aisles that present some concerns for use by handicapped persons.

5. Control mechanisms (e.g., lights, heat) in classrooms are often installed in a manner that does not allow a person in a wheelchair to use them. This can be a most relevant barrier for handicapped teachers.

6. Blackboards, bulletin boards, or similar items are not always placed at heights that allow persons in wheelchairs to use them.

7. Entryways into classrooms are often too narrow.

8. Placing certain instructional areas in parts of the building that cannot be reached by a handicapped person is a potential barrier.

9. Improperly designed libraries (e.g., stacks too high, deep-pile carpeting) are often overlooked as a barrier.

D. *Food Service Areas.* Food service areas are an important component of a school building. Common barriers found in this part of the educational environment include:

1. Cafeteria tables that do not have sufficient height to accommodate wheelchairs.

2. Cafeteria tables that have attached seating are barriers unless certain segments are designed to accommodate the non-ambulatory or semi-ambulatory.

3. Entryways, aisles, and food service lines are often too narrow to accommodate wheelchairs.

4. Facilities for returning trays are often too high to allow persons in wheelchairs to return their trays.

E. *Restrooms.* Another area of a school building that is used by everyone is the restroom complex. Common barriers in this part of a school include:

1. In multi-story buildings, restrooms for both sexes are not always provided on each floor.

2. Inadequate size for water closets prevents persons confined to a wheelchair from using the facilities.

3. Installation of vestibule areas (common in school buildings to provide privacy) can be too narrow and/or short.

4. Sinks placed too high are a common barrier.

5. Placement of soap and towel dispensers do not always reflect proper design consideration for the handicapped.

6. Improper design of water closets (e.g., no grab bars, toilet too low) is a common barrier.

7. Control mechanisms are not always designed to allow handicapped persons to use them.

F. *General Safety Features.* Other interior barriers involve the general safety features of a school building. Common problems in this category include:

1. Alarm systems that do not provide adequate warnings to persons with severe hearing handicaps is a common barrier (e.g., lights blinking on and off).

Figure B.3
Selected Data Concerning Use of Wheelchairs

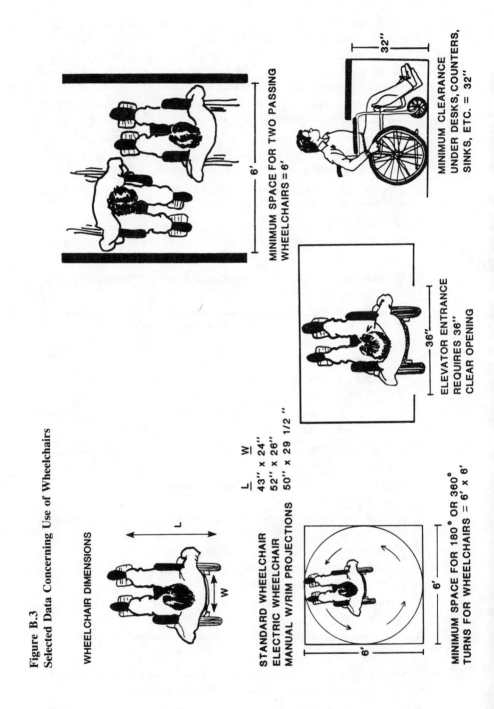

WHEELCHAIR DIMENSIONS

| | L | W |
|---|---|---|
| STANDARD WHEELCHAIR | 43" x 24" | |
| ELECTRIC WHEELCHAIR | 52" x 26" | |
| MANUAL W/RIM PROJECTIONS | 50" x 29 1/2" | |

MINIMUM SPACE FOR TWO PASSING
WHEELCHAIRS = 6'

MINIMUM CLEARANCE
UNDER DESKS, COUNTERS,
SINKS, ETC. = 32"

ELEVATOR ENTRANCE
REQUIRES 36"
CLEAR OPENING

MINIMUM SPACE FOR 180° OR 360°
TURNS FOR WHEELCHAIRS = 6' x 6'

Figure B.4
Selected Data Concerning Use of Crutches

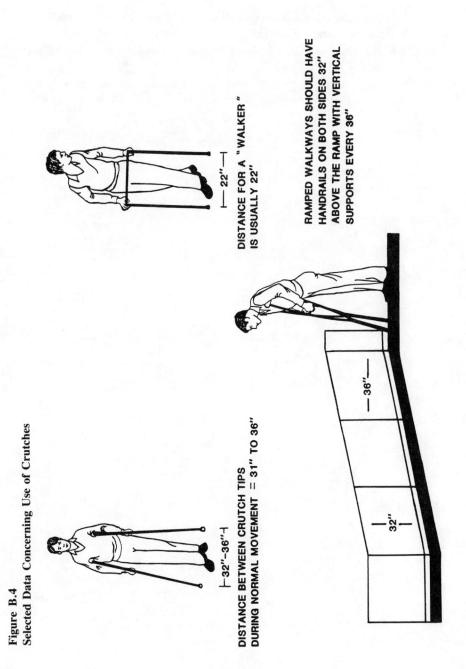

├─32″–36″─┤

**DISTANCE BETWEEN CRUTCH TIPS
DURING NORMAL MOVEMENT = 31″ TO 36″**

├─ 22″ ─┤

**DISTANCE FOR A "WALKER"
IS USUALLY 22″**

**RAMPED WALKWAYS SHOULD HAVE
HANDRAILS ON BOTH SIDES 32″
ABOVE THE RAMP WITH VERTICAL
SUPPORTS EVERY 36″**

├─ 36″ ─┤

├ 32″ ┤

2. Exit signs that are improperly placed or do not use good color combinations present a potential hazard.

3. Emergency exits are not always designed to accommodate all types of handicapped persons.

4. High risk areas (e.g., boiler rooms, shop areas) are not always properly identified for persons with visual problems (e.g., raised lettering on the doors).

# BIBLIOGRAPHY

Abramson, P. (1981). The superintendent of buildings and grounds: His job, his status, his pay. *American School and University,* 54 (2), 66–71.

Affleck, K., and Fuller, B. (1988). The integration of programming and educational specifications. *CEPF Journal,* 26 (6), 9–12.

Alexander, W., and Kealy, R. (1969). From junior high school to middle school. *High School Journal,* 53, 151–63.

Allison, J. (1988). Relocatable classrooms: An alternative to permanent construction. *School Business Affairs,* 54 (1), 24–25.

Alspaugh, J. (1981). Accuracy of school enrollment projections based upon previous enrollments. *Education Research Quarterly,* 6 (Summer), 61–67.

American Association of School Administrators. (1974). *Declining enrollment: What to do.* Arlington, VA: American Association of School Administrators.

American Institute of Architects. (1987). *You and your architect.* Washington, DC: The American Institute of Architects.

Anderson, L., and Van Dyke, L. (1963). *Secondary school administration.* Boston: Houghton Mifflin Company.

Arnett, D. (1987). Orlando creates "educational city of future." *Education USA,* August 10, (364).

Ashley, D. (1987). Utilizing computer-aided design (CAD): A new tool for facilities planning. *CEPF Journal,* 25 (6), 11–17.

Association of School Business Officials of the United States and Canada. (1981). *Custodial methods and procedures manual.* Park Ridge, IL: Research Corporation of the Association of School Business Officials of the United States and Canada.

Baker, J. (1982). *Microcomputers in the classroom.* Bloomington, IN: Phi Delta Kappa Educational Foundation (Fastback no. 179).

Baldwin, G. (1988). Fixed assets: Disposing of property and resulting funds. *Journal of Education Finance,* 13 (3), 274–89.

Bensen, M. (1988). From industrial arts to technology education. In R. S. Brandt (ed.),

*Content of the curriculum.* Alexandria, VA: Association for Supervision and Curriculum Development, 167–80.

Blackburn, J., and Campbell, J. (1988–89). Public Law 99-457: Concerns and challenges for public education. *National Forum of Educational Administration and Supervision Journal,* 6 (2), 124–28.

Boles, H. (1965). *Step by step to better school facilities.* New York: Holt, Rinehart, and Winston.

Borowski, P. (1984). Maintaining a computerized building file. *CEPF Journal,* 22 (5), 18.

Bowers, J., and Burkett, C. (1989). Effects of physical and school environment on students and faculty. *CEPF Journal,* 27 (1), 28–31.

Boyer, E. (1989). Buildings reflect our priorities. *Educational Record,* 70 (1), 24–27.

Brookfield, S. (1986). *Understanding and facilitating adult learning.* San Francisco: Jossey-Bass.

Brooks, K., Conrad, M., and Griffith, W. (1980). *From program to educational facilities.* Lexington, KY: Center for Professional Development, College of Education, University of Kentucky.

Brubaker, C. (1988). These 21 trends will shape the future of school design. *The American School Board Journal,* 175 (4), 31–33, 66.

Brubaker, J. (1947). *A history of the problems of education.* New York: McGraw-Hill.

Butts, R., & Cremin, L. (1953). *A history of education in America.* New York: Henry Holt and Company.

California State Department of Education. (1986). *Administration of maintenance and operations in California school districts: A handbook for school administrators and governing boards.* Sacramento, CA: California State Department of Education.

Campbell, R., Corbally, J., and Nystrand, R. (1983). *The introduction to educational administration* (6th edition). Boston: Allyn & Bacon.

Carnegie Forum on Education and the Economy. (1986). *A nation prepared.* New York: Carnegie Forum.

Carter, M., and Rosenbloom, C. (1989). Compensation survey for school and university administrators. *American School and University,* 61 (5), 21–38.

Castaldi, B. (1987). *Educational facilities: Planning, modernization, and management* (3rd edition). Boston: Allyn & Bacon.

Castetter, W. (1981). *The personnel function in educational administration* (3rd edition). New York: Macmillan.

Chan, T. (1988). The aesthetic environment and student learning. *School Business Affairs,* 54 (1), 26–27.

Chick, C., Smith, P., and Yeabower, G. (1987). Last in; First out maintenance budgets. *CEPF Journal,* 25 (4), 4–6.

Christopher, G. (1989). 10 trends for future educational design. *CEPF Journal,* 27 (1), 15.

Clark, T. (1984). Monitoring and conserving energy usage in existing educational buildings. *CEPF Journal,* 22 (3), 21–22.

Coley, J. (1988). A practitioner's perspective on school facility problems. *School Business Affairs,* 54 (8), 20–24.

Collins, G. (1987). Facilities outlook: School design then, now . . . and soon to be. *American School and University,* 59 (4), 12–13, 17–18.

Cooper, H. (1985). *Strategic planning in education: A guide for policymakers.* Alexandria, VA: National Association of State Boards of Education.

Cope, R. (1987). *Opportunity from strength: Strategic planning clarified with case examples.* ASHE-ERIC Higher Education Report No. 8. Washington, D.C.: Association for the Study of Higher Education.

Council of Educational Facility Planners. (1978). *Surplus school space—The problem and the possibilities.* Columbus, OH: Council of Educational Facility Planners.

———. (1985). *Guide for planning educational facilities.* Columbus, OH: Council of Educational Facility Planners.

Council of Educational Facility Planners, International. (1980). *Energy use in community schools.* Columbus, OH: Council of Educational Facility Planners.

Dale, C. (1986). How to set maintenance priorities. *American School and University,* 58 (9), 128, 130.

Davis, J. (1973). *The principal's guide to educational facilities.* Columbus, OH: Charles E. Merrill.

———. (1988). Playground safety. *American School and University,* 61 (2), 43–44.

Davis, J., and Loveless, E. (1981). *The administrator and educational facilities.* Washington, DC: University Press of America.

DeRoche, F., and Kaiser, J. (1980). *Complete guide to administering school services.* West Nyack, NY: Parker Publishing.

Drake, T., and Roe, W. (1986). *The principalship* (3rd Edition). New York: Macmillan.

Earthman, G. (1986). Research needs in the field of educational facility planning. *ERIC,* Document ED 283 301, 12 pages.

Eisner, E. (1985). *The educational imagination* (2nd edition). New York: Macmillan.

Erekson, T. (1980). Identifying, removing architectural barriers. *NASSP Bulletin,* 64 (432), 102–8.

Ficklen, E. (1988). Design for learning: New looks in school architecture. *The Washington Post Education Review,* November 20, 4–5.

*Future directions for school financing* (1971). Gainesville, FL: The National Educational Finance Project.

Garrett, D. (1981). "The impact of school building age on the academic achievement of high school pupils in the state of Georgia." Unpublished doctoral dissertation, University of Georgia.

Ginsburg, S. (1989). Caveats and cautions. *Educational Record,* 70 (1), 46–48.

Glass, T. (1984). Planned maintenance programs: A memorandum to facility officers. *CEPF Journal,* 22 (3), 13.

———. (1987). Demographic sources and data available for school district planners and architects. *CEPF Journal,* 25 (2), 7–13.

Goldblatt, S., and Wood, R. (1985). Construction management for educational facilities: Professional services' procurement and competitive bid statutes. *ERIC,* Document ED 268 670, 18 pages.

Goodman, L. (1976). A bill of rights for the handicapped. *American Education,* 12, 6–8.

Graves, B. (1985). Facility planning: School closings—Never easy. *American School and University,* 58 (1), 111.

———. (1986). Facility planning: What do teachers want? *American School and University,* 58 (8), 8.

———. (1989). Why long-range plans should be in loose-leaf binders. *American School and University,* 61 (6), 20.

Greenhalgh, J. (1978). *Practitioner's guide to school business management*. Boston: Allyn & Bacon.

Guthrie, J. (1988). Educational finance: The lower schools. In N. Boyan (ed.), *Handbook of Research on Educational Administration*. White Plains, NY: Longman, 373–89.

Guthrie, J., Garms, W., and Pierce, L. (1988). *School finance and education policy* (2nd edition). Englewood Cliffs, NJ: Prentice-Hall.

Hansen, S. (1986). Energy management: The cost of delay. *American School and University*, 58 (12), 28–32.

Harris, C., and Byer, D. (1989). Salvaging tomorrow's higher education facilities today. *Educational Record*, 70 (1), 34–39.

Harris, D., Burrage, P., and Smith, W. (1986). Local insights keep enrollment projections on the money. *The Executive Educator*, 8 (11), 20–21.

Hawkins, H., and Lilley, H. (1986). *Guide for school facility appraisal*. Columbus, OH: Council for Educational Facility Planners.

Hawkins, H., and Overbaugh, B. (1988). The interface between facilities and learning. *CEPF Journal*, 26 (4), 4–7.

Henson, K. (1988). *Methods and strategies for teaching in secondary and middle schools*. White Plains, NY: Longman.

Hentschke, G. (1986). *School business administration: A comparative perspective*. Berkeley, CA: McCutchan.

Hessong, R., and Weeks, T. (1987). *Introduction to education*. New York: Macmillan.

Hill, F. (1989). *Tomorrow's learning environments*. Alexandria, VA: National School Boards Association.

Hill, J. (1972). *How schools can apply systems analysis*. Bloomington, IN: Phi Delta Kappa Educational Foundation (Fastback no. 6).

Hodgkinson, H. (1985). *All one system: Demographics of education, kindergarten through graduate school*. Washington, DC: Institute for Educational Leadership.

Holloway, C. (1986). *Strategic planning*. Chicago: Nelson-Hall.

Hoy, W., and Miskel, C. (1982). *Educational administration* (2nd edition). New York: Random House.

Hudson, C. (1988). Financing public elementary and secondary school facilities in Nebraska. *Journal of Education Finance*, 31 (3), 338–41.

Hughes, L., and Ubben, G. (1984). *The elementary principal's handbook* (2nd edition). Boston: Allyn & Bacon.

Jarolimek, J., and Foster, C. (1981). *Teaching and learning in the elementary school*. New York: Macmillan.

Johnson, D., Johnson, R., Holubec, E., and Roy, P. (1984). *Circles of learning: Cooperation in the classroom*. Alexandria, VA: Association for Supervision and Curriculum Development.

Jordan, K. (1988). Financing capital outlay and debt service in Arizona. *Journal of School Finance*, 13 (3), 290–96.

Jordan, K., McKeown, M., Salmon, R., and Webb, L. (1985). *School business management*. Beverly Hills, CA: Sage Publications.

Justis, R., Judd, R., and Stephens, D. (1985). *Strategic management and policy: Concepts and cases*. Englewood Cliff, NJ: Prentice-Hall.

Kauffman, D., and Lamkin, C. (1985). Designing schools for tomorrow's technology. *Education Digest*, 50 (7), 54–57.

Kluenker, C. (1987). Construction management and local contractors: A good team for the owners. *School Business Affairs,* 53 (1), 22–23.

Kluenker, C., and Haltenhoff, C. (1986). How to hire a construction management company. *School Business Afffairs,* 53 (5), 58–62.

Knirk, F. (1979). *Designing productive learning environments.* Englewood Cliffs, NJ: Educational Technology Publications.

Kowalski, T. (1981). Organizational patterns for secondary school curriculum. *NASSP Bulletin,* 65 (443), 1–8.

———. (1982). Organizational climate, conflict, and collective bargaining. *Contemporary Education,* 54 (1), 27–30.

———. (1983). *Solving educational facility problems.* Muncie, IN: Accelerated Development.

———. (1988). *The organization and planning of adult education.* Albany, NY: State University of New York Press.

———. (1988). Variety consulting. *American School and University,* 61 (1), 360–61.

Kowalski, T., and Fallon, J. (1986). *Community education.* Bloomington, IN: Phi Delta Kappa Educational Foundation (Fastback no. 243).

Kowalski, T., and Weaver, R. (1988). An analysis of attitudes of leading superintendents toward community education. *Community Education Research Digest,* 3 (1), 9–17.

Lane, M., and Lane, K. (1988). Design considerations for microcomputer laboratories. *CEPF Journal,* 26 (1), 10–11.

Lane, K., and Betz, L. (1987). The principal new to a school—What questions to ask about the facility. *NASSP Bulletin,* 71 (502), 125–27.

Laszlo, E. (1972). *The relevance of general systems theory.* New York: George Braziller.

Lawrence, J. (1984). Energy-conscious design. *American School and University,* 56 (12), 43, 46, 49–50.

Ledford, B. (1981). Interior design: Impact on learning achievement. In P. Sleeman and D. Rockwell (eds.), *Designing learning environments.* White Plains, NY: Longman, 160–73.

Leu, D. (1965). *Planning educational facilities.* New York: Center for Applied Research in Education, Inc.

Lewis, A. (1989).*Wolves at the schoolhouse door: An investigation of the condition of public school buildings.* Washington, DC: Education Writers Association.

Lieberman, M. (1986). *Beyond public education.* New York: Praeger.

Lindbloom, K., and Summerhays, J. (1988). School security. *American School and University,* 61 (1), 50–55.

Lows, R. (1987). Enrollment projection: A methodology for eras of growth and decline. *CEPF Journal,* 25 (2), 4–7.

———. (1987). School tax referenda: A case study of the relationship between referenda outcomes and demographic variables. *Journal of Education Finance,* 13 (1), 30–44.

McClelland, J. (1985). An analysis of building replacement costs. *CEPF Journal,* 23 (2), 6–9.

McGovern, M. (1989). Asbestos, the law. *CEPF Journal,* 27 (1), 18–21.

McNamara, J., and Chisolm, G. (1988). The technical tools of decision making. In N. Boyan (ed.), *Handbook of Research on Educational Administration.* White Plains, NY: Longman, 525–68.

McNeil, J. (1985). *Curriculum: A comprehensive introduction* (3rd edition). Boston: Little, Brown and Company.

Madden, M., and Coughlin, T. (1985). Selection and compensation of architectural services for school facility construction: Guidelines for school districts. *Resources in Education*, June, ERIC document no. ED 267 485, 47 pages.

Meyen, E. (1978). *Exceptional children and youth: An introduction.* Denver: Parker Publishing.

Millett, J. (1981). Planning: The current context. In H. Kaiser (ed.), *New directions in higher education: Managing facilities more effectively.* San Francisco: Jossey-Bass, 7–12.

Moody's Investment Service (1988). *Moody's industrial manual.* New York: Moody's Investment Service, Inc.

Moore, D. (1989). A new approach to selecting architects. *CEPF Journal.* 27 (1), 35–37.

Morris, J. (1981). Developing a small scale preventive maintenance program. *American School and University,* 53 (8), 15.

Mullin, P. (1985). Outlook on roofing systems. *American School and University,* 58 (4), 42, 44.

Murk, P., and Galbraith, M. (1986). Planning successful continuing education programs: A systems approach model. *Lifelong learning,* 9 (5), 21–23.

Mutter, D., and Nichols, W. (1987). What do we fix first? A step-by-step plan for an inhouse maintenance audit of school buildings. *CEPF Journal,* 25 (4), 6–9.

Nelson, N. (1972). "Performance specifications: Determining space requirements." Unpublished paper, Purdue University, West Lafayette, IN.

Nimtz, P. (1988). Metal roofs—Cost-effective alternative. *School Business Affairs,* 54 (12), 50–55.

Noyes, K. (1987). Surplus schools can serve the community. *Aging,* 356, 13–16.

Ornstein, A. (1989). Controversy over size continues. *The School Administrator,* 46 (4), 42–43.

Paoletti, D. (1989). Acoustical and audiovisual design considerations. *CEPF Journal,* 27 (1), 22.

Perrone, V. (1985). *Portraits of high schools.* Lawrenceville, NJ: Princeton University Press.

Peterson, L. (1986). Continuity, challenge and change: An organizational perspective on planning past and future. *Planning in Higher Education,* 14 (3), 6–15.

Piccigallo, P. (1989). Renovating urban schools is fundamental to improving them. *Phi Delta Kappan,* 70, 402–6.

Plante, P. (1987). *The art of decision making.* New York: American Council on Education and Macmillan.

Plumley, J. (1978). "The effect of school building age on the academic achievement of pupils from selected schools in the state of Georgia." Unpublished doctoral dissertation, University of Georgia.

Pullum, T., Graham, S., and Herting, J. (1986). How to forecast public school enrollments, *American Demographics,* 8 (10), 52, 54.

Quindry, K. (1979). The state–local tax picture. *Journal of Education Finance,* 5 (1), 19–35.

Rankin, J. (1987). Energy—A force for change. *CEPF Journal,* 25 (1), 7–8.

Reecer, M. (1988). When students say school makes them sick, sometimes they're right. *The American School Board Journal,* 175 (8), 17–21.

Roberts, A., and Cawelti, G. (1984). *Redefining general education in the American high school.* Alexandria, VA: Association for Supervision and Curriculum Development.

Rondeau, E. (1989). The future of facility management. *CEPF Journal,* 27 (1), 9–14.

Rowe, D. (1987). Healthful school living: Environmental health in the school. *Journal of School Health,* 57 (10), 426–31.

Rublin, L. (1985). Asbestos fallout: It can be hazardous to a company's financial health. *Barron's,* February 11, 6–7, 22, 24.

*San Antonio Independent School District v. Rodriguez* (1973). 411 U.S. 1.

Sawyer, G. (1986). Making plans work: Administering and controlling strategic plans. In J. Gardner, R. Rachlin, and H. Sweeny (eds.), *Handbook of strategic planning.* New York: John Wiley & Sons, 8.1–8.19.

Schubert, W. (1986). *Curriculum: Perspective, paradigm, and possibility.* New York: Macmillan.

Shepard, G., and Ragan, W. (1982). *Modern elementary curriculum* (6th edition). New York: Holt, Rinehart and Winston.

Simko, E. (1987). Proactive maintenance saves money. *American School and University,* 59 (7), 31–38.

Simoter, D. (1988). Limiting asbestos liability. *American School and University,* 61 (3), 225–27.

Skypeck, W. (1988). Why ask for CADD? *CEPF Journal,* 26 (6), 6–8.

Smith, E., Stevenson, K., and Pellicer, L. (1984). Follow these nine steps to select the architectural firm that can design a new school to your exact specification. *The American School Board Journal,* 171 (5), 36–37.

Smith, M., and Zirkel, P. (1988). Pauley vs. Kelley: School finances and facilities in West Virginia. *Journal of Education Finance,* 13 (3), 264–73.

Soupon, R. (1985). Lower energy costs, same comfort. *American School and University,* 57 (11), 13.

Spencer, D. (1988). Implications for facility planners at the elementary and secondary level. *CEPF Journal,* 26 (2), 16–17.

Spring, J. (1985). *American education* (3rd edition). White Plains, NY: Longman.

Standard & Poor's Corporation (1988). *Standard and Poor's,* 49 (18). New York: Standard & Poor's Corporation.

Stewart, G. (1987). Confirming enrollment projections in rural districts. *CEPF Journal,* 25 (2), 16–17.

Stollar, D. (1967). *Managing school indebtedness.* Danville, IL: The Interstate Printers and Publishers.

Stronge, J. (1987). The school building principal and inventory control: A case for computerization. *CEPF Journal,* 25 (6), 4–6.

Sylvester, T. (1988). Relocatable and modular classrooms: Booming business. *School Business Affairs,* 54 (1), 22–27.

The National Commission on Excellence in Education (1983). *A nation at risk.* Washington, DC: U.S. Government Printing Office.

Theobald, R. (1987). *The rapids of change.* Indianapolis, IN: Knowledge Systems, Incorporated.

Thompson, D. (1988). Providing for capital improvement projects in Hawaii. *Journal of Education Finance,* 13 (3), 302–11.

Thompson, D., and Camp, W. (1988). Analysis of equity in capital outlay funding mechanisms in Kansas. *Journal of Education Finance,* 13 (3), 253–63.

Toll, M. (1988). Choosing an asbestos abatement contractor. *American School and University,* 61 (3), 219–20, 225.

Tougaw, T. (1987). The view from here. *CEPF Journal,* 25 (4), 2.

Uhler, S. (1988). Scrutinizing architectural contracts. *School Business Affairs,* 55 (12), 57–58.

United States Department of Education. (1988). *Targeted Forecast* (April). Washington, DC: Center for Education Statistics.

United States Department of Labor. (1980). *Monthly Labor Review, 1980.* Washington DC: Bureau of Labor Statistics.

Venter, B. (1985). Buying maintenance. *American School and University,* 58 (12), 30–36.

Waldron, L. (1988). The map to cost effective roofing. *School Business Affairs,* 54 (12), 21–22, 47–48.

Walker, D. (1985). Curriculum and technology. In A. Molnar (ed.), *Current thought on curriculum.* Alexandria, VA: Association for Supervision and Curriculum Development, 91–102.

Weinert, R. (1987). Construction management: A sensible alternative when building new schools. *School Business Affairs,* 53 (1), 16–21.

Wiles, J., and Bondi, J. (1984). *Curriculum development: A guide to practice.* Columbus, OH: Charles E. Merrill.

Wlodowski, R. (1985). *Enhancing adult motivation to learn.* San Francisco: Jossey-Bass.

Worell, J., and Stilwell, W. (1981). *Psychology for teachers and students.* New York: McGraw-Hill.

Worner, W. (1981). Small school districts and the high cost of energy. *Journal of Education Finance,* 6 (3), 297–309.

Yeager, L., and Bilbo, D. (1983). Asbestos: A present hazard in education. *CEPF Journal,* 21 (3), 20–21.

Young, D. (1987). Roof management program—Three steps to success. *CEPF Journal,* 25 (4), 14–15.

# AUTHOR INDEX

# SUBJECT INDEX

## ABOUT THE AUTHOR

THEODORE J. KOWALSKI has been a teacher, principal, and superintendent in the public schools of Indiana and Illinois. Currently he is dean of Teachers College at Ball State University. Prior to accepting his present position, Dean Kowalski taught at Purdue University and served as professor and director of educational leadership studies at Saint Louis University. The author of over 125 professional publications, his recent books include *Solving Educational Facility Problems* (1983), *Community Education: Processes and Programs* (1986), *The Organization and Planning of Adult Education* (1988), and *Case Studies on Teaching* (1990). He serves on the editorial boards of three professional journals.

Dean Kowalski works extensively as a planning consultant with educational institutions and private industry. His work focuses on strategic planning, the development of facilities, and program planning. He also is a noted speaker and conducts workshops throughout the United States. His recent work has focused on long-range planning for organizations facing uncertain futures.

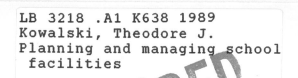